CYBORG

CYBORG

DIGITAL DESTINY AND HUMAN
POSSIBILITY IN
THE AGE OF THE
WEARABLE COMPUTER

STEVE MANN WITH HAL NIEDZVIECKI

DOUBLEDAY CANADA

Doubleday Canada and colophon are trademarks.

National Library of Canada Cataloguing in Publication Data

Mann, Steve, 1962–
Cyborg : digital destiny and human possibility in the age of the wearable computer

ISBN 0-385-65825-7

1. Mann, Steve, 1962– .   2. Wearable computers.   3. Cyborgs.
I. Niedzviecki, Hal, 1971– .   II. Title.

QA76.2.M35A3 2001   004.16   C2001-900752-3

Jacket and text design: Daniel Cullen
Printed and bound in the USA

Published in Canada by Doubleday Canada, a division of
Random House of Canada Limited

Visit Random House of Canada Limited's website: www.randomhouse.ca

RRD 10 9 8 7 6 5 4 3 2 1

TO MY WIFE, BETTY,
AND MY PARENTS, BILL AND RUTH

CONTENTS

*why should you care about
the wearable computer?*

■■■ t is traditional for a book about technology to open with an earnest
■■■ fictional scene depicting the grim future. Whether the book goes
on to discuss technology in general, or some particular technological
advance, the bleak tone reminds us that nothing short of "life as we know
it" will be at stake in the coming pages.

In beginning this particular book about a particular kind of technology
— wearable computers and other personal electronic appliances — I could
not help wondering about the effectiveness of the standard apocalyptic-
scenario opening. After all, how can we continue to sound the alarm
when, according to every best-selling future shock tome since technology
made book printing possible, we should already be living on a wasted
planet populated solely by robot roaches? And if we do sound a warning,
won't that cry be lost in the aural pollution of alarms, cellphones, bleating
pop tunes, and car horns? How many times can the alarm be sounded

before we start to ignore it? What story can I tell you that will cause you to seriously reassess not just the technologically altered future but also the looming present?

It's not that I am an incompetent science fiction writer. Instead consider it this way: as many of the technologies discussed in this book will make clear, science fiction has been eclipsed by reality; thus any book that successfully hopes to chart the intertwined paths of technology and the future must be prepared to take its cues from actuality rather than fantasy. Hidden cameras, instantaneous Web broadcasts, corporate tracking devices, virtual friendships — that stuff isn't new, is it? When discussing a technology as wide ranging as the wearable computer, or a concept as vast as the cyborg, we start to wonder — What already exists? What is in the making? And what has been with us since the beginning?

The truth is always more complicated than the shocking opening. The book harping on the dangers of the latest technological trend starts by painting a truly ugly picture, then disintegrates into hypothetical eventualities that could be good or bad, depending on this, that, or the other thing. Ten years later, the books are usually wrong anyway. Thus, I have deliberately left out of these opening remarks the final scenario, so terrifying, so removed from the way we live, that there can be no question: the very fabric of our lives is at stake in the pages to follow. But if I'm not trying to scare you into paying attention to the rest of this book, I suppose the question becomes: Why read on? Why *should* you care about the wearable computer?

To fully answer that question, I would have to find some way to quickly and simply define what a wearable computer is and could be. I would have to explain the potent meaning of the cyborg, and conjure up some quick image of how these intertwined ideas function in the world today and will function in the world tomorrow. I would have to summarize the complicated series of questions I attempt to address and answer — as well as they *can* be answered — throughout the course of this book. In other words, I can't begin to tell you what you need to know about wearable technology in these waning opening pages. All I can do is assure you that the cyborg is not to be found in the realm of hypothetical eventualities and hyperbolic horrors — it is real; it is now. Each scenario in this book encounters wearable technology; each scenario postulates a new interface, a new relationship, between the human being and technology; each scenario demonstrates how present day extensions of human ability through technology affect the shape of society; and each scenario speaks to the way we live our lives now, as opposed to the way we can expect to live our lives in some potentially disastrous future.

As you read this book you will, I suspect, become more intrigued — and perhaps alarmed — by the "reality" depicted, than by any pseudo-parable I could have constructed. In reality, substantive societal change occurs incrementally, moment by moment, inch by inch, run-of-the-mill triumphing over spectacle. One moment you swipe your card; the next moment you are faced with an improvement: simply wear a wristband that will automatically open the door; then, sometime later, the wristband becomes an implanted microchip that can keep track of what floors you are permitted to access, how many pens you've picked up from the company supply depot, and exactly how many seconds every day you spend in the company toilet.

One moment you are capable of communicating with other countries instantaneously via the computer stationed on your desk. Two weeks or two months or two years later, you find yourself capable of sending your brain, or your gaze, or your virtual image, anywhere at any time from any place.

Why should you care about the wearable computer? Not because it is some dangerous new bugaboo with the potential to destroy all life on the planet with the flip of a switch, but for precisely the opposite reason: Because it is everywhere, as ubiquitous as it is invisible, capable of changing the everyday minutiae of how we go about our lives, permeating our consciousness, altering fears, desires, and ways of being. You should care because the wearable computer is at once strange and familiar, alien and domestic, a dangerous foe and your new best friend. You should care because, unlike the doomsday opening scenario you might have been expecting, soon our lives will be dramatically changed by the wearable computer. But the world will look pretty much the same — *and most of us won't even notice.*

INTRODUCTION

the reluctant cyborg

"IN THE ELECTRIC AGE WE WEAR ALL OF MANKIND AS OUR SKIN."

"THE COMPUTER [IS] THE MOST EXTRAORDINARY OF MAN'S TECH-
NOLOGICAL CLOTHING; IT IS AN EXTENSION OF OUR CENTRAL
NERVOUS SYSTEM. BESIDE IT THE WHEEL IS A MERE HULA-HOOP."
— MARSHALL MCLUHAN, *WAR AND PEACE IN THE GLOBAL VILLAGE*

hen Marshall McLuhan wrote those passages in the late 1960s, it was taken for granted that the social seer was speaking metaphorically, abstractly. But read his aphoristic predictions today and they have an entirely different connotation. In the twenty-first century, we could easily argue that McLuhan was predicting, not theorizing. We could say that he was pointing the way to a very real time when we would use the computer not as an entertainment accessory, not as a vehicle to take us from one place in so-called cyberspace to another, not even as a problem-solving and data-storage device, but as an extension of the self in the same way clothing is an extension of the skin.

These are strange days for humanity. Extending the mind and body with computer prostheses is not something one does without a sense of risk and confusion. Inventions and innovations are announced at an almost daily rate. Technology changes individual lives and whole societies, and then changes us again, before we've even begun to grasp the implications of such systemic alterations to our daily fabric. Fuelled by the rapacious needs of consumer society, technology is evolving faster than our ability to harness the energies of technological metamorphosis. As a result, the dawn of the twenty-first century is also a crossroads in the history of humanity. We are entering the post-human age. In this age, biology is no longer limited by the genetic codes of evolution. Today, we can rebuild ourselves, transcend the supposed limitations of the human form — both physical and mental. This, of course, gives rise to all manner of ethical and ontological considerations. As the present eclipses the speculations of even the most brilliant of our past theorists, we must remind ourselves that though the *idea* of extending the human being through technology is not a new one, actually putting that concept into action remains relatively untried and untested. How will we post-humans grapple with the awesome powers to reinvent humanity and society that technology has bestowed on us? To what extent are individuals free to alter their own bodies and minds? To what extent will individual mind/body alterations affect other members of society?

Although many commentators and thinkers have tried to grapple with these issues, there are certain questions one can only answer through experience. In equipping myself, over the past thirty years, with a second skin, an extended central nervous system, I have sought to understand what the post-human world could look like. Using technologies that will be described to you in the coming pages, I alter my perceptions and states of being. Every morning I decide how I will see the world. One day, I give myself eyes in the back of my head. On other days I add a sixth or seventh sense, such as the ability to feel objects that are not touching me. Things appear different to me than they do to other people. I see everyday objects as hyper-icons I can click on and bring to life (similar to the way you click on an icon on a Web site). I can choose stroboscopic vision to "freeze" the motion on the spinning wheels of a car going a hundred kilometres an hour, allowing me to count the grooves in the tread. I can block out the view of particular objects — sparing myself the distraction, for example, of the vast sea of advertising that surrounds us.

In my everyday existence, I live in a videographic world: I see the entire world, even my hands and feet, through a camera lens. A simple way to describe it would be to say that it's as if I am watching my entire life as a television show. However, unlike the passive television watcher, my goal is not to tune out reality. In fact, the device I wear — which I have called WearComp since I began to make wearable computers as a teenager — has quite the opposite effect: equipped with WearComp, it is up to me how and what I see, how and what I choose to focus on or exclude; this freedom heightens my sensitivity to the flow of information that exists in a perpetual swirl all around us. It also allows me to, in effect, liberate my imaginative space from much of the visual detritus that confronts and distracts us in the form of billboards and flashing neon signs.

Functioning daily in tandem with WearComp does more than simply provide me with "special powers." The wearable computer allows me to explore my humanity, alter my consciousness, shift my perceptions so that I can choose — at any given time — to see the world in very different, often quite liberating, ways. By exploring what it means to be a human being permanently connected to a computer, I have made a choice as to which road I would like to walk. As someone who refuses to deny the attraction, the strange beauty, of expanded human potential through wearable computer prostheses, I am seeking to demonstrate that the individual can have a role in shaping the coming cyborg society. But I am also choosing to wander down a dangerous path. In refusing to sit down at the fork of the road and passively accept what others decide my role should be in an electronic world increasingly hostile to the free agent, I explicitly condone alterations of the human through technology. Where will this path lead us? I accept and seek to implement the awesome power of technology to alter human life. However, I also believe that the individual — whether human, post-human, or cyborg — must be able to make his or her own decision. The road forward demands that we aggressively encounter and counter technology. We must, as I will argue throughout this book, use the monster of technological excess against itself. We must confront technology with technology put to different purposes and ends. In doing so, we will clear roads previously blocked to us — we will turn off the highway of blind progress that encourages us to speed toward a future destination fuelled by technologies we are asked not to understand.

Over the years, I have been described as both "the world's first cyborg" and "the inventor of the wearable computer." These are two radically different concepts. But these dual roles have made me increasingly aware of the challenges inherent in being at once an inventor and an experimenter, a calculating scientist and a human being. Since I began building wearable computers, I have functioned repeatedly as my own primary test subject. My work and my life have merged, leaving me to wonder where humanity begins and machinery ends. In inventing, designing, building, and actually wearing WearComp in a variety of ordinary day-to-day settings (as opposed to the lab), I have learned that the technical feat of getting the machines to work can only be considered a starting point. The wearable computer provides unique challenges in engineering, but also in morality and human ontology. Beyond design and construction, I have had to grapple with a plethora of complicated issues, the most obvious of these being the effects, often undesirable, that the apparatus has on the wearer and the wearer has on other people.

When I began building wearable computers I had little or no insight into the social dynamics the wearables would carry with them. I thought the weight on my shoulders was simply the load of carrying around pounds of hardware, all of it adapted from the rather bulky technologies available to me in the late 1970s. The fundamental philosophical issues that relate to wearable computing came to the fore only after actually wearing the apparatus in a wide variety of real-life situations for many years. How could I have known that, as a cyborg, I was opening myself up to be insulted, snubbed, even physically assaulted? How could I have known that the cyborg life would be a solitary one fraught with self-imposed dangers, including flashbacks and visual confusion disorder and, perhaps more meaningfully, a profound loneliness as I struggled both to traverse and to maintain the boundaries of where I began and my computer ended?

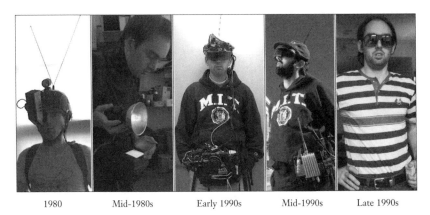

| 1980 | Mid-1980s | Early 1990s | Mid-1990s | Late 1990s |

WearComp through the decades as modelled by Steve Mann.

This book is about my invention of devices that have allowed me to become computer, camera, telephone, videophone, and, of course, myself — all in a single entity. This book is also about an attempt to harness technology as a way to take back some of what technology has caused us to lose. For this reason, I often think of myself as a reluctant cyborg. Though

I use the WearComp system in my everyday life and, indeed, cannot imagine how I would function without it, I also know that my decision to confront technology with technology is accompanied by significant consequences to both myself and society at large. This is invasive, powerful technology, and its use changes not just how I scribble down an idea or send an e-mail but how I think and feel.

In the past two decades, I have designed and built more than a hundred different kinds of wearable computer systems. One of my original impetuses for constructing these systems was a desire to alter and extend personal reality through the use of technology. Gradually, as both myself and my inventions matured, my intentions changed and the systems became concerned with the more general issue of personal autonomy in an era of increased automation and ever-more-invisible technologies. Today, the WearComp outfit is no longer a cumbersome weight. The latest version is, in fact, quite sleek, the only visible hardware being an ordinary-looking pair of bifocal eyeglasses. Even when fully rigged, one can still play an acceptable game of squash. The number of people who would consider wearing the WearComp system will soon be on the rise. In fact, it is just a matter of time before many of you will have the opportunity and means to join me in the cyborg world. But the smaller the WearComp system becomes and therefore the more the physical burden of being a cyborg is alleviated, the heavier the metaphorical burden of life as a cyborg becomes.

One day we will all feel naked without our wearable computers. I say this not with glee but with a certain amount of cautious optimism. The wearable computer is not just another gadget, in the same way that the personal computer cannot be dismissed as just another technological trinket. Certain technologies change the fundamental underpinnings of our lives. The car is one example. The personal computer is another. And the wearable computer will be yet another (one that, perhaps, will combine the mobility and liberation aspects of the car with the processing power of the computer). At the same time, I don't feel altogether comfortable as a predictor of the future. This book is rooted in the past and present — not the future. The cyborg age is upon us now, and is no longer some science fiction fantasy or fashionable gimmick. The question is not: Will we have wearable computers? or Will we become cyborgs? The question is: What kind of cyborgs are we now?

The more I fuse with the machine, the more I am aware of the extent to which our society and our individual lives are fused with technology that is out of our control. As I was developing new ways to live through and with technology, I was also developing an ambivalence — even a fear — of technology's place in our lives. I was in the process of becoming a cyborg — at a crossroads in my personal pilgrimage to the post-human world. But did that also mean I was legitimizing a vast array of controlling technologies — from surveillance cameras to corporate-endorsed "smart" suits? The reluctant cyborg is an individual determined to harness technology's potential, but not at the expense of freedom and singularity. We can use wearable computers to enhance our lives, we can create a permanent connection to borderless cyberspace communities, we can permanently interface with the machine, so long as we retain our awareness of how our choices will affect our selves and our world.

1

HOW WEARCOMP WORKS

The WearComp (wearable computer) is a data processing system attached to the body, with one or more input and output devices. The primary input/output device consists of a technology called EyeTap. This allows the user to view the world as images imprinted onto the retina by rays of laser light controlled through several linked computers. The WearComp user "sees" through miniature cameras, with the image filtered into the computer system before finally being projected into the eye. The EyeTap allows the eye to function as both a camera and a display with text and graphic capabilities. In this way, eye and camera, mind and computer, are joined. The user is at once in constant contact with the surrounding world, and in constant contact with a data processor tailored to personal specifications. This allows for all the standard functions of a desktop computer — e-mail, Web browsing, word processing, data processing, etc.— plus constant mediation of visual input, and, of course, total mobility. In this kind of wearable computer the laser output projection is always perceptible regardless of the particular task or body position. One does not turn the computer on or off. Rather, one functions at all times through the computer. The computer runs continuously and is always ready to interact with the user. Unlike a laptop computer, the wearable computer does not need to be opened up or turned on prior to use. One's vision is, in fact, constantly mediated through the computer.

One can change the instructions of the WearComp at any time, in the course of everyday activity. To input into the system there is a pocket "keyer" that allows the instruction set that determines how the computer will operate to be easily modified. The smallest keyer is a push-button switch you can press for a short time (a "dot") or a long time (a "dash") to key letters using a code, such as Morse code, at maybe fifteen words per minute if you have some reasonable degree of experience. A single push-button keyer is sufficient to allow the experienced WearComp user to send and receive e-mail, take photographs, make calculations, and instruct the computer to screen out all ads for cigarettes. Currently, in my lab we are doing research on systems that function not by keyer but by reading brainwaves — thus allowing the wearer to interact with the computer without hand or voice input. We have been somewhat successful: By various modes of thought we can take a picture, tune the brightness, and change the contrast on the EyeTap system, all hands-free. However, complete hands-free control over WearComp is still somewhat in the future.

Unlike in traditional computing, the wearable computer sits in the background; it is ever-present, but rarely the primary task. Instead, the wearable computer provides constant mediation of one's surroundings. The effect is to allow the wearable to function as a portable, sustained, yet non-monopolizing, controllable entity, much more akin to, say, having the television on in the background while you eat dinner and talk to your family than to working on a desktop computer that demands your constant, undivided attention.

The most important difference between my invention and the many different wearable technology prototypes in various stages of development is the generality of purpose that is inherent to the wearable computer design. Just as McLuhan predicted, WearComp functions as an overlay, as a second skin, not as a tool to be turned on and off. This diversity of function is the system's greatest strength. What makes the wearable system so powerful is that it is not designed for any one specific task. The technology can be re-purposed for uses a manufacturer never imagined. This is a significant advance over past and present "personal technologies," from eyeglasses to the wristwatch to the pacemaker to the computer shoe designed to monitor your workout.

Often, we are discouraged from experimenting with potentially liberating cybernetic technologies by the notion that only corporations and government bodies can safeguard our health in a technologically complex world. It is assumed that WearComp must be more dangerous to the user than other already-sanctioned electronic devices. I am repeatedly asked about WearComp's potential effect on the user's health. People will say, "Isn't shining that laser into the eyes harmful?" To the contrary, because my eye can focus anywhere it wants to, the image of what I see can appear to hover in space at any distance my eye chooses to focus on. And after years of experimentation, I've learned how to direct light into the eye with zero eye strain.

People also ask, "Isn't the radiation from the antenna harmful?" Despite the fact that concern for electromagnetic radiation is a recent phenomenon, I've been thinking about these issues for many years. I've tried everything from dyeing my hair with copper and plating it with aluminum, so that my whole body would act as a Faraday cage when fitted with a conductive hat, to designing special clothing with conductive threads. While many of my designs could best be described as crazy, and many of the solutions were hardly as glamorous as an aluminum hairdo, the process of invention has led to some very practical embodiments that address the physical problems we will face when many of us decide to become cyborgs. Which is to say that I no longer receive unexpected jarring shocks, and have been able to device new methods of protecting my brain from potentially damaging radiation that do not involve hair dyes and metal hats.

I'm not going to tell you that, at this point, there are no health risks associated with the wearable computer system; what I will argue is that wearing such a system is likely to prove no more or less risky than spending prolonged periods talking on a cellular phone or even sitting in front of a standard desktop computer. However, because exposure to the wearable computer is ongoing, the effect is more intense and immediate: I have, in the past, experienced disorientation and flashbacks upon severing my connection with the system. There is no doubt that, just like clothing, one must gradually adapt to requiring the EyeTap system for everyday sight. Nevertheless, I am more comfortable wearing the wearable system I have built myself than I am with a whole host of technological appliances designed and built in corporate laboratories under lock and key. As with much of our technology, from pharmaceuticals to genetically modified crops to cellular phones, only time will be able to fully determine how the wearable computer might ultimately alter our physiology and our society.

THE EVERYDAY CYBORG

The WearComp system I envisioned as a teenager and now wear in everyday life is more than just nifty new hardware. The longer I have lived in tandem with the system, and the more time I have spent enhancing its operations, the more I have come to realize the profound changes to society and even humanity that a multi-purpose wearable computer/videographic perspective suggests. Topics including education, privacy, autonomy, community, democracy, and even reality are among the issues that the wearable computer directly affects and, in the process, seeks a new moral consensus concerning. How will we define and understand what it is to live the unobserved life when it comes to pass that everyone and anyone could be secretly recording and even broadcasting? How can we protect ourselves from oppression and totalitarianism when wearable technologies that monitor our every move are issued to workers around the world? Will our capacity to be in constant communication with the cyberspace world of the Internet erode our ability to function in what we now call "real" life? The features of the wearable computer and the possibilities for change that they present indicate just how many of the pressing and conflicting themes of postmodern life are raised by cyborg technology.

Does my description of the wearable computer sound mundane compared to the fantasy? Or is it, rather, even more disconcerting than anything dreamed up in the movies? Depending on who you are, and what you consider to be the limits of human-technological interface, the answer is undoubtedly one or the other — but few respond impartially to the technologies I am describing. In fact, when people hear of my work, they often imagine a very strange apparatus. One finds oneself conjuring up images of circuits fused to scalps, antennas protruding from ears, eyes pulled out to make room for telescopic lenses. If we discount surgery and physical implants, the wearable computer summons up images of mini-necklace keyboards and wristwatch LED screens. Functionality often seems to take a back seat to the imagination: sleek designs and Star Trek–inspired mirages. Those who have not yet been exposed to the reality of personal cybernetic technology imagine implications that transcend even our wildest sci-fi fantasies; or else, they immediately conclude that personal cybernetic systems will connote another instalment in a long list of inventions that have served to further debase our hopes for a technology that can give us better, freer lives.

One reason for the proliferation of vague statements and irrational design concepts is that wearable computing, like so much new technology jargon, is a seemingly clear idea made murky by the huge number of pre-conceptions attached to the concept. These are preconceptions that come to us in the form of science fiction, corporate propaganda (one day soon you'll tuck your child in by phone, according to a telephone company television commercial), and, of course, the histrionics of media that consistently infuse wearable technology systems with some vague sense of super-capability that is almost never defined.

Many articles have hyped the arrival of this new technology, but few have taken the time to convey long-term implications and possibilities. The media, for instance, occasionally latch onto my wearable computer project and write articles that manage to at once combine an appreciation for what they suppose is my entrepreneurial daring with a blanket dismissal of my efforts as the work of a "freak" or a "weirdo."

Not that one can hold the media completely responsible. The pace of change is exponential. We must include the wearable computer as part of a larger wave of technological innovations that — with the advent of the personal computer in the late 1970s — has swept over us first as a fad and a joke, then as business accessories, and then, suddenly and inexplicably, as social forces transforming vast swaths of our lives. In twenty years, the Internet went from a text-based research tool to a visually driven populist fantasyland with portals in bars, bedrooms, and universities. Even relatively conservative commentators such as Don Tapscott, author of *The Digital Economy*, argue that: "Today we are witnessing the early, turbulent days of a revolution as significant as any other in human history. A new medium of human communications is emerging, one that may prove to surpass all previous revolutions — the printing press, the telephone, the televison, the computer — in its impact on our economic and social life."[1] Tapscott's rhetoric is by now familiar to us, as it echoes the prescient cries heard as early as the 1960s from such prophetic figures as Norbert Weiner (who coined the term *cyborg*) and Marshall McLuhan. Today, almost everyone seems to be trumpeting the horn of technology. We are faced with many different kinds of thinkers applying many different agendas to the already confusing process of technological change. Given such an environment, it is hardly surprising that wearable computing often comes across as just another bewildering, even frightening, idea.

The actual embodiment of cybernetics as it appears in wearable computing technology is a different matter. Though the wearable computer does embody many of the premises of the B movie, its existence as a relatively mundane entity with functions in everyday life comes as a surprise to anyone who expects super-beings and dramatic sci-fi scenarios. The advancing wave of cyborgs will not be noticeably less human; they will continue to have jobs, families, and "normal lives."

Nonetheless, just as many resisted McLuhan's vision, many have resisted my concrete approximation of what McLuhan predicted thirty-five years ago. That fact is, people find me and my wearable computer peculiar. They think it's odd that I spend most of my waking hours wearing eight or nine Internet-connected computers sewn into my clothing. They are surprised when I wear opaque wraparound glasses day and night, inside and outdoors. They find it strange that to sustain wireless communications during my travels, I will climb to the hotel roof to attach an antenna and Internet connection. They wonder why I sometimes seem detached and lost, but at other times exhibit vast knowledge of their specialty. A physicist once said he felt that I had the intelligence of a dozen experts in his discipline; a few minutes later, someone else commented that they thought I was mentally handicapped. Despite the peculiar glances I draw, I wouldn't live any other way.

WearComp has allowed me to develop new methods of learning about the world around me, liberating me from the traditional barriers society imposes in the separation of trades, of work and leisure, of everyday life and artistic expression. With WearComp, I can be a scientist and photographer, an engineer and an abstract painter, a philosopher and a broadcaster. WearComp forces us to reconsider ideas around creativity and work by challenging not only the limits of physical possibility, but also the divisive strictures that separate communities and mentalities, the computer programmer from the painter, the news reporter from the on-line diarist. WearComp has the potential to free us from all manners of invasion — it can protect physically, but it can also protect mental space by guarding from invasive advertising and unwanted surveillance.

The wearable computer also provides me with new ways of communicating — both to those closest to me and to those farthest away. In addition to having the Internet and massive databases and video capture and recall at my beck and call, I am also available to others. While I am grocery shopping, my wife — who may be at home or in her office — can see exactly what I see and help me pick out vegetables. She can imprint images onto my retina while she sees what I see. This kind of visual simultaneity is one of the most powerful functions of the WearComp system. It allows the individual to fully enter — to communicate and be a substantive part of — the videographic world of images that dominates everyday existence. The WearComp user, at once a recorder and broadcaster, has a much greater capacity to control the flow of information all around him. This allows for increased interactivity with society and humanity, despite the many reports to the contrary. As comfortable in the grocery store as in cyberspace, the cyborg is not necessarily a post-human evil abomination. My daily life is arguably no more surprising — or mundane — than the daily life of anyone else who lives, as we all do, at the beginning of this new century's grand experiment in mass communication and social engineering.

VICARIOUS SOLILOQUY: IMAGING THE CYBORG

In recent years, as demands on my time have increased, I have developed a new way of delivering speeches. It is a method of making "personal" appearances without actually being physically present in an auditorium. It is also a method that allows those in the audience to, in effect, become me. What I have dubbed the Vicarious Soliloquy system arose quite naturally out of delivering lectures. I'd typically use a video projector, and plug the projector into a computer, which would then have a link to my WearComp system. Most of my presentations were prepared as links to my main Web pages, so that giving a presentation was a simple act of showing the audience a series of Web pages. Since I wear (or, in the more existential sense, "am") an embodiment of my WearComp apparatus, one of the Web pages I showed would allow the audience to see the world from a cyborg perspective. At this point in a lecture, I would broadcast, on the screen facing the audience, my real-time view through the WearComp device. The effect on the audience has always been quite impressive, with many shocked audience members achieving an instant introduction to life as mediated through the wearable computer. The high point of my appearance, though, would usually arrive during the question-and-answer period, when I would walk around in the audience talking to people one on one, my view of the conversation (whatever I was looking at, usually the person's face) being shown on the screen at the front of the room. I would also hold onto a small notepad, write on the notepad, and, of course, the whole audience would see the notepad as I was writing. When someone asked a question, I would project the picture on the screen and point my cursor at the person I was looking at. At these talks, I would become the camera, and the audience would have the experience of being at once spectators and participants in the event's main "entertainment."

Often during presentations, I would pace, walk into the audience, and even sit down in a chair, as if I were a member of the audience — all while giving a keynote talk at a conference or symposium. Sometimes I would leave the room while I was giving the address — delivering the speech to myself, so the audience could no longer see me. Naturally, the audience could still hear me speaking over the PA system, which was responsive to an output of my wearable apparatus, and, of course, the audience could still see through my right eye, which was "tapped" and transmitted to the screen. Having delivered this type of lecture multiple times, I began to wonder why I was physically present at the conference site, particularly when the number of invitations to give talks was growing. I came up with the idea that I'd do exactly the same thing as before, with one minor difference: Only my connection would be there — not my face, my avatar, or any other part of me, just the existential aspect of facilitation by which the audience could vicariously be me rather than see me.

Thus, the lecture would be a Vicarious Soliloquy. It's not really a soliloquy, in the sense that the audience isn't watching me talk to myself from an external viewpoint, but rather, is vicariously experiencing me giving the talk to myself. The existential aspect of the apparatus of the invention puts the audience, in effect, inside my head to share a first-person perspective. In this scenario, WearComp causes the eye itself to function much like a document camera or an overhead projector. Now, normally, for the main speaker at a conference not to be in actual physical attendance at the event would be considered a half-measure at best. However, in the case of this particular twist on video-conferencing, audiences have responded with excitement and fascination. In looking through my eyes at themselves, the audience senses — in a single instant — what it is like to live a videographic existence. A conventional two-hour lecture could never convey that feeling. The fact that my body is hundreds of miles away from the site of the conference only serves to underscore the changes in perception and in community interaction that will be part of the cyborg age.

There are other, perhaps more substantive, reasons for wanting to give an audience the experience of *being* me, as opposed to just *seeing* me. Beyond this technique's function as an interesting option for public speaking — one that makes for a vibrant (non)appearance — the idea of the Vicarious Soliloquy has allowed me to explore the relationship between learning and experience. Developing the Vicarious Soliloquy system brought me to a point where I realized that much of WearComp's potential has to do with facilitating the act of being instead of doing. This may seem like an odd pronouncement, but, in fact, it is an idea at the heart of my philosophy of technology; a philosophy that has guided my attempts to explore the implementation of personal cybernetic systems into society. In exploring the Vicarious Soliloquy as a cinematographic genre, I was able to explore the way that technology in many cases predisposes us to certain ways of first doing and then being. When we have new technology, we also have new possibilities to be.

Some years ago, I was asked to give the keynote address at the DEFCON~7 convention (an annual gathering of hackers and digital radicals held in Las Vegas) using the Vicarious Soliloquy model. I presented the address at DEFCON~7 as a lecture to myself, which I gave from my office thousands of miles away while walking around writing on a notepad. After I finished speaking, the audience was invited to pose questions. An audience member asked if I had a mirror I could look into so the group could see my physical appearance. Not expecting to be seen by anyone, I was wearing one of my ancient experimental rigs containing parts more than ten years old. Having worn it for so many years, it's become quite comfortable, like an old pair of jeans. Nonetheless, I found a beamsplitter (a transparent material with a thin optical coating on it), which I held up in front of myself. Suddenly, the audience could both "be me" and "see me" at the same time.

A second interesting moment at the same conference occurred when someone asked why I use paper, pens, and pencils to give my lectures. Without thinking, I replied glibly, "I'm a Luddite." The audience — surprised — laughed. But in coming up with that reply, I had also surprised myself. What did I mean?

So two questions arose out of this experience, both of them indirectly addressing the central issue of how the human's "being" is changed and retained in the course of developing cyborg innovations. Both questions also reveal a bias in our current understanding of how today's and tomorrow's electronic "communication" apparatuses will alter society.

First, there's the question of why someone such as myself — delivering a highly sophisticated, technologically advanced Vicarious Soliloquy to a group of futurists — would nonetheless use pencil and paper to illustrate a point or outline a basic design schematic. The assumption behind this question is that in all cases current technological innovation is superior to previous technological innovation. Surely, the audience member is asking, there must be a better way for me to convey my information than with, shudder, a pencil?

This assumption — that the cyborg will not communicate in conventional forms — is also the assumption of the last two hundred years of technological innovation. Each time a new method to do something is discovered, it is assumed that the old way was a poorer version that should be automatically discontinued. But this is not always the case. In fact, such thinking is what allows technology to steal away the human aspects of our daily lives, including the simple (practical) pleasure of the tactile feel of pencil on paper.

The WearComp device, and my approach to cyborg technology, stems not from a desire to subvert or debase humanity, but from my love for humanity's diversity and capacity to appreciate a multiplicity of options and realities. Just because I am a cyborg does not necessarily mean that I believe every single aspect of human technology needs to evolve and become a complicated process only available through computers. The fact remains, for instance, that the easiest way to show an audience a simple visual diagram or text is to write it out on a chalkboard or — as in the case of the Vicarious Soliloquy — write it down on a pad of paper.

However, the asking of this question made me realize how skewed our perception of technology is. The idea is always to manufacture the illusion of progress, even in the many cases when "progress" is actually a backward step. What we need, I could have told the audience at DEFCON~7, is a new approach to technology. It's not just that I am a cyborg Luddite, it's that we should all be cyborg Luddites. Embodying — and inventing — cyborg technology is more than just a mechanical process. One must also consider the applications for this technology — not just what we can now do differently, but how the process of doing is itself permanently altered as a result of cybernetic developments. The question of the utility of one's inventions in society shouldn't be an abstract one. Free-spirited implications — from new ways of giving lectures to altering the entire educational process — should be considered both abstractly as hypotheses and concretely as applied experiments. The worth of personal cybernetic innovations in particular depends on their ability to encounter society in unpredictable but exciting ways that challenge what has come before on a level of substance, not surface.

Such considerations should be the central issue, uppermost in the minds of any inventor working in the field of wearable computing. As the range of innovations expands and the impact on human life becomes increasingly extreme, it is no longer enough just to invent a device and turn it into a product. Rather, devices must be turned into particular products — products devised in a way that enables not just doing, but being. Mark O'Brien, a severely disabled writer and commentator who relies extensively on cyborg-like technologies, put it this way in a seminal late 1980s issue of the *Whole Earth Review* titled "Is the Body Obsolete?": "What I, as a disabled person, need," he wrote, "is what we all need — better devices under our conscious control, not the abolition of our consciousness."[2] O'Brien's sentiments guide my attempts to approach the wearable computer not as a replacement technology but as a technology that enhances and communicates with the essential workings of our being.

WEARTEL AND "REAL" CONNECTION

Another important facet of the human condition is our ongoing need for "real" connection regardless of changes in our communication infrastructure that might challenge customs and mores. When, at the DEFCON~7 conference, I was asked to look in a mirror so the audience could "be me" and "see me" at the same time, I learned something about the nature of the Vicarious Soliloquy process. I learned that it functions as a clever tool, but does not ultimately replace my actual attendance at the event. In terms of performances and even talks like the ones I give, it is worth remembering that an audience does not attend an event to see a video of a performance or even a "live" broadcast. We come for the "real" thing (which is why lip synching is considered a questionable practice — after all, from lip synching you can move quite easily to simply having look-alike actors pretend to be performing, thus negating the need for the actual performer to tour at all). Quite simply, neither real-time video nor phone connections can adequately replace a human being's physical presence. The conference call and the video connection allow for scattered individuals to gather in a central location and exchange information. However, as anyone who has tried to conduct a meeting in which several of the participants attend via long-distance connection knows, the method has serious limitations. That kind of connection is fine for a brief meeting, but utterly fails when we depend on it to link geographically scattered individuals in a meaningful way. If you were conducting an important business deal — a merger, say — you probably would not rely solely on a conference call to assess the CEO of a company. A face-to-face meeting would be considered necessary.

In another derivation of the Vicarious Soliloquy technique that I call the WearTel phone, the users — each fitted with EyeTap — see each other's point of view. Traditional video-conferencing merely provides a picture of the other person. But because most of the time we call people we already know, WearTel is far more useful in allowing us to exchange points of view. The miniature laser light source inside the WearTel eyeglass-based phone scans the retinas of both parties and swaps the image information, so that each person can see what the other person is looking at. By letting others put themselves in your shoes and see the world from your point of view, a very powerful communications medium results. And, as with the Vicarious Soliloquy, there are significant applications for the technology as it now stands. Just as the Vicarious Soliloquy would greatly improve certain kinds of presentations, WearTel might allow scientists to better and more accurately discuss their findings with their peers in other cities and countries. It would be, as they say, the next best thing to being there.

Cybernetic technologies such as the wearable computer should enhance — not replace — human capability. These technologies should recognize our desire — our right — to encounter that which confirms our visceral need to be ourselves in the company of others. It is my hope that cybernetic systems that can challenge technology's tendency to homogenize and reduce difference for the sake of conformity and universality will be the greatest legacy of the cyborg age. Wearable technologies conceived and constructed under such a framework may yet return us to our individuality, even as we discover new ways to enjoy community and collectivity. WearTel allows you to be in the head of another person, at least nominally. Still, the question of what we look like, the interest in the surface appearance, pervades, despite any technological interface we could construct to change the situation. Being me, rather than seeing me, does not — as we might have suspected — lessen our anxiety about our existential status as individuals alone on a crowded planet. In fact, WearTel and the Vicarious Soliloquy emphasis our individual exteriority (or aloneness) even as we are experiencing, in a totally new way, the simultaneity that vision confers upon humanity. As Margaret Morse writes in *Virtualities*, "In an era when cameras can travel under the surface of the skin, the desire to experience, interact, even touch the image in an apparently mediated way refuses to stop at the screen itself."[3]

And yet, despite the realizations that these projects enabled, I have to admit to finding the question of my physical appearance quite a frustrating one. Why would anyone care what I look like? Isn't the process of being "inside" someone else's head much more interesting? A stint on the

WearTel system may be useful to exchange important information, but it wouldn't replace a tour of the company, or dinner with a loved one. Could we, then, imagine that as more people start to form links with others that allow them to "be" in each other's heads, seeing what someone else sees, our innate desire for the physical (or at least the sense of the physical) will dissipate? However, the fact remains that, as human beings, we don't want to "be" other people. We want to connect with others, find some common territory, share space in a way that is mutually meaningful. We want to "be," but not if that means we can't be ourselves.

Eventually, we will live in an interconnected cyber-environment that will confirm our tangible urge to "be" fully ourselves while relishing the possibilities of a life of communal interaction liberated from the limits of the body. However, that is a vision I will leave for later in this book. Though not without their practical applicability, clearly WearTel and the Vicarious Soliloquy are only a beginning. We cannot create in a vacuum, pretending that human society has no impact on the intent of our inventions, particularly when those inventions have already been met with both intense aversion and impassioned attraction.

I AM A CAMERA

The well-known phrase bordering on cliché states: "I am a camera." That is literally the truth where the WearComp-equipped cyborg is concerned. And yet, I am not a camera, and no technical enhancement I invent can truly turn any individual into a mere data prosthesis. English writer Christopher Isherwood, who penned the famous camera aphorism in his 1939 collection *Goodbye to Berlin*, wrote of the subjective and arbitrary nature of a human experience that nevertheless seems to endlessly repeat itself. His opening passage has lingered in my consciousness over the years:

I am a camera with its shutter open, quite passive, recording, not thinking. Recording the man shaving at the window opposite and the woman in the kimono washing her hair. Someday all this will have to be developed, carefully printed, fixed.[4]

This surreal yet somehow detached portrayal of anonymous lives recognizes the contradiction of the modern spirit, our ceaseless attempts to become what we can never be. In Isherwood's narrative, the act of fleeting memory — a "someday" that will never arrive — is juxtaposed with the act of "developing," "fixing" the instantaneous mechanical memory of the camera. The phrase "I am a camera" becomes one of ambiguity and lament, revealing the profound weakness inherent in self-awareness: a human being cannot be a camera. We cannot function as "passive, recording, not thinking." We are betrayed by that which makes us human — our inability to be the impassive chroniclers of our own fleeting precious moments. Isherwood's problem — the problem of the human machine as separate from the human spirit — is my problem, our problem, the dilemma of the human race as we stumble into the twenty-first century.

Throughout my life as an inventor, I have attempted to preserve and enhance human spirit and individuality. But I have done so through the very mechanisms that, in the last hundred years, have been such useful tools to those who would threaten our individuality, our primal sense of ourselves as autonomous human beings. And yet, as the paradox of the I-as-camera metaphor suggests, and as my own success at achieving an extension of my physical and mental capabilities through personal cybernetics confirms, we can no longer ignore Isherwood's paradigm. For our future as individuals to be assured, we must explore the contradiction that my life as a cyborg embodies.

In the twentieth century we sought ways to move from the impossibilities of the subjective I-am-a-camera — the human being as an emotional, informal, tenuous recorder of memory — to the seemingly infinite possibilities of the human being as machine, methodical chronicler of factual absolutes. I think of this transformation as a progression in which the metaphor is shifted away from the unstable "I" and toward the "eye." Thus, the history of twentieth-century technological innovation takes us away from the romantic "I am a camera" and toward the more factual "Eye is a camera." The eye is cornea, pupil, light refracting into lens. The eye is a machine. But the "I" is subjective, subconscious, shifting currents of personality and memory and society, light moving into shadows in unpredictable blurs.

However, the twentieth century has also revealed our substantive error in approaching technology as a way to control human experience. When we are all just "eyes," what will be left to see? Isherwood's observations, coming on the eve of a Nazi brutality unlike anything the world could have imagined, are all the more prescient for their positioning of the fleeting, impotent glance as the enduring strength of a fragile humanity.

And yet we cannot deny the power of the technologically inspired gaze to transform us into mere mechanisms. How, then, to reconcile technology to humanity? The answer is not to retreat to a spartan cabin in the wilderness, or to bemoan at length the fate of communities and environments flattened under the steamroller of technology. We must, instead, begin a new search for ways to bring the "eye" and the "I" together.

I started my search for this possible fusion in the 1970s when I developed a technique that causes the eye to behave as a camera, recording selected moments of the gaze for a cold technological posterity so different from the permeable shifting impossibilities of memory. I came to realize that such a personal imaging system not only takes pictures of what the eye sees, but also empowers the individual with a videographic memory prosthesis. In essence, not only does your eye function as a camera, but your "I" also becomes the camera — the "eye" and the "I" fuse together — the human brain and the camera/cybernetic extension of the eye become inextricably linked. As a result, a new kind of memory is made possible — in which the human being as a whole takes on the role and responsibility of the camera. The individual is then technologically enhanced but not freed of the responsibilities that human life entails: technology is no longer an amoral force no one can control or be held responsible for. In our society, we excuse invasive technologies as long as they are "required," no matter how ludicrous or invasive such technologies may be. However, as soon as the technologies proliferate to the general population, authorities seek to control individual use (pharmaceuticals and firearms, for example). This to me is very telling. We accept the right of a faceless invisible entity to make decisions and violate our personal space, but we do not accept the accountable human being in front of us and his or her right to use technology in similar ways. As with the hidden camera, we prefer fatalistic out-of-view inevitability to overt recognition of the realities of the situation.

At the beginning of the twenty-first century, no one is immune to the daunting, oppressive forces of "progress." At the same time, machinery and technology do not necessarily represent all that is wrong with the world. The list of benefits that technological innovation has imparted to the human race are many. These benefits, though, have required gradual realignments in our understanding of the human condition. As I have merged with the machinery I am constantly reinventing and reconsidering, my relationship to technology has become ever more complicated. This is to be expected, and is hardly a revelation. More surprising, perhaps even more fascinating, is the clear way that my relationship to the "I" — to my humanity and to the humanity of those around me — has evolved. I, too, have been in the process of reconsidering the human, not abstractly, not through studies of the forces of history, but through more than twenty years of experiments performed on my own body.

My project is not just one of shrinking circuits and ever-more-minuscule power sources. Underlying the search for technical innovation is the search for a way to re-establish the essential essence of humanity — the "I" — at a time when the mechanically enhanced "eye" sees only the functionality of a human body to be improved and enhanced. This book about the invention of the wearable computer is also, then, a book about finding a way to position the human being at the crux of technological "improvements" that can reassert freedom and individuality.

In marrying the body with the computer, we have a new approach to technology, to mechanism, and ultimately to memory and being. This approach has informed — even driven — my creation of personal cybernetics systems. Can we extend our projection and memory storage capabilities without reducing what makes us, ultimately, human? I believe we can, and have sought to do so with my inventions. I also believe that my approach, so different from current ways of thinking about technology and human interaction, can alter the shape not just of the far future but of today.

Equipped with a continuously "remembering" camera merged with the subjective gaze, the human being is saddled, at last, with the responsibility of technology. We are no longer able to deny our complicity in the project of developing hidden technological extensions of self that challenge our humanity by eliminating our longing for a "someday" when shifting, slippery memories can be instantly "developed" and "fixed" for eternity. Someday is today — the eye is a camera and I am a camera.

2

REAL INTELLIGENCE

██ common goal in the field of artificial intelligence (AI) is to
██ create "smart" machines that can replace human functions,
perhaps to the point where we will no longer be able to do things for ourselves. AI includes everything from rooms that automatically adjust
their environment according to human
presence — illumination, temperature
control, etc. — to cars that drive themselves, to toilets that flush automatically
once they "see" that you have finished. I
have always been a skeptic when it comes
to artificial intelligence. Technology critic
Natalie Jeremijenko notes that "When we
started calling things smart, smart cards,

The "smart" sensor above this urinal
lets it know when it's time to flush.

smart buildings, smart everything, we started referring to ourselves as dummies. Simultaneously, that yellow series of Books for Dummies appeared: *Quicken for Dummies*, *The Web for Dummies*, *Personal Finance for Dummies*."[1] Her argument is similar to my own: What we need are not technologies that predict and replace human activity, but systems and technologies that expand and enhance human possibility.

With AI, we devise gadgets that can replace human interaction with "smart" instantaneous pre-programmed interaction. We are robbed, then, of our ability to interact and respond to the decisions technology makes about what we want. I believe that we need another model with which to approach the project of technologically enhanced human capacity: humanistic intelligence (HI). Under the HI model, the users of a given apparatus can take control any time they wish. The technology is responsive to the users — we shape the computer's behaviour, as opposed to the computer causing us to shape our activities to correspond to its pre-programmed assumptions. Do we want to wake up to a world where only the computer knows how to drive the bus? Suppose we wake up to find that central navigation has gone awry and the bus is hurtling the wrong way down a one-way street, but we have long since forgotten how to drive? We are passive, unable to get the computer to respond to the situation. Rather than "smart rooms," "smart cars," "smart toilets," etc., I would like to put forward the notion of "smart people."

In an HI framework, the goal is to enhance the intelligence of the human race, not just its tools. "Smart people" means, simply, that we should rely on human intelligence in our development of technological infrastructure rather than attempt to take the human being out of the equation. An important goal of HI is to take a first step toward a foremost principle of the Enlightenment, that of the dignity of the individual. This is accomplished, metaphorically and actually, through a prosthetic transformation of the body into a sovereign space, in effect allowing each and every one of us to control the environment that surrounds us. This process has little or nothing to do with subsuming perfectly functional technologies — such as writing with a pencil on paper — into more complex, less adaptable technologies.

Rather than trying to emulate human intelligence, a humanistic framework for computing recognizes that the human brain is perhaps the best neural network of its kind, and that there are many new applications within the domain of personal technologies that can make use of this excellent, but often overlooked, processor. This might not sound like such a radical idea, but if you look at the fundamental direction that research in robotics, artificial intelligence, and even wearable technology has taken over the last fifty years, you'll find it is in opposition to the idea of working *with* the human brain. The goal, it seems, has been to replace the human, as opposed to enhancing or empowering it. The robotics expert Hans Moravec, for instance, writes of eagerly looking forward to the inevitable day when the computer will perform the estimated ten trillion calculations per second that will finally allow a processor to operate at brain speed.[2] But with HI, devices are not merely intelligent signal processors a person might use to replace his or her own ability to think. Instead, devices function by turning the user into part of an intelligent control system. One of the founding principles of developing technology under the HI system is that the user must be an integral part of the discourse loop. The wearable computer allows for new ways to be, not just do.

We often hear about certain countries or areas being more "advanced" societies because they use more cellphones or because they pay for things with smart cards or chip implants, but if we are to accept such reasoning we have to say that there are communities of dogs, pigs, and cattle that are more advanced than us because they have microchip implants, electronic tags and genetically engineered attributes that allow them to carry out "transactions" automatically. Thus we must ask the question: Does being a user of technology make one a more advanced being? In other words, does simply using a technology cause a person to be more advanced? Perhaps pigs or cattle are more advanced than some communities because they are "being digital" (being branded, having digits branded onto their bodies).

A humanistic intelligence approach is to develop technology that doesn't simply turn us into technologically "advanced" cattle, but rather maintains and enhances the essential element of human existence — our autonomy. Keeping that in mind, here are three attributes that set the WearComp system apart from today's array of "smart" competitors:

CONSTANCY: The computer runs continuously, and is "always ready" to interact with the user. Unlike a laptop computer or handheld personal digital assistant, it does not need to be opened up and turned on prior to use. The signal flow from human to computer, and computer to human, runs continuously to provide a constant user interface.

AUGMENTATION: Traditional computing paradigms are based on the notion that computing is the primary task. Wearable computing, however, is based on the notion that computing is *not* the primary task. Wearable computing assumes that the user will be doing something else at the same time as doing the computing. Thus the computer augments both the intellect and the senses.

MEDIATION: Unlike hand-held devices, laptop computers and PDAs, the wearable computer can encapsulate us. It doesn't necessarily need to completely enclose us, but the concept allows for a greater degree of enclosure in an individually created system than traditional portable computers. There are two aspects to this encapsulation. The first is solitude: The wearable can function as an information filter and allow us to block out material we might not wish to experience, whether we wish to avoid offensive advertising or simply desire to replace existing media with different media. In less severe manifestations, it may simply allow us to alter our perception of reality in a very mild sort of way. The second aspect is privacy:

Mediation allows us to block or modify information entering or leaving our encapsulated space. In the same way that ordinary clothing prevents others from seeing our naked bodies, the wearable computer may, for example, serve as an intermediary for interacting with untrusted systems, such as third-party digital anonymous cash "cyberwallets."

Constancy, augmentation and mediation are the main attributes of the wearable computer, giving rise to a lengthy list of possibilities when it comes to establishing how the cyborg actually functions in everyday society. If you were to visit a wearable computer showroom and were accosted by a gentleman in a plaid sports jacket who assured you that he "uses one himself," you might leave with a brochure that highlights the following features:

UNRESTRICTIVE TO THE USER: It is ambulatory, mobile, roving, "you can do other things while using it"(for example, type while jogging, etc.).

NON-MONOPOLIZING OF THE USER'S ATTENTION: It does not cut you off from the outside world like a virtual reality game. You can attend to other matters while using the apparatus. It is built with the assumption that computing will be a secondary activity rather than a primary focus of attention. In fact, ideally it will provide enhanced sensory capabilities. It may, however, mediate (augment, alter, or deliberately diminish) the sensory capabilities.

OBSERVABLE BY THE USER: It can get your attention continuously if you want it to. The output medium is constantly perceptible to the wearer.

CONTROLLABLE BY THE USER: Responsive. You can grab control of it at any time you wish. Even in automated processes you can manually override to break open the control loop.

ATTENTIVE TO THE ENVIRONMENT: It is environmentally aware, multi-modal, multi-sensory (as a result, this ultimately gives the user increased situational awareness).

COMMUNICATIVE TO OTHERS: It can be used as a communication medium, individually or on a mass basis, as per direction of the user.

EXPRESSIVE: Allows the wearer to be expressive through the medium, whether as a direct communication medium to others or as means of assisting the production of expressive media (artistic or otherwise).

This may seem like an abstract list of the properties of an abstract system. Nonetheless, this list lies at the heart of what I believe technology should and could do for us. In the past, technology has seemed to act on our lives sporadically, passively, in fixed spaces (such as offices), and in secret. The WearComp system seeks to allow for a different relationship between technology and the individual. The features of this relationship include constancy, interactivity, mobility, and protection from secret violations of our physical and mental space. These are not just features on a gadget, but principles — even rights — that will take on ever-greater significance in the coming age. The wearable computer can then be understood as a crucial beginning to a new phase of technological development that not only extends human senses but, more importantly, allows us, the (post) human beings, the cyborg Luddites, to reassert our autonomy over technology wherever and whenever we choose.

THE SOFTWARE VIRUS

I reject operating systems such as Microsoft Windows and the software developed for it. Here is a perfect example of a system designed to function independently of us. We do not need to know how it works, we only need to apply our needs to its functions. But what happens when something goes wrong? Our total ignorance means we cannot sharpen our own pencil. There is a gap in what should be a closed loop. Microsoft allows us to operate only on the principle of a straight line: either the computer tells us what to do, or we tell it what to do. Our intelligence and understanding — our being — are not enhanced by this system. If you want to change Windows to operate in a fundamentally different way, you cannot. When our pencil snaps, we must hire someone to come and sharpen it for us. Though we might easily acquire the knowledge to make our own repairs and improvements, we are only permitted to function in the way the Microsoft system wants us to. We are trapped in a "desktop prison."

Essentially, such software should be thought of as a kind of virus. I use the term *virus* to denote systems (hardware, software, etc.) in which there is deliberate obfuscation of the true functionality in order to keep certain aspects of the system hidden from the end user. In the case of computer programs, this might comprise an executable computer program that comes with neither the program source code (the human-readable form of the program instructions) nor an open disclosure of everything the program does or may do. Basically, a software virus comes in a form that encourages us to "trust me, run this executable program." For the purposes of the humanistic intelligence framework, a virus can be defined as hardware or software that may have hidden functionality, that does something the user does not know about or cannot confirm (such as software that, upon installation, automatically sends information to the parent company about the buyer). In the software business, this kind of hidden functionality is regularly implanted, and it is known not as a virus but as a Trojan Horse. (A term that, nevertheless, acknowledges the subterfuge involved.) However, to the extent that wearable technology ideally functions as a part of the individual (and has the potential to change the way the individual "is"), I find myself using more virulent language than the software industry typically employs. After all, a viral wearable computer — one that contains software performing functions unknown to the primary user — directly affects the individual's self-determination and mastery over his or her own destiny. Pervasive systems such Windows are also viruses, based on the way they spread. A friend creates a document in Microsoft Word and sends it to you; you then need to buy Word to open the document, and so you need to buy Windows to run Word, hence the virus has spread to you. Now you start learning Word and you create documents in Word and send them to your friends so you then become a "carrier" of the disease.

It takes some effort to learn how to read and write, to learn basic mathematics, and to master various trades that might, for example, involve learning how to use specialized machinery. Why should a computer be any different? Various companies sell a "user-friendly" vision of computers — a computing environment in which the user doesn't need to think. We could advocate the same approach to learning how to read and write. Instead of literacy, we could simply have talking signs everywhere and multimedia televised bookware. The Internet could replace television, and books as well. If everyone wore a "user-friendly" computer, the computer could even read signs to us, so we'd never have to learn how to read. Just point and click! Unless you're a software "developer." There's something seriously wrong with this vision. It hearkens back to the Middle Ages, a time when only a few elite individuals had the ability to read and write and the vast majority were kept illiterate. It has been argued that the consumer is better off "protected" from having to learn even the basics of computer programming. This, of course, is the self-serving argument of software monopolists. Perhaps it is true that many of us don't wish to learn detailed new skill sets simply to function in everyday life. But, then again, if we are not given the option to learn and contribute, if, indeed, we are prevented from viewing how most of our programs work, the argument that this is done for our own benefit seems dubious at best. Why not plant the seeds for everyone to contribute to humankind's knowledge? The distinction between "developer" and "end user" needs to be redefined. We should be encouraged to learn and understand how computers work, and we should be allowed to modify and adjust software and hardware according to the needs of both ourselves and our particular communities.

This process should begin early. When our public primary schools adopt proprietary "user-friendly" computers tied to particular commercial vendors, we tie our children's education to commercial proprietary standards. Imagine that instead of teaching children how to read and write we taught them only how to understand the world through some specific brand of language interpreter, in which the language would change over time, so that those taught this system would become dependent on commercially sold updates. In some ways this is like a drug dependency — we desperately need it to function, and we have no control over the supply or the content. (This could also be compared to large multinationals that sell farmers "suicide seeds" that can only be used once, forcing farmers to buy new seeds every year and turning them all into serfs enslaved to proprietary technology.) In the coming era of personal cybernetics, we will need to learn a new set of basic skills. If all we learn is how to put on our "user-friendly" eyeglasses, preloaded with advertisements, and multimedia spectacles, we may simply become addicted to a mind-numbing thought-free existence. This is an existence in which we will be prevented from asserting our right to personalize and conceptualize our own relationship to technology. In the future, we should all be thoughtware developers (without having to buy a thoughtware kit).

It's not that everyone must be able to do their own programming and fix their own computers, but that, in a humanistic intelligence framework, everybody should have the option to modify their own programming and tinker with their own hardware if they wish to do so. This should be as fundamental and sensible a right as the right to renovate our own house as we see fit. "More advanced" should mean understanding and controlling how our systems work. We should define computer literacy as understanding source code and how the kernel works, not simply being a user of computers. Pigs and cattle are users of computers, they have a "user-friendly" interface to the various electronically controlled feedlots that fatten them before the slaughter. Does this mean that pigs and cattle are computer literate? We should distinguish between "livestock literacy" and a more meaningful operational literacy. With most software today, we cannot modify operations, even if we are willing to study the programming and learn how. This is an example of a dumb "smart system" that benefits the technology (or the corporatology) more than the end user. It is a system of technological hierarchy that is smart for the small handful of software moguls, because it ensures that the vast majority of human beings remain dumb to the possibilities of the system.

There are alternatives to Microsoft's domination, in particular the open-ended GNU/Linux operating system in which programming can be free and improvements and new applications can be made by anyone who wishes to do so. Of course, operating systems such as Linux and its applications (including WearComp) are not designed to work on the flick of a switch. Devices embodying HI often require that the user learn a new skill set, and are therefore not necessarily easy to adapt to. Just as it takes a young child many years to become proficient at using his or her hands, some of the devices that embody humanistic intelligence have taken years of use before they began to truly behave as if they were natural extensions of the mind and senses. In terms of human-computer interaction, my goal is not just to construct a device that can model (and learn from) the user, but, more importantly, to construct a device in which the user is given the opportunity to learn from the device.

In the coming decades, we will live in an age of shared realities and new levels of cultural discourse. No longer confined to our role as passive participants in a ratings shell game, culture will be freed from the constraints of commerce and entirely new paradigms exploring the relationship of art and entertainment and employment and daily life will manifest themselves, challenging many of the ways of being we currently take for granted. But the move toward a human-friendly technology that, first and foremost, connects and joins communities and individuals (as opposed to disconnecting and alienating) will not be a simple one. My experience has shown me that even far less complicated technological advances carry unexpected consequences and force us to reassess our assumptions about how a technology will be used and what it will be used for. We must constantly reassess the effects of communication technology on our capacity to "be ourselves," even as we strive to establish methodologies that can navigate the ever-shifting eddies of innovation.

SAFEGUARDING OUR HUMANISTIC PROPERTY

Just as we protect our intellectual property — both foolishly and fairly, depending on circumstances and personal opinions — we must also begin to think about protecting our humanistic property. Humanistic property is the mental space that surrounds us, that we occupy and thus own. It is what we see, what we hear, what enters our senses. Formerly, it has been free for others to steal. However, one of the things that WearComp does is begin to safeguard this humanistic property, essentially the right to think free of distraction and obstruction. In concrete terms, this means, for instance, that in the future individuals will decide what advertisements they would like to see or not see. This is done using one of the applications of the WearComp system, something I call the Visual Memory Prosthetic. In this function, visual information — what I see — is temporarily recorded in a memory buffer. This allows me to then instruct the computer to block out all images of that nature in the future. WearComp's Visual Memory Prosthesis can help us forget or not see at all, as well as remember and enhance vision. It can, effectively, filter out unwanted visual detritus through the EyeTap. The technical process by which this is done is relatively simple: I can take an electronic snapshot of an ad and tell my computer to block that ad from my vision in the future. Or, I can generalize, telling the computer not to show me visuals that contain certain words, images or shapes. In this way, I can set my programming to delete any advertisements for cars, cleaning products, or condoms — any of certain selected advertisements placed into a kill file. If I prefer, I can use the WearComp system simply to eliminate all specified billboard advertisements from my vision. Of course, the less specific one gets, the more difficult it is to present the proper set of instructions to the computer. However, when a greater community of WearComp users begins to share programming and kill files, the project of removing ads from everyday experience will be much less time consuming. I simply will not "see" them; they will not enter my consciousness and take up space in my mind. I do not believe this will lead to the end of advertising, just to the end of *unwanted* advertising — the end of theft of our visual attention, our humanistic property.

There are other aspects of the memory application: If something atypical happens, sensors pick up the sudden change in the user's heart rate and the video record of the event will be pulled from the buffer into permanent storage. This represents an advance in the relationship between human and machine. In the Visual Memory Prosthetic, your brain is using the machine as a second brain, and the machine is using your brain as a second central processing unit (CPU). It's a two-way street. My machine modifies me and I modify it. This is a collaborative model that allows the human being to be "smarter" through the computer, but does not itself endow the computer with any replacement technologies: I do not necessarily count on the computer to remember everything for me; I do not *replace* human memory with computer memory.

I personally use the Visual Memory Prosthetic as an artist's sketch pad of sorts, useful for taking down visual "notes" and helping me overcome my visual memory deficiency. By supplementing part of the brain with computer memory accessible on the Internet, there is no reason why one should ever need to forget what someone looks like. And, of course, with biosensors we can extend memory even beyond matters of simple recall — we can ensure that memories of significant events of our lives are permanently fixed. By applying the HI framework to memory and emotional state, the wearable computer will bring out the best in both human and machine and, in the future, have applications that might include alleviating the impact of diseases that cause gradual memory loss.

Memory is fragile and temporary, and this is part of the tragic beauty of human life. We cannot replace memory with a Visual Memory Prosthetic. We can complement memory, and empower ourselves to have a record of important moments, the same way we take snapshots at graduations, weddings, and reunions. All I'm suggesting here is that we extend memory, not by negating it (selling it, replacing it, forgetting it) but by complementing it. To delve deeper into the implications of the Visual Memory Prosthetic and the HI philosophy applied to its development is to argue that the central human function of memory is not challenged by this process, though it is augmented, mediated, or made smarter. Which is to say that there are basic human experiences that should never be renegotiated — our inalienable right to have and preserve our own memories (whether through snapshots or any kind of memory prosthesis) is certainly one of them. At the same time, we must remember that what comprises memory should not be considered immutable — a new way to remember promises a new way to think, leading to new ways of "being."

CYBORG COUNTERPOINT

Wired magazine once described my work as "a counterpoint to the military-industrial complex." The article suggested that my approach was in contrast to the majority of more recent developments in the wearables field, which, not surprisingly, have occurred at the behest of large multinationals, often funded by armies and governments. Again, we return to the crossroads that humanity faces as we embark on our journey toward the post-human age. Though I am far from the only person to have recognized the utility of the wearable computer and set about developing such a system, the goal to develop a wearable system designed to empower, not conquer, is not always as evident within the "military-industrial complex." The vision of many of those developers working for some of our biggest and most powerful government and corporate institutions is in contrast to my original attempts to personalize and humanize technology. Which road will we go down? The road on which wearable computers create and foster independence and community interaction? Or the road on which wearable computers become part of the apparatus of electronic control we are ever more subject to and unaware of?

Moving parallel to my inventions — in the opposite direction — has been the steady development of invasive systems that reduce human personal space. Hidden cameras monitoring us on our streets and sidewalks, in our schools and stores, in our pools and fitting rooms; extensive databases collecting our addresses and interests; advertisements plastered on everything from the sides of houses to screen-savers to buses to garbage cans are just the visible elements of what amounts to a sustained attack on human individuality. We must also face the encroachments that misapplied wearable technologies will soon bring to the fore, everything from implanted chips that monitor whereabouts (ostensibly for criminals on parole) to advanced eavesdropping devices that will be able to analyze brain wave patterns and ferret out false statements. To put it simply, the environment we live in today allows us neither physical privacy nor mental solitude. Margaret Morse warns in *Virtualities* that

If the future promises to be an "augmented" reality, an animistic, artificial world supported by ubiquitous computing in which the material and virtual are distributed indeterminately in mixed environments and in which we interact with undecidably human and/or machine agents in what only appears to be "real time," and in which virtual space itself is a surveillance agent, then this will be a world that television has prepared for us by pretending to be talking *to you*.[3]

This strongly worded caution reminds us that a society already steeped in the familiarity and virtuosity of technology is far closer to blindly accepting limiting and potentially dangerous wearable computers. The television, long our "friend," long an ally in the corporate battle to penetrate our homes and minds, may well be just the precursor to more dramatic interventions into our personal space and every waking moment. While I have sought ways to filter out the mental garbage that distracts and dehumanizes us, the bulk of technological innovations in general and in the wearable computing field in particular have sought ways to increase that uncontrollable flow of "information" into our minds and lives. This "accidental" information flow, with its pseudo-interactivity and pretend chumminess (the television talking especially to you), leaves us vulnerable to the even more intrusive penetrations into our personal space that the wearable computer age could bring. So, it is with considerable urgency that I continue to explore ways in which technology can be used as a means to counter repression and enhance freedom.

ENGWEAR: CYBORG FOR SALE

The struggle for human freedom today is not about access to goods and products. It is, rather, about access to information, essentially the ability to communicate with each other. The wearable computer is useful only inasmuch as it allows us to reclaim our right to both private communication between individuals and to mass communication between the individual and the community. As we become more and more reliant on information that a select few own and control — whether it be information on the damage our town's factory is doing to our river or our next door neighbour's candidacy for mayor of the city we live in — we become increasingly vulnerable to oppression. The wearable computer's capacity to instantly disseminate information while preventing spurious invasions in the form of propaganda and surveillance is a tonic for an increasingly divisive, secretive age.

The common approach to wearables today is to build what I think of as smart uniforms — computerized uniforms meant to enhance the doing of a certain task, often at the expense of personal liberty. The smart uniform may allow the soldier of the future to access instantaneous information about enemy movements and capabilities, but it will also surely have a mechanism that prevents defection or treason and limits access to alternative reports about the conflict at hand.

Clearly, it would be naive of me to assert that WearComp will turn back this tide and alter the history of the twentieth century (a curious epoch in which individual freedom was seemingly prized above all other values, even as it was reduced and relegated at every turn). There has always been a dark side to wearable devices. Simple examples of wearable technology that enslave rather than liberate the individual include handcuffs, leg irons, and any other implements that the individual wears but does not have control over. More recently, the beeper, the cellular phone, the PalmPilot — all these innovations can be viewed not just in terms of their liberating possibilities, but also in terms of their capacity to reduce freedom. So, too, might the wearable computer be misused and become part of the apparatus of control.

In an age that equips possibly corrupt armies, police forces, secret services, and commercial corporations with further extensions of their ability to limit and possibly violate our freedoms, can we afford not to move forward with technology like WearComp? As a non-violent deterrent to control and repression, I welcome efforts to commercialize general-use wearable computers. Just as the Internet has provided us with unprecedented opportunities to communicate with each other and counter official mediations of reality, WearComp will extend our communicative capabilities, allowing us another defence from those who would hoard knowledge for profit or power.

One of my long-term goals has always been to make the wearable computer design available on the mass market. I hope to sell some form of the WearComp system on the open market in years to come. At the same time, I constantly ask myself: Will we truly be better off when the WearComp system is commercially available?

Only open and free access to technology can advance the cause of individual freedom. Only by ensuring the widespread proliferation of technologies do we, if nothing else, ameliorate their impact by making them available to as many people as possible. We cannot go back. Too much of our living (collectively and individually) takes place in technologically mediated spaces (such as television and the Internet and even the high-rise office tower, not to mention the coming "smart" buildings currently in development) over which we have only nominal control. We must go forward. The WearComp system will allow us to reclaim and develop these spaces. It is only when we all have equal access to information creation technologies that we can be free of the power of invasive technologies currently occupying all aspects of our lives.

One example of a WearComp application that could allow the individual to reclaim communal information space is what I call the ENGwear system (Electronic News Gathering wearable system). This is a wearable videographic system for use by reporters and news agencies worldwide that will allow for real-time broadcast and reporting in a variety of media. Perhaps more importantly, ENGwear will also allow individuals and smaller groups to broadcast instantaneously across the world. The implications of creating a level playing field in the broadcast medium of television will be enormous. I will discuss these implications at a later point in the book, but for now it is sufficient to note that with ENGwear, for the first time since the invention of long-distance communication technology, from the telegraph to the telephone to the television, there will be the potential for the individual to have more control over communication technology than the corporation and the government.

In accessing this control, will we take another step away from what is understood as quintessentially human, face-to-face, communication? Again, we must decide in which direction we will travel. The broadcast cyborg communicates in a different way than the human being. Perhaps the cyborg, outfitted to broadcast twenty-four hours a day, is an incarnation of the desire for community and connectivity? It is also possible, however, that the broadcasting cyborg is post-human in a way that reduces and negates the capacity for individual human contact; just as McLuhan postulated, the medium becomes the message: when we adjust our physiology to create a broadcast-friendly being, are we also adjusting what we will be able to broadcast, what we are capable of communicating?

RESEARCHING THE CYBORG

Ordinarily, when engaged in research, students and employees (the roles are blurred in the corporate-university system) sit in front of university-owned computer consoles and use software provided by the university or corporation — software in a computing environment maintained by a central information services department. However, in my case, I was my own personal computer, my own system administrator, and my own research lab. As a Ph.D. student at the Massachusetts Institute of Technology, rather than use the laboratories, my experiments took place in and comprised aspects of my own real life. I was a voltmeter and I was also an oscilloscope. A probe hanging from my clothing allowed me to monitor voltages of signals and store these quantities on my clothing-based computer. Instead of using one of the lab voltmeters like the other students, who would read the voltages and copy these numbers onto a sheet of paper for later entry into university-owned computers, I simply read the voltage into my "body." In this way I never had to copy down the numbers onto scrap paper and retype them later.

By subverting the traditional system of research, I was implicitly challenging the right of the institution to own my work. In an age when almost all research funding in technology at the university level comes from corporations who expect a share of the pie when something marketable comes about, my tendency to work both within and outside the university structure was a serious challenge to a system that, today, is ingrained and perpetuated at universities across the world, despite its serious flaws. We live in an age when students can be jailed by their alma mater for attempting to claim ownership over their own discoveries. In his book *Owning the Future*, Seth Shulman discusses, for instance, the case of researcher Petr Taborsky, who was arrested and convicted of theft in a dispute with the University of Florida over a patent on a new kind of kitty litter. Concludes Shulman:

> Long viewed as fertile havens for nurturing and cross-pollinating ideas that would be profitable only in future generations, the nation's research universities have come to be seen by corporate sponsors as tempting orchards of unclaimed conceptual fruit for the picking. This . . . gravely erodes the conceptual commons and impoverishes the university's fundamental educational mission.[4]

In 1997, U.S. companies spent $1.7 billion on university-based science and engineering research. If your work hasn't already been pre-sold to corporate sponsors, there's always the Bayh-Dole bill, passed in 1980, which gives educational institutions in the United States ownership of inventions created with federal funds. Even in Canada, once a bastion of public higher education, the trend is toward corporate-directed research. As a *Globe and Mail* report states: "More and more researchers are combining publicly funded academic work with the drive to profit from their discoveries or do contract work for large . . . companies."5

The struggle between for-profit research and individual experimentation is in keeping with the legacy of the history of cyborgs and cybernetics, which has always grappled with two similarly contrasting visions — that of the possibilities of human freedom in the cyborg age versus the corporate/institutional approach to developing the computerized "smart" uniform. When I first arrived at MIT, many people were engaged in research on the ubiquitous "smart room" concept, essentially designing interiors that would automatically react to our needs. The by now familiar concept is one in which sensors, cameras, and microphones respond to our physical requirements — if we are hot, the room is cooled; if it gets dark, the lights come on; if we suffer a heart attack and collapse on the carpet, an ambulance is summoned.

The smart room is a retrograde concept that empowers the structure over the individual, imbuing our houses, streets, and public spaces with the right to constantly observe and monitor us for the purported benefit of ensuring we are never uncomfortable or forced to get up from the armchair to switch on a lamp. Is it any wonder that I first encountered hostility with regard to the direction my research was to take? The very essence of my research was antithetical to the corporate-approved smart room concept. WearComp contests the utility of ubiquitous computing, forcing us to reconsider the current research trend toward cameras and microphones everywhere in the environment watching and listening to us in order to be "helpful." Indeed, part of my motivation for furthering my WearComp invention has always been my revulsion at the "intelligent butler" (smart room) model, built on top of a ubiquitous surveillance network. My opposite approach clashed dramatically with MIT's research thrust — a corporate-directed set of priorities that privileges things over people. I don't reject all work done on smart objects. I simply believe there must be a compromise between what we wear and what we rely on the environment to provide. Countless theorists — from scientists to science fiction writers — have recognized the inevitability of computers being integrated into everyday life while fearing the position of the human being in the feedback loop of an automated society. There are and will continue to be certain tasks or capabilities better served by wearable technology than environmental technology, and vice versa. I like to think that personally relevant "light current" (information, etc.) will be more in the wearable spirit, while infrastructural, non-personal "heavy current" (electricity for lighting the environment, charging batteries, etc., as well as general non-person-specific information) will be more in the environmental spirit. This suggests "smart" materials for personal information should be situated on the body and "dumb" materials (infrastructure in its most raw form) in the environment. This "smart people/dumb environment" paradigm offers an alternative to "smart rooms" and other environmental intelligence-gathering infrastructure. Moreover, the "smart people/dumb environment" framework solves privacy issues, as well as customization and user-preference issues, by allowing each individual to "own" his or her personal "bits" and set forth and customize a personal protocol for interacting with the world. A simple example is that of heating and cooling controls and other such matters that have recently become the domain of "smart buildings" and intelligent occupancy sensors. A "dumb" building that merely "obeyed" commands wirelessly sent from the occupant (for example, "I'd like light turned on now," or "I'm too cold") would be far less invasive in terms of the privacy of the occupant and would not need to second-guess the occupant's true internal physical or preferential state or know the occupant's identity.

AI REVISITED: TOWARD THE FLESH MACHINE

The obsession with smart things as opposed to smart people is hardly a new one, of course. Since the beginning of modern research, the quest has been not to empower humans by extending their individual and connective capacities, but rather to replicate humans or, failing that, to harness humans. The research emphasis on robotics and artificial intelligence seems to be a "natural" progression — the culmination of an industrial revolution that has always put stuff before life. Artificial Intelligence (AI) was the moniker given to the effort, spearheaded in 1956 by soon-to-be MIT professors John McCarthy and Marvin Minsky, to make computers think. Explains robotics professor Hans Moravec: "Traditional artificial intelligence attempts to copy the conscious mental processes of human beings doing particular tasks."6 Critic O.B. Hardison, Jr., puts it a little more cautiously: "AI is the investigation of ways in which computers can be coaxed to emulate what would be considered intelligent behaviour in humans."7 *Mind Children* author Moravec goes on to posit that what we need to "take advantage" of human mobility and computer calculating power is a "high-tech" wardrobe that will eventually lead to the conscious computer.8 Note the move from a cyborg concept that could allow the human to explore new ways of being, to a computer creature that could simply replace the human being as the more perfect citizen of the police state. These are the defence department and company-sponsored thinkers at the frontline of robotics who, in their enthusiasm for creating robot servants to do our bidding, utterly fail to encompass the future of human possibility that sees the cyborg as an end, not a means by which humanity can be bypassed or enslaved.

Computers have yet to be endowed with the common-sense ability to think. Robotics reached a peak and is now in a downward spiral, perpetually unable to solve the problem of consciousness. Thus attention is being turned toward other ways in which docile populations of easily controlled workers might be attained. These ways centre around the smart stuff concept of which many at MIT were — and still are — so enamoured. Smart rooms may have become smart uniforms, but the end result is the same. As the radical New York–based Critical Arts Ensemble hyperbolically puts it, "the body is on the verge of being placed under new management, and like all exterior cultural phenomenon, it will be to function instrumentally so that it may better fulfill the imperatives of pancapitalism (production, consumption, and order)."[9]

What was at first an emphasis on AI and robotics has turned into an emphasis on wearable/implantable technologies. The Critical Arts Ensemble, at the farthest nexus of paranoia, apocalyptically call this transformation The Flesh Machine. They write:

> The Flesh Machine is a heavily funded liquid network of scientific and medical institutions with knowledge specializations in genetics, cell biology, biochemistry, human reproduction, neurology, pharmacology, etc., combined with nomadic technocracies of interior vision and surgical development . . . It has two primary mandates — to completely invade the flesh with vision and mapping technologies . . . and to develop the political and economic frontiers of flesh products and services.[10]

Would I put it quite that way? Probably not. Nonetheless, I see the Critical Arts Ensemble's point. The shift of attention away from AI and robotics and toward "the flesh" can be frightening and potentially devastating. We react to this shift with a fear that is quite understandable given our seemingly limited range of options and perspectives. In his political history of the space age, Walter A. McDougall argues: "We want to believe that we can subsume our individualism into the rationality of systems yet retain our humanity still."[11] Technology, no longer something developed by the beneficent government in a big lab to help win wars against fascist despots, is in the home and in everyday life. The flesh is under threat. Rational systems pervade. Our humanity is threatened. But what is the true nature of the threat? Who is being threatened, and how? One of the fascinating aspects of technology in society is that it creates an undercurrent of unease, though the precise fears of the society are hard to articulate or pinpoint. Thus, it's helpful to talk not just vaguely about our fears, but to address specific concerns related to specific technologies. For instance, in the wearable computer model generally promoted by governments and organizations, the project is to create smart uniforms to "assist" in the accomplishing of specific tasks. This is, and will continue to be, a source of anxiety in society. Will we soon be required to wear computers at work? If so, do we get to take them off for lunch? What if we need to go to the bathroom? How is our autonomy threatened? How will our minds be invaded?

CYBERNETICS: INVENTING THE CYBORG

The unease most of us feel in regard to technology has its roots in early speculative writings dealing with computers and their integration into society. In 1948, the mathematician Norbert Wiener developed a new theory of information and the way it interacts. He published a book about this theory and called it *Cybernetics*, from the Greek word *kubernetes*, meaning "steersman." He defined cybernetics quite simply as the "study of messages as a means of controlling machinery and society."[12]

What Wiener basically did was give a name to the feedback or closed loop by which information is processed in the human being and in the computer. Which is to say that our brain-body functions are cybernetic in their operation. They are self-regulating and feedback is the means by which a body regulates itself. Similarly, the computer functions cybernetically, with information entering, responses to that information exiting, and information feeding back as a result of what has occurred. Wiener used the process of reaching out and picking up a pencil as an illustration of cybernetic behaviour, although his actual theories on the application of cybernetics were far less prosaic. In fact, Wiener was interested in how the computer would be introduced into society and what kind of feedback loop would arise from the process. He speculated that we would want our computers to be smart, but not too smart, making an analogy to a Roman slave owner and his Greek slave. The slaveholder wants an intelligent but subservient slave. Alas, Wiener wryly notes, "complete subservience and complete intelligence do not go together."[13]

The work of Norbert Wiener allowed for a new understanding of information processing and put forth the intriguing idea that the human being would, in the future, exist in tandem with the computer as a single cybernetic system. Then, in 1960, at a time when the U.S. space race with the USSR was well underway, two American visionaries, Manfred E. Clynes and Nathan S. Kline, riffed off the idea of cybernetic systems to coin another related word that would spawn an entirely new way of thinking about human/computer interaction. In the typically inscrutable language of the scientist, they wrote: "For the exogenously extended organizational complex functioning as an integrated homeostatic system unconsciously, we propose the term 'cyborg.'" Cyborg, not incidentally, came from a merging of the terms *cybernetic* and *organism*. Inspired by a NASA conference on the possibility of humans living in space, and then published in the space travel magazine *Astronautics*, the duo's article "Cyborgs and Space" essentially hypothesized that human beings would have to be physically/chemically altered if space exploration was ever to be successful. In essence, they were arguing that humans could become part of a cybernetic loop that would function unconsciously to extend certain predetermined processes. Kline and Clynes showed none of Wiener's skepticism. They spoke of the cyborg having "robot-like problems . . . taken care of automatically and unconsciously," thus "leaving man free to explore, to create, to think and to feel."[14]

And so, two words, two radical concepts, gave birth to today's struggle to incarnate and determine the nature of the cyborg age. Now, at the beginning of the twenty-first century, we must try to realize the vision made abstractly possible by the cybernetic concept and made tangible by the hypothesis of Kline and Clynes. But the two concepts — however much dependent on each other — also represent a contradiction that continues to haunt cyborg reality. From the outset, the cyborg was imbued with contrary ambiguity — boundless optimism about the possibilities of human freedom versus caution and even despair over the extent to which technology under the auspices of corporate control could alter human life. Today, we see this polarization repeatedly, from *The Six Million Dollar Man* to *The Terminator*; from a horrific vision of a totalitarian corporate Flesh Machine to Donna Harraway's muted optimism that "Cybernetics is all about feedback loops and adjustments; we don't know what social and political potential humans have when they are (arguably) freed from the more insidious interpolations of identity, gender and one-way representation."[15]

The astonishing speed with which the cyborg has gone from imaginary utopian space traveller to earthbound entity fraught with the contradictions of everyday life testifies to the urgent need to address what lies between enthusiasm and skepticism, totalitarianism and anarchy. As a cyborg, I stand in the ebbing current between freedom and entrapment, adapting and applying the histories of the cybernetic/cyborg discourse to a paradigm of invention I hope will make good on the Clynes/Kline promise even as it addresses the uncertainty of Norbert Wiener. However, the path to developing a cyborg future that bridges Wiener's sly understanding of technological entrapment and Clynes/Kline's fantasy optimism isn't as apparent as it may seem. A promising direction can easily become a dead end.

A BRIEF HISTORY OF THE WEARABLE COMPUTER

Naturally, I'm not the only inventor who has worked in this field, nor am I the only thinker to wrestle with the problem of expanding the feedback loop in a way that will redefine rather than obliterate human participation. There are those who argue that wearable computing has been around since the beginning of time, whether in the form of the wristwatch (which computes time), or eyeglasses (which mediate visual perception of reality with optical computing, no less!). Is a slide rule or a pocket calculator a wearable computer? After all, they perform computations, and can be worn in a shirt pocket. Is a one-transistor timing circuit a wearable computer? Is a pocket radio from the 1950s a wearable computer? It had timing circuits, as well as multipliers (superhet mixer) and adders. It was definitely wearable, and it could even be used while being worn. Even before the important terminology of cybernetics and cyborgs was established, work was being done on portable technologies, some of which we might loosely define as wearable computers. Of course, all this simply underscores the difficulty of exploring the history of the development of the wearable computer. Though today there are hundreds of start-ups, established corporations, university labs, and government-funded experiments, all working on designing wearable computers of various utilities and sizes, the past reveals that confusions of intent, purpose, and utility have always been apparent in the development of personal cybernetic systems. Accordingly, though we might talk about a history of the wearable computer, it is just as meaningful to talk about the history of personal technologies in general, many of which have allowed far more spontaneity and exploration of the interconnections between society and community than do today's "smart" suits imbued with limited use and function and developed with motives contrary to a humanistic philosophy.

At MIT, Ed Thorp and Claude Shannon invented a wearable timing device as early as 1961. Although not a computer, it was an example of the direction in which wearable technology would move. Slightly bigger than a wristwatch, it was a concealed time calculation apparatus intended to predict roulette wheels. The significance here is not so much the technical accomplishment, but the fact that as early as 1961 wearable technologies were initiating the paradigm shift that involves using technology against technology. Here we have an early example of individual experimenters employing hidden handmade technologies to be used to oppose the interests of a larger technological environment — in this case, the casino.

Roulette wheel prediction systems, in fact, became a kind of obsession with those exploring humanistic technology — at least two other notable improvements on the initial design followed on the heels of that initial experiment. The first was a microprocessor-based timing circuit concealed in a camera case built in 1972 by Alan Lewis at CalTech. The second was a microprocessor-based timing circuit concealed in a shoe that had nine solenoids to provide a range of tactile outputs. The invention of this shoe, put together by a ragtag group of disaffected grad students under the guise of Eudaemonic Enterprises, was chronicled in Thomas Bass's book *The Eudaemonic Pie*.

In the late 1970s the Eudaemons designed and built a wearable shoe system for purposes of assisting a roulette player predict where the ball would land. Rather than attempting to predict the exact number on which the ball would stop, the experimenters divided the wheel into eight octants and attempted to predict in which octant the ball would land. It was not necessary to predict this outcome with high accuracy; it was sufficient to *occasionally* (with probability only slightly better than pure chance) know in which octant the ball would land. In this manner, the apparatus was successful in providing a small but sufficient increase in betting odds, for purposes of winning money at the game of roulette.

While at MIT, I had the chance to use my WearComp system to photograph the noteworthy shoe, loaned to me by the Eudaemons. Using a unique photographic technique called lightspace (to be discussed at length in the next chapter) I bathed the Eudaemonic shoe in a high-contrast purple videographic glow. Looking at the resulting photos, the shoe took on new meaning for me. I realized that the profound nature of the

Eudaemon shoe comes not from its small size or ingenious design, but from its function as a covert humanistic device designed to time the ball on a spinning roulette table. This was an important contribution to the notion

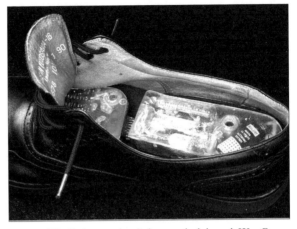

The Eudaemon shoe I photographed through WearComp.

of existential technology; for example, the humanistic technology of self-determination dedicated to the individual spirit. Not only was this an early free-spirited example of humanistic technology, it was also one that took place in one of the most restrictive environments outside of prison — the gambling casino. It was remarkable that the free will of the individual could manifest itself amid an environment of technological repression and surveillance.

What appeals to me about the Eudaemons is their spirit both as inventors and as individuals willing to take personal risks to confront corporate and/or criminal authority. Some may say they were breaking the rules or violating laws, but to me, the casino is a perfect example of a cybernetic system in which humans are mere functionaries in a loop; in that sense, it is the casino and those who maintain its operations that could more fairly be accused of criminal status. The Eudaemons simply wanted to pit humanistic technology against institutional technology, thereby changing the feedback paradigm to benefit the individual over the corporate. Like my early WearComp system (designed to function as a "photographer's assistant" — more on that in the next chapter) the Eudaemon system was largely of singular functionality. Yet in both inventions there was the sense of human possibility coupled with excitement about manipulating the manipulators. Perhaps, these fledgling attempts suggested, the "system" could be confronted on its own terms. The Eudaemon shoe did not lead to constant jackpots; it did not even improve the odds by very much. In fact, according to Bass's official account, the shoe was never successfully used in the Las Vegas casinos to recoup even the cost of constructing it. However, as with the "Photographer's Assistant" (which also relied on the random nature of human experience), the human was given the opportunity to inject himself into an otherwise predetermined, and often unfriendly and sterile, environment.

TOWARD AND AWAY FROM THE WEARABLE COMPUTER: EARLY HUMANISTIC INVENTION

Much of the early work done on wearable technologies shared this sense of spirit, innovation, and promise. Hubert Upton, in 1967, designed an eyeglass display as an aid for lipreading. Ten years later, in 1977, C.C. Collins developed a wearable camera-to-tactile vest for the blind (you'll encounter my own variation on this, the Vibravest, in a later chapter). And, of course, in what would prove to be a landmark move with implications that are still being wrestled with today, 1979 saw the arrival of the Walkman from Sony, the first commercial wearable entertainment device.

However, if you dig deeper, you'll find that the tendency to make communication technologies portable and personal begins as early as

1947, the year Motorola released the first-ever suitcase television. In fact, television has a long history as a portable communication device. Following the suitcase TV came the 1965 Sony TV4-203 UW, the world's

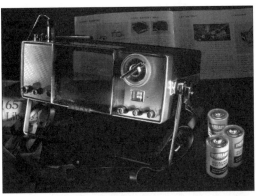

first "wearoperable" TV. This battery-powered TV had an antenna built into a neckstrap so that it was wearoperable (that is, could be worn while in use). A ten-centimetre screen provided direct viewing without the need for a magnifier. It ran on 12 to 13.5 volts from nine 1.5 volt "C" size batteries inserted into the back of the set, or on a car battery; one of its optional accessories was a car mount antenna. In 1980, only a year after the Walkman, we got the world's first pocket television and, in 1982, Seiko built the first wristwatch television. Sixteen years later, in 1998, I designed and built the world's first Linux-based wristwatch/video conferenc-

Portable televisions, precursors of personal technologies to come.

ing system, a watch that can display full-colour broadcast-quality video. (Similar to the Vicarious Soliloquy concept, the wearer of the watch can

The wristwatch/video-
conferencing system I
invented in 1998.

receive a broadcast from the perspective of the WearComp user — for example, the watch can show what the broadcaster is watching.)

Clearly many early wearable devices and technologies were not computers. What separates computers from portable entertainment devices, resistor-capacitor timing circuits, digital timers, modulators, mixers, and the like, is the fact that the computer can transmogrify itself into nearly anything at the mere change of a program. Its purpose is determined by its machine instructions, whereas the shoe timer or radiowear has to be torn apart and rebuilt to make it do something else. This ability to change into any one of a wide variety of things is really at the heart of the computer revolution. It is the ability to do things the manufacturers never intended that separates computers, and the coming wave of wearable computers, from single-use devices such as the Walkman or even the Eudaemonic shoe. Nonetheless, the limited-use approach has been predominant in the overall methodology of designing wearable technologies. In the majority of wearable developments since the Eudaemon's shoe, rote functionality has triumphed over possibility. Unlike the desktop computer, the approach to personal wearable technology continues to emphasize limited function. My own struggle to develop a different kind of wearable technology with a wide range of applications has been, thus, not only a technological challenge but also an institutional challenge: the wearable computer I eventually built stands in direct contrast to the overall tendencies of what has now become a personal technology "industry."

Keeping in mind that it's almost impossible to survey all the research currently being done on wearable technology (and that by the time you read this, unlike the fundamental ethical principles of wearables, this material will, no doubt, already lag slightly behind current innovations), it's worth looking at some recent wearable technologies that are now or will soon be available to the consumer. A T-shirt that monitors vital signs was developed at Georgia Tech's school of textile and fibre engineering, research financed by the U.S. navy. (This idea of putting monitoring devices in clothing is all the rage: shoes, pants, hats are all under development.) Then there's the virtual keyboard, designed at the University of California Berkeley, which employs ten minuscule silicon chips glued to fingernails that then track your finger movements on invisible keyboards. The information is transferred to a processor via low-power radio waves. You can type while you wait in line, while you drive, or while you lie in bed. Not to be outdone by the U.S. navy, the army has long been interested in wearables, and has several items ready to go, including an infantry interface (more on that shortly). The U.S. air force has the infamous Pilot's Associate, developed by some of the world's biggest corporations, including McDonnell Douglas, Texas Instruments, and General Electric. The Pilot's Associate is meant to function as a combat pilot's interdependent interface, a way to marry the pilot to the plane, thereby enhancing functionality.

The United States Department of Defence has been a leading player in wearables research ever since the founding of the department's advanced research project agency (DARPA), which came into being in 1958 after the Russians beat the U.S. into space with Sputnik. The purpose of DARPA has always been to invest heavily in future technologies to avoid future embarrassments. In 1988, a deputy director of DARPA proposed funding of $400 million over eight years for neural network research, with the goal of producing a machine "approaching the intelligence" of a bee. That project, however, soon gave way to the more realistic goal of cyborg soldiers. In 1994, DARPA started the Smart Modules Program to develop wearable and miniature computers. In 1996, DARPA sponsored one of the earliest known conferences on wearables, a workshop titled "Wearables in 2005." That same year, Boeing, a company closely tied to the American military, hosted a wearables conference in Seattle. A visit to DARPA's Web site yields another look at the promised infantry integration outfit, known on the site as the "special operations combat management system," which will

> demonstrate advanced wearable computer technology by developing an integrated soldier information system to augment and enhance mission execution of the Special Operations soldier. . . . This system will provide a hardware and software solution to manage complex mission data in the chaotic battlefield environment, and provide increased situational awareness through visualization and automated information management.[16]

DARPA has also funded the development of Diplomat, a wearable technology being developed at Carnegie-Mellon University that will offer speech-to-speech translation (with obvious military and industrial applications).

However, as with the stirrup and gunpowder before them, wearable technologies have gradually made their way out of the military-industrial complex and into the mainstream consumer electronics arena. Compared to the gun, the proliferation of wearable computers has occurred on a much faster time scale. While it took hundreds of years for guns to make their way out of the army and into closets and trunks and behind the counters of mini-marts everywhere, the spread of computer technology must be measured in computer years. We are entering an era in which consumer electronics is surpassing the technological sophistication of some military electronics. Since technology now develops at a much faster rate than typical military hardware, the military has lost its edge. Today, on-sale technology begins to challenge, and in some ways exceed, the technical sophistication of its limited-production military counterparts. WearComp and other innovations developed outside of the military-industrial complex rival military accomplishments and shift the paradigms through which we are introduced to wearable technology. The fact that most people think of wearable computers in terms of their application as instruments of war is, no doubt, representative of the way in which wearables have been developed and presented to the public. However, a closer look at the picture suggests that consumer technology has already brought about a certain degree of personal empowerment, from the portable cassette player that allows us to replace the ads and music piped into department stores with whatever we would rather hear to small hand-held cameras with the potential to capture police brutality and human rights violations. Clearly, wearable computing is just beginning to bring about a much greater shift in social mores, a shift that may well be equivalent to the mass production of the firearm. Moreover, this levelling of the playing field may, for the first time in history, happen almost instantaneously, should the consumer electronics manufacturers beat the military to developing a fully functional wearable computer ready for mass production.

It's interesting to look not just at what wearable technology is being developed, but also at what has been abandoned. For instance, the jetpack, a popular image of the future in the 1950s, actually reached a point in the late 1960s when a prototype was ready for production. However, the military declined to produce it, and no further advancements into jetpack technology have been undertaken. Is this an example of a potentially liberating technology that was, perhaps, just a little too far-reaching in its extension of the abilities of the individual? Although the jetpack is not a wearable computer, it is wearable technology with the potential to increase individual mobility and liberty. Indeed, if one could get one's hands on a present-day incarnation, the individual might very well expect to have their personal mobility enhanced considerably. Although the argument slips into the deepening groove of militia-like conspiracy paranoia, one can certainly imagine drawbacks to developing something like the jetpack, which would allow people what militaries and governments may well consider to be an unthinkable level of freedom of movement. Did the jetpack, like the fully functioning wearable computer, gradually appear less as a useful war-making tool, and more as an impediment to population control?

FASHIONABLE CYBORGS

Putting aside speculation bordering, for some, on *X-Files*–like paranoia, it's clear that developing new modes of personal travel — whether mental or physical — is hardly a priority of the military-industrial complex. So far, the only mass-produced wearables have, not surprisingly, been designed for the workplace and the battlefield. Xybernaut Corporation recently released the fourth generation of its Mobile Assistant, a wearable computer used in manufacturing situations where workers not only need to use computers but also must be able to move around the factory or have both hands free for their work. The United States army is testing prototypes that map a soldier's location, show where the enemy is hiding, and enable the soldier to aim and fire a weapon without being exposed to the enemy. The army is also testing a T-shirt made of cotton woven with fibre optics that can relay medical information from wounded soldiers. (There's that T-shirt again!) Clearly, the wearable computer could be big business. Research in the field is sponsored not just by Microsoft and IBM, but by Nike, Levi-Strauss, and Swatch. In fact, electronics multinational Philips and clothing manufacturer Levi-Strauss have developed a jacket with built-in mobile phone and MP3 player, to be marketed to what they call "urban nomads." Sony owns the rights to the name WebMan, and is planning a consumer version of the wearable computer. Companies such as Nokia, Motorola, Hewlett-Packard, and Samsung are also interested in the concept. These companies, of course, are less interested in human freedom than in lifestyle technologies that turn computers into fashion accessories.

THE MICROMANAGED CYBORG

It is apparent that the struggle to humanize technology is almost as old as the impetus toward technological innovation. Norbert Wiener's hesitation and Clynes/Kline's enthusiasm suggest that the age-old conflict between the individual and the aggregate (government, corporate, or religious entity) becomes increasingly pronounced as more technological resources become available to both people and their institutions. Where personal technologies are involved, contradictions are always paramount: we might pass laws against personal ownership of guns, and instead appoint a centralized authority to have power over us and keep us safe. We might also request that central authority watch over us with video surveillance cameras to guard us from crime. We want to use technology to keep ourselves firmly absorbed in the collective, our goods guarded, our way of life protected by a surveillance infrastructure we implicitly support. But then, we also want to use technology to enhance our ability to announce and protect our individuality, and we bristle when laws are passed requiring us to register our guns or when we find out that the government intends to install motion-detecting cameras on our highways to catch us speeding.

In today's world, control is attained through information. Surveillance and mass media have become the preferred instruments of social control. Department stores are protected by security cameras rather than by owners with shotguns under the counter or armed guards. So it is that technology first creates an uneven playing field and then levels it, only to have the process begin all over again. These days, it is relatively easy to get a gun. However, few people today have similar access to the surveillance infrastructure. In the coming cyborg future, though, more and more of us will be able to maintain our own surveillance program. This is not necessarily a good thing, nor does it have to mean the end of life as we know it. Certainly, it represents our endless treadmill race to keep up with technological forces that, in liberating us, change the parameters of power and threaten our freedom. No wonder it has always been a common refrain to argue that "technology diminishes man; its tendency toward greater wealth, better goods, speedier communications and transportation is finally more than offset by its reduction of man to its own terms."

This argument about technology's propensity to reduce humanity can be connected to the gradual shift over time toward less physically severe punishments inflicted with greater certainty, as documented in Michel Foucault's famous text *Discipline & Punish*. Foucault describes how, in the Middle Ages, the lack of sophisticated surveillance and communications networks meant that criminals often escaped detection or capture, but when they *were* captured punishments were extreme and public. Gruesome corporal punishments where criminals might be crucified, or whipped, branded, drawn and quartered, or burned at the stake, were quite common. The evolution from punishment as a spectacle, in which people are tortured to death in the village square, to incarceration, in which people are locked secretly in a cell, marked the first step in a shift toward less severe, but more precise, punishments. Combined with improved forensic technologies such as fingerprinting, this reduction in the severity of punishment came together with a greater chance of getting caught. As technology enables the power structure to engage in ever-expanding surveillance schemes, punishment becomes ever more methodical, secretive, and complicated — at once raising the ante of law and order in democratic societies that deliberately obscure surveillance networks and their implications.

More recently, with the advent of "boot camps," to which delinquent youths are sent for mandatory military-style training, the trend continues by addressing social problems when they are still relatively minor. This requires greater surveillance and monitoring, but at the same time is characterized by less severe actions taken against those who are deemed to have broken the law. If we extrapolate from this trend, what we arrive at is a system of social control characterized by surveillance and punishment. At some point, the forces applied to the subjects of the social control are too weak to even justify the use of the word *punishment*; we might do better to refer to this process as "micromanagement."

This "micromanagement" of society may be effected by subjecting the population to mass media, advertising, and calming music played in department stores, elevators, and subway stations. It has to do with influencing every aspect of our lives: what food we eat, where we live, and what we think about. As the invisible technology/surveillance network continues to spread with little impediment, we find our lives ever more managed, prepackaged, and monitored — all for the sake of our own happiness and comfort. The American president Calvin Coolidge, speaking at the dawn of the great age of advertising, said, "Advertising is the most potent influence in adopting and changing the habits and modes of life, affecting what we eat, what we wear and the work and play of the whole nation."[17] So it is that, through advertising (abetted by a ubiquitous surveillance network that provides "market information"), through subtle forms of punishment and control, micromanagement spreads into areas that were generally private in earlier times. Cameras move from banks to department stores to fast-food restaurants. They first appear above cash registers to discourage robberies, but then move into the aisles and spread throughout the store to deal with petty theft and collect information on our browsing patterns. The trend continues: more technology to deal with lesser inconveniences, all in the endless pursuit of perfecting the social order.

One particularly subtle form of social control that uses similar technology is the new hands-free electronic showers first developed for use in prisons where inmates would otherwise break off knobs, levers, and push buttons. These showers are beginning to appear in government buildings, health clubs, and schools. The machine watches the user, from behind a tiled wall, through a small dark glass window. When the user steps toward the shower, the water comes on, but only for a certain length of time, and then it shuts off. Obviously the user can step away from the viewing window and then return to receive more water, thus defeating the time-out feature of the system, but this need to step away and move back into view is enough of an irritant to effect a slight behavioural modification of the user. Thus, what we see is that technology has swept across all facets of society, but is being used to deal with smaller and smaller problems. From dealing with the destructiveness of mass murderers and bank robbers to law-abiding people who threaten cost effectiveness or the environment by taking long showers, the long arm of surveillance has reached into even the most private of places, where we might once have been alone. The solitude of the shower has been intruded upon, not with a major punishment, but with a very minor form of social control, too small in fact to even be called a punishment.

These surveillance and social control systems are linked together, and often to central computer systems. Everything from surveillance cameras in the bank to electronic plumbing networks are being equipped with fibre-optic communications networks. Together with the vast array of medical records, credit card purchases, buying preferences, etc., stored on computers, we are affected in more ways, but with lesser influence. We are no longer held at bay by mounted cavalry. Rather, we are influenced in very slight, almost imperceptible ways through, for example, a deluge of junk mail, marketing, advertising, or a shower that shuts off after it decides we've been standing under it for too long.

While some may argue that a carefully managed society results in maximization of happiness, others argue that the homogenization of society is unhealthy and reduces humans to cogs in a larger piece of machinery, or at the very least results in a certain loss of human dignity. Moreover, just as nature provides biodiversity, many believe that society should also be diverse, and that people should try to resist ubiquitous centralized surveillance and control. Some argue that micromanagement and utilitarianism, in which a person's value is measured in terms of his or her usefulness to society, is what led to eugenics, and eventually to the fascism of Nazi Germany.

So the question remains: Must all technologies reduce and dehumanize? Or can we imagine ways to introduce technology into society that will have the opposite effect and re-humanize? The advent of the personal computer has allowed individuals to communicate freely and easily among themselves. No longer are the major media conglomerates the sole voice heard in our homes. The World Wide Web has ushered in a new era of underground news and alternative content. Thus centralized computing facilities, the very technology that many perceived as a threat to human individuality and freedom, has given way to low-cost personal computers that many people can afford. This is not to say that personal computers will be as big or as powerful as the larger computers used by corporations or governments, but simply that if a large number of people have a moderate degree of computational resources, there is a sense of balance in which people are roughly equal in the same way that two people, face to face, one with a .22 calibre handgun and the other with a Colt .45, are roughly equal. A large bullet hole or a small one, both provide a tangible and real risk of death or injury. Modern cryptography makes this balance even more pronounced, for it is so many orders of magnitude easier to encrypt a message than it is to decrypt it. Accordingly, many governments have defined cryptography as a munition and attempted, with only limited success, to restrict its use.

Information is power, seeing is believing, and institutions believe in power — power over individuals. But the tables are turning. The very miniaturization that has made it possible for police to hide cameras in shopping mall washrooms has also made camcorders small and light enough for average citizens to carry around and capture events such as human rights abuses by the Canadian armed forces in Somalia. Miniaturization and mass production inevitably turn the technology into an equalizer, even if said technology begins as an oppressive tool. However, we cannot rely on optimistic assertions that it will all balance out in the end. I've argued in this chapter that the optimistic vision of the liberated cyborg is being undermined by the movement — at universities such as MIT, in corporations, in military/government labs — to implement repressive single-purpose "smart" technologies more in line with Norbert Wiener's muted warnings. The emphasis, unfortunately, continues to be on subtle control. Often, we barely notice how this control is manifested. The forces of hegemony show themselves as relatively innocuous control systems instituted to maintain social order, much like the obedience collars worn by dogs. Obedience collars are described by their manufacturers as producing an "electrical corrective signal" when the dog deviates from its confined space. In addition to being a pleasant euphemism for "painful electric shock," the notion of a "corrective signal" describes quite well the dehumanizing "control theory" approach to maintaining social order. The "control theory" approach might, at first, appear to maximize happiness for all, but at some point one must ask: Where does micromanagement lead? Is our idyllic world a prison? Perhaps the prison grows around us so slowly we don't see it until we hit the walls of our cell, like Jim Carrey's character in *The Truman Show*? Truman sails to the edge of the earth and crashes into its wall, suddenly discovering his confinement vessel — the television studio as a cell with a window of freedom; a micromanaged, technologically-enabled prison one cannot see until it's too late. Discovery is something the makers of the confinement vessel never envisioned. Crashing into the wall reveals truths that are otherwise shrouded in lies manufactured by the control/containment system. The accident comes when we harness the technologies of control to individual ambitions. In learning first-hand what it is to be on the other side of the camera, we begin to understand how much of our lives have been spent under observation, and the extent to which that unease permeates our humanistic mental property. We also understand how desperate we are to hear our own voices in a system that only pretends to celebrate the individual.

It is the ability of personal technology to be owned, operated, and controlled by the user that makes it worthwhile. When the goal is to remove the humanistic from the human being (as in AI-powered super-robots or smart uniforms), the sense of a future that can be improved by personal technology falls by the wayside. As David Channel writes in his essay "The Vital Machine,"

> A bionic ethic must take into consideration both the mechanical and the organic aspects of the cybernetic ecology in order to maintain the system's integrity, stability, diversity, and purpose-fulness. Neither the mechanical nor the organic can be allowed to bring about the extinction of the other.[18]

We cannot assume that all wearable technologies will be empowering. The ease with which researchers, sniffing the winds of technological change, switched from smart rooms to smart clothes (all the while maintaining what can only be described as a corporate ideology,) clearly indicates the danger of blanket assumptions concerning the benefits of wearable technology. One can envision many wearable systems that, unfortunately, will take us in the other direction — away from personal freedom. Chris Hables Gray and Steven Mentor write in their essay "The Cyborg Body Politic and the New World Order" that

> Cyborg technologies can be restorative in that they restore lost functions and replace lost organs and limbs, as most are in medicine, or they can be enhancing, which is what most military and industrial research aims for. These latter projects seek to

construct everything from factories controlled by a handful of "worker-pilots" to infantrymen in mind-controlled exoskeletons to the realization of that very important dream many computer scientists have of downloading their consciousness into immortal computers. Cyborg advances in entertainment offer the possibility of more ambiguous changes that neither enhance nor restore humans but just alter them, or perhaps even degrade them into addicts of direct neurostimulation or more virtual thrills.[19]

Gray and Mentor cover the gamut of cyborg innovations coming soon to a store near you — computer uniforms, addictive reality simulations, computers with the minds of people — all of these are on the wish list of corporate society. Within this beguiling swirl of possibilities, there is the sense that, once again, any progress is superior to what came before it. If we put our mind in a computer, we do so to advance to a "new level" of humanity — the immortal god. No mention is made, however, of what may be lost in the process.

WEARING AWAY AT PERSONAL FREEDOM: WEARABILITY AND EXISTENTIALITY

The stakes in the personal technology sweepstakes are high, even, in some cases, a matter of life and death. Wearable technology has recently been proposed as a mechanism for imprisonment in the form of remote-control obedience cuffs worn around the ankle for tracking, and sometimes pain-giving, purposes. Waist-worn obedience belts have been proposed and used in the United States as well as other areas. Amnesty International is currently calling for a ban on such telematic torture devices. "Teletorture" devices raise the spectre of a totalitarian society, or at least threaten to undermine individual freedom. Obedience devices have two attributes: the ability to observe (through some means of surveillance or tracking) and the ability to control (through teletorture). This combination of observability and controllability gives rise to a pre-programmed punishment algorithm that enslaves the wearer in the feedback loop of an automated process. Even technologies that contain only one of these two channels (cellular phones that track the whereabouts of the user at all times) suggest a disturbing trend.

My concerns about the possible effect that wearable technologies could have in a totalitarian environment are justified, I believe, by the lessons the past has taught us. Technology — from the stirrup to the gun — has been held over our heads, used to dominate and control vast populations. Of course, it doesn't have to be that way. We are at a unique stage in history, a time when it is possible to facilitate a dispersal of personal technologies that could counteract repression through ubiquity and diffusion. This opportunity to enhance human possibility is the reason why we must insist that wearable computers not be uniforms tied to specific functions but rather overall systems that include human beings in the cybernetic loop. Despite the institutional/corporate direction to the contrary, the wearable computer should and could combine the obsession with increased efficiency and connectivity with a significant increase in our personal empowerment.

The fact that we seem to be entering an era of unprecedented, technologically enabled micromanagement is a potent answer to critics who ask: Why wear a computer at all; why not just have an intelligent environment that responds to your wishes? These critics argue that the WearComp apparatus could be replaced by simply having environmental technology everywhere (the "smart" room of cameras and microphones in every room of every building connected to a massive computer network), so that the functionality of WearComp could be summoned from "intelligence" placed within the environment. They argue that a centralized intelligence infrastructure could recognize our faces and control devices, functioning as an "intelligent butler" in the user's environment. What these critics overlook (whether deliberately or through unawareness) is the fact that wearable technology is superior to all smart environment models, as long as it takes its directives from a single user. If the aim is to enhance personal freedom, the technology should be decentralized and adaptable — not tied to the whims of head office.

However, as we have seen, wearable computing does not always create personal space, and in fact may itself become a "double agent" working against the user. Rather than just assume that any wearable technology is superior to any previous technology, I like to evaluate new wearable technologies on the basis of two very particular attributes: wearability and existentiality.

Wearability denotes how much free movement an individual has when utilizing a personal technology system. A system has wearability if it allows independence through freedom of movement (including the ability to "put on" and "take off" the technology). A walkman has wearability, as does an artificial heart, but an iron lung or a mainframe computer lacks wearability. Wearability, of course, does not automatically mean that the wearer will actually have autonomy in action and thought.

Existentiality is a term I've devised to denote the degree to which the individual has control of the technology — does it allow the creation of sustainable personal spaces? Although there is a strong correlation between wearability and existentiality, not all wearable technology provides existentiality, and vice versa. For instance, if someone had a computer implanted in their head that automatically recorded and transmitted their thoughts, that implant would allow for the highest degree of wearability but would severely restrict existentiality.

The fundamental issue in wearable computing is that of personal empowerment, through the equipment's ability to provide the individual with a personalized, customizable information space owned, operated, and controlled by the wearer. While personal computers have gone a long way toward empowering the individual, they only do so when the user is at home. They do facilitate a strong degree of existentiality, but tied as they are to the domestic environment, they lack the capacity to truly empower with regard to wearability. Since the home is perhaps the last bastion of space not yet touched by the long arm of public surveillance, the personal computer's capacity to change our lives is not nearly as profound as that of the wearable computer will be, as it allows us to transport our personal space, our existentiality, out into the world. As we take a closer look at the development of the wearable computer over the course of the twentieth century, we should also maintain a vigil for the features of wearability and existentiality, the two essential attributes that will transform the computer age into the age of personal cybernetics.

REMODELLING THE REACTIVE ROOM

There are holes in the ceiling of my office at the University of Toronto. Many times, while working at my desk, I have looked up over the mountains of scattered reports, transducers, and wires and contemplated the punctures in the ceiling peering down at me. The holes come from my predecessor, the previous occupant of this little corner of the electrical engineering department. The holes formerly housed cameras, part of Bill Buxton's project to test what he called the "reactive room." Buxton, like some of my professors at MIT, sought to develop smart spaces — "non intrusive," "invisible," and "integrated into the general ecology of the home or work place"[20] is how he put it in a 1995 paper. In that paper, Buxton expressed concern that "the integrity of the personal space of the occupant [be] preserved" under his designs. Nevertheless, the gaping holes in the ceiling where the cameras once were speak to me of a different story, a tale of micromanagment, of perpetual observation, of possible invasion.

I wonder: Does my predecessor ever ask himself how we can be sure that "invisible" and "integrity" will work together? When the smart uniform is slipped over our street clothes, how can we know we'll be able to take it off? It is time to ask and act on these questions instead of waiting passively for the next showroom model to tell us how we will live. Do we really need smart offices and the increased "efficiency" they promise? Or is it rather the opposite, that what we need — what the future will inevitably bring us — is an integration of life and work that will look profoundly inefficient to us denizens of the age of officiousness?

When I look at the holes in my ceiling, I think of the paradoxical history of a still-burgeoning cyborg age, a history that began in 1948 with no guarantees, no assurances, just wildly optimistic expectations countered by profound disappointments. Unlike many other technologies, wearable technology is very personal. The insertion of technology into the prosthetic territory of the individual can be either a substantial violation of individual and community space or a true enhancement of existential capability and possibility. Either way, the widespread uses of wearable technology will serve to alter the paradigm of our understanding of power and its possibilities for decentralization in the age of the cyborg. We are not far from a time when many versions of the wearable system will be widely available. Soon, many of us will live in a collaborative computer-mediated reality. We will no longer distinguish between cyberspace and the real world. We will form new kinds of societies and communities. On one side street, hopefully not too far from the main drag, we will use WearComp and similar inventions to challenge those who would lock us into smart uniforms that, in the process of keeping track of our productivity, turn us into products. There are those who shudder at the prospect of a population of wearable computer users — cyborgs — roaming the streets. However, I don't fear the company I will keep in a world of cyborgs. On the contrary: I fear The Company in a world in which I remain the solitary cyborg dissenter.

3

CYBORG ENVY, CYBORG FEAR

▢ ver the years, I've been met with all kinds of hostile attitudes to my presence. Even today, I meet people who seem to instantly dislike me based on how I look and what they think I represent. So many preconceptions and prejudices swirl around my work and my person that I have often felt like an exile from the places and institutions I was meant to be part of. Much of this has had to do with the fact that my work is me — I am an embodiment of my invention, and, in many ways, I am my own solitary institution. Thus, intensely personal reactions were to be expected, as my literal presence is an assertion of complex forces in the world. My appearance twenty years ago forced confrontation, unveiled hidden biases, and asked questions that could not easily be answered. Though today the WearComp I wear is all but undetectable, I have never sought to turn away from the question of how the cyborg should or could function in society. I have spent a significant amount of time exploring the different ways the cyborg is understood in society, assuming roles as a cyborg photographer, cyborg performance artist, and cyborg sculptor. The results of my social and cultural experiments, far from being secondary to my work as an engineer and teacher, have instead enhanced my perception of the way the cyborg in particular, and personal technologies in general, have come to be feared, or at least not always welcomed.

So I have sought to be not just an inventor, but also an explorer surveying the complicated terrain of a society at once in the throes of, and horrified by, its own technological contrivances. This is, at times, an awkward marriage. A textbook I wrote on intelligent signal processing was accepted for publication only on the grounds that I remove my philosophical musings, evidently not appropriate for graduate-level engineering and computer science students. Yet when I teach, I end up teaching not only the principles of engineering that involve the building of computers, but also the underpinnings of my philosophical stance, which sometimes calls into question the corporate-controlled invisible technological society we currently live in. The crossroads that society faces is not just a hypothetical idea, but one I feel every day when my work as an engineer competes and even interferes with my commitment to exploring the moral ramifications of cyborg technologies as something more than just a new wave of product for us to play with.

In truth, many of us would rather not be confronted by a entity that makes the invisible hardware of day-to-day life a personal reality. Such confrontations, after all, are the stuff of myths and legends — Frankenstein, the Golem of Prague, and later the Terminator — all incarnations of our fear that we will one day transcend and endanger our humanity through technology. As Donna Harraway writes, "A cyborg is simultaneously a myth and a tool, a representation and an instrument, a frozen moment and a motor of social and imaginative reality."[1] I know all too well the way one can stand in flux between horror and fascination, desire and disgust, one's very existence reduced to either "myth" or "tool." And yet, neither state is particularly desirable for the autonomous human being. My presence as a functioning cyborg forces me to confront and attempt to understand — and alter — the hostility I encounter wherever I go. Neither myth nor tool, the challenge is to make it clear what I am and what I intend to continue to be: a human being seeking to reclaim the essential attributes of the individual through greater control over and integration with wearable technologies.

I have come to realize that hostile reactions have less to do with who I am and much more to do with how I am perceived: as an embodiment of corporate and bureaucratic control over a frightening, changing world; a kind of walking, talking technological slave — the invisible chains binding us to machinery made suddenly apparent to all. Or perhaps, I have reasoned, hostility stems from what Joseph Dumit has termed "cyborg envy," described as "existing alongside stressful fears of the human species being outpaced by the world." In "cyborg envy" Dumit theorizes that individuals "dream of . . . technological redemption" even as they come to think of their bodies "as somewhat deficient cyborgs."[2] In other words, it is not just those who fear becoming cyborgs that react with antagonism to my presence, it is also those who resent the fact they are not yet full-fledged cyborgs.

Cyborg envy and cyborg fear stem from society's overall failure to implement and explain technology as something that human beings develop and control. As a cyborg, I have sought to confront not just the random outbursts that reflect the understandable insecurities of a society navigating extreme change, but also the systemic apparatuses that perpetuate our widespread anxiety over technology. Which is to say that my everyday, unplanned encounters with the hidden technologies that modulate and direct human life constantly remind me that, for many of us, the cyborg persona is a horrifying one simply because we lack control over so much of the technology that determines important aspects of our lives. We are used and controlled by our technologies at least as much as we use and control these same technologies. As a result, our social consensus seems to be that technology is mysterious, inherently dangerous, a creature to be controlled only by the specialists and the experts. Someone who purports to walk around in everyday life wearing a computer is breaking the rules, challenging sacrosanct assumptions.

Of course, most people do nothing overt to indicate their disapproval or discomfort with the way I defiantly mix the hidden trappings of a technological society with the mundane activities of every day. But then, the vast majority don't have to say anything; they know that in our "free" society they can count on the agents of corporate control to raise countless objections to my existence. Rote responses from managers, security guards, customs officials, airline employees, and various governmental functionaries have served to demonstrate why the cyborg is so very suspect in a society that outwardly seems only too comfortable with technology. The truth, as evidenced by countless encounters with agents of authority, serves to illustrate a bias that I have long suspected: technological innovation is welcome only insofar as it can be controlled and regulated in ways that subjugate the power of the individual to corporate purposes.

Let's take flying to another country as an example. When travelling by air, I am almost invariably informed by a customs agent or security representative or airline steward that I must remove my wearable gear (which does not affect the functioning of the airplane in any way). I have become increasingly unwilling to accede to such demands, as there is no real reason for me to remove the apparatus — no statute or law — and no prohibition of bringing WearComp across a border. Arguments that I could be, for instance, a walking bomb are patently ridiculous — a hijacker does not show up at check-in with a stick of dynamite taped to his forehead. It may seem reasonable to the reader that those charged with protecting the plane from terrorism would be wary of my gear. At the same time, the often unprecedented levels of belligerence I encounter suggest an institutionalized cyborg hostility; the airline representative's hostility is the same hostility I've encountered in the department store, in the subways of big cities, and even in universities I've attended such as MIT and McMaster. If I am not accosted or shunned, people will often want to know who is doing the experiment on me, as if to suggest that I am merely the product of a large corporate vision. The proverbial tip of the iceberg, this hostility is just a small manifestation of the hostility toward anyone who attempts to use technology for purposes that fall outside the parameters of our system: You can't do/wear that. Why? Because you can't.

Unlike Obi-Wan Kenobi, I do not yet have the force at my disposal — in response to such situations there is no gizmo I can use to change the minds of those hired to maintain the unstated social norms that govern technological use. Thus I have relied on extreme reactions to safeguard my right to wear and operate technology that is unimposing on those around me and allows me to go about my work while on a long flight (after all, WearComp at its simplest is just another version of the portable computer: I may edit a piece of writing, I may answer e-mail, I may read an article).

In the 1980s I responded to continual demands to remove my WearComp system by growing my hair through fine mesh in a skull cap and then "locking" it on the other side (hair-locking may be accelerated by teasing in beeswax to cause the hair to tangle together permanently). I had already been using conductive/metallic hair dyes to help make my hair form part of a ground-plane for a transmitter, so my hair was sufficiently "damaged" to allow it to lock quite easily. The skull cap formed a substrate upon which other devices could be mounted. In this manner, I could not reasonably be asked to remove the apparatus, because that would require cutting it off my hair. This necessary subversion of the body provided a reasonable barrier to the constant requests by others that the apparatus be removed.

A more recent variant of this same approach depended on modifying the brain rather than the body. Since WearComp allows me to computationally augment, diminish or otherwise alter the perception of reality for the purposes of attaining a heightened sense of awareness, including compensating for visual/spatial/mental deficiencies that cannot be corrected with ordinary prescription eyeglasses, I could argue that I had medical requirements that necessitated wearing the system. Removal of the apparatus could result in my inability to see properly, as well as in sensations of nausea, dizziness, and disorientation. Since WearComp involves deliberate modification of the visual system — the development of alternate neural pathways through the process of certain kinds of very long-term visual adaptation — I would explain that I have attained a permanent or semi-permanent bonding with the apparatus, in the sense that others cannot reasonably ask that it be removed.

Coupled with this argument, I might also make the kind of legal argument that almost always frightens authority's representatives: using the rules and regulations of hierarchical responsibility against itself, I would point out that because requiring me to remove my device amounts to a violation of my physical space — my body — the agent must be prepared to accept legal responsibility for any brain damage or onset of flashbacks that might result from a sudden re-instantiation of the old (temporarily or semi-permanently weakened) neural paths. Thus, when asked to remove the apparatus — if in fact it even could be removed (if it were not permanent or semi-permanent) — I might present the representative with a form to sign declaring that they (the agent and the entity on whose behalf the agent acts) accept all responsibility for any damage their demands could do to me.

In such public situations, I have confronted cyborg hostility with my own attempts to show this hostility is really hostility directed against the hidden prognostications of technologies that seem to rule our lives through prophecy and mystery. Increasingly, technology seems to hide behind the walls of the corporate logo — it works that way because head office says it has to work that way. Similarly, I am denied my right to challenge the way technology works or even to wear my own technology as I see fit because, again, according to the "powerless" clerk confronting me, that's the way "management" or "head office" says it has to be. Experiences of cyborg hostility — essentially the result of an anxiety-ridden populace subjugated to the misguided use of invisible technologies — have informed my development of a different social agenda and inspired the "performance" interventions into society that I will shortly describe to you. Over the years, such a philosophical stance has alleviated the solitude I have experienced and the hostility I have encountered — from people who know nothing about me and my work — wherever I have gone.

CHILDHOOD CYBORG

Growing up in Hamilton, Ontario — an industrial city on the western tip of Lake Ontario, located roughly halfway between Toronto and Buffalo — I always felt the urge to create and build all manner of electrical contraptions. As a young child during the 1960s and early 1970s, technological innovations were coming at a rapid rate (from a man on the moon to microcomputers to video cameras with miniature televisions for viewfinders) and I was constantly inspired by the possibilities of change I saw all around me. I came by this inclination naturally; in the early 1950s, my father, a life-long tinkerer and experimenter, constructed a wearable radio. He revelled in all things mechanical, and taught me quite a bit about electronic circuits even before I had mastered reading, writing and arithmetic.

Needless to say, I inherited his fascination with circuitry. My brother (now an associate professor in artificial intelligence) and I rigged up various contrivances, including an early warning system that would let us know if our parents were coming toward our room and a bugging system that allowed us to listen in on their private conversations about us. As a child, I removed the stereo head from a large cassette deck and installed it in a specially modified portable battery-operated dictating machine. Then I added two high-quality sound reproduction amplifiers so I could listen to music while walking or jogging. (The world's first Walkman?) While many people scoffed at this invention, I quickly realized its possibilities not only as a portable music device, but also as a way to drown out the distractions of what was becoming an increasingly hostile world. I no longer had to hear blaring ads, roaring car engines, or meaningless conversations. I could use the portable cassette deck to preserve and enhance my personal space and drown out the increasingly pervasive hum of a muzak society.

The concept of personal space protection continued to develop for me, just as invasive ways to penetrate personal space were being honed by the hucksters and marketeers who, today, threaten to dominate our mental environment. While still in my teens, I began to daydream about an entity that could do more than just mediate my perception with song. I began to think about different ways to reclaim — to mediate — my personal space, my personal sense of reality. I came up with a concept I called "lightspace." The goal of lightspace was to experience an altered perception of reality, of what I could see, by exploring a large range of possible forms of illumination while observing a scene or object from different viewpoints. Lightspace was essentially a photographic project. I sought to somehow capture the essence and possibility of altered perceptions by trapping momentary shifts in perception through the medium of photography. To do so, I needed to create a link between mind, body, and camera that would also allow for the ability to program complex sequences of events. It was my work with lightspace that led to the invention of the WearComp system.

In the 1970s, obsessed with the relationship between camera, eye, and mind, I built a wearable digital computer from a large number of electronic components salvaged from an old telephone-switching computer. I did a great deal of this experimentation in the basement of a television repair shop where I spent much of my childhood as a volunteer fixing TV sets. The TV repair shop, then known as York Radio and TV, on King Street in Hamilton, was a small independent shop run by its owner, Antonin Kimla. As a young child, I was fascinated by television and its inner workings, and gravitated toward television repair shops and the like. Being too young to work legally (I had yet to reach my sixteenth birthday), I asked Antonin if he needed a volunteer to help fix televisions, and I expressed my desire to learn more about how televisions operated.

From his reaction, it was clear that he didn't think that a kid barely in his teens would know anything about fixing televisions, but I was persistent. I returned to his shop three or four times, each time reminding him of my desire to help. One day, he put me to a test, showing me a television set he asked me to try to repair. He had already turned it around on the workbench, so the back was facing outward (the front of the TV set facing the wall). He had taken off the back cover and bypassed the safety interlock so that it was running and all of the vacuum tubes ("lamps," as he called them) were glowing. I could see that the filaments in the picture tube (cathode ray tube) were glowing, as were the filaments in all the other tubes. However, I listened for the horizontal oscillator, which seemed absent, and with my voltmeter, confirmed the absence of the twenty thousand volts or so that should normally be under the suction cup on the side of the picture tube. That act alone probably persuaded him, since not too many children carry around voltmeters complete with a homemade high-voltage probe. I measured other voltages at various points around the television circuit, and within a few minutes noticed that there was voltage across the on/off switch at the back of the volume control. So, I told Antonin that the problem appeared to be with the on/off switch. He was impressed by how quickly I had located the difficulty, and we both laughed at the simplicity of the problem: he had simply switched the television off. You see, those were the days of vacuum tube circuits, which normally took a long time to warm up. However, manufacturers incorporated a feature known as "instant on," in which the tubes remained at half wave when the set was turned off so they would stay warm and come on right away when the set was turned on. Antonin created a beautiful puzzle by simply switching the set off and then turning the front against the wall to hide the on/off switch, while opening up the back of the set and pulling out the television chassis, with all the tubes still glowing.

I spent many hours at Antonin's shop learning about televisions and related appliances. I became particularly fascinated by the miniature cathode ray tubes inside the viewfinders of some television cameras. Some of these small tubes were low voltage (less than ten thousand volts, as compared to the twenty thousand or so volts of regular televisions). Because of their low power, I discovered that these small tubes could be run from a battery. Thus I had the perfect answer for a viewfinder for my computer and photographic gear, all of which I had altered to run off batteries.

WearComp0 was portable limited-function technology of the kind that is now pervasive in our society, no different than the PalmPilot, the digital camera, or the cellular phone, though, of course, much heavier, cumbersome, and unsightly. It was, to put it plainly, a far cry from the wearable computer that I envisioned. Undeterred, I continued to refine WearComp0 and its evolutionary successors. After further years of work, I came up with various embodiments of a new family of WearComps I referred to as WearComp2 (second generation). WearComp2 was field programmable, with an input device (a keyer and joystick for cursor control, both built into the handle of an electronic flashgun), text and graphical displays, sound recording and playback (crude home-brewed analog-to-digital and digital-to-analog converters), and a wireless data connection to provide links to other computers. I completed this system in 1981 when I was in my late teens.

Though an advance over my earlier prototype, WearComp2 was still a burden to lug around. I wanted to reduce its bulk and make it look more normal. This goal led me in 1982 to experiment with building components directly into clothing. I learned how to make flexible circuits that could be sewn into ordinary fabric. This work enabled versions of WearComp that were not only more comfortable to walk around in but were also less off-putting to others than the earlier ones.

In spite of these successes, my life as a cyborg remained mostly solitary. I did connect, quite literally (by serial data cable), with an understanding woman during my freshman year at McMaster University in my home town of Hamilton. We faced unusual challenges in this configuration, such as having to choose which public rest room to use when we were electronically as well as mechanically joined. Thinking back, I imagine we must have made a comical sight, trying to negotiate doorways without snagging the cable that tethered us together.

Such relationships were rare, though, and it was seldom that I could get others to wear my seemingly strange contraptions. People were unable to get past my technological shell, which they found more than a little daunting.

Around 1984, I noticed the first of many subtle changes in society's attitude toward personal technology. This was the year I met Betty, my future wife, and it was also the year I began to feel more confident about my emerging cyborg identity. The "new wave" androgyny movement was in full swing, and its aesthetic of reinvented persona and sexual ambiguity spoke to novel ways of understanding technology's intimate relationship with the body. I recall a group of us going to see the movie *Liquid Sky* at the Broadway Cinema in Hamilton. The movie, today a new wave cult classic, features aliens addicted to the chemicals produced in the human brain at the moment of orgasm. The aliens follow around models, waiting for them to have sex, so they can kill their partners at the crucial moment. Anne Carlisle stars as both the female and male model leads, emphasizing the sense of the body in flux and change. I remember that immediately after the movie the four of us — Chris and Terry (appropriately androgynous names) and Dan (who would often disappear for long periods into the women's washroom to fix his makeup) — went out on a lightspace expedition to create a series of cybernetic pictures around downtown Hamilton. In the fringe culture at the time, there was much blurring of the divisions between male and female. There was also a growing sense of personal technologies — particularly the home computer — entering our lives not just as appliances but as potential extensions of self. This was a pop culture–infused era fraught with ambiguity and confusion. It was also an era that was permissive when it came to exploring the limits of the physical — suddenly I was just one of many who were thinking about altering or enhancing the body in some way. Perhaps it was the successful lightspace outing afterwards, but despite the obvious camp of *Liquid Sky* I still remember feeling a new sense of confidence after that night: important aspects of my perspective — however distant they remained from the mainstream — had been articulated. For the first time, I no longer felt totally out of place as a cyborg. A year later, I would finally convince Betty to try WearComp. She has been wearing the system on and off ever since, and after more than fifteen years is almost as much of a cyborg as I am.

CYBORG PH.D.

In the late 1980s, while pursuing my master's degree in Engineering at McMaster University, I worked with two supportive professors, Ghista Nandegopal and Hubert deBruin (who still teaches at McMaster). They provided valuable input into my quest to add biosensors to the WearComp so it could monitor my heart rate (as well as the full EKG waveform) and other physiological signals. Around the same time I also came up with an early version of what I called the Vibravest — a garment studded with radar transceivers and vibrating elements. I would close my eyes and walk down the hallway, confident that any wall or other obstacle would be felt as warning vibrations on the appropriate side of the vest. This is accomplished by a radar system that establishes a far-field electromagnetic wave pattern whose output is used to drive tactile transducers connected to my body. If someone sneaks up behind me, I can feel them "pressing" against my body. The closer they get, the stronger I feel them, a cramming sensation against my body. In addition to the assistance this technology may one day provide to the visually impaired, I found that by being able to close my eyes and spare myself the cognitive load of processing all that visual information, I was able to think more clearly.

Wishing to pursue further adaptions to WearComp technology and explore my developing understanding of the nature of human-computer interaction, in 1991 I took my inventions with me to the Massachusetts Institute of Technology (MIT) as a Ph.D. student. First, I secretly climbed onto the rooftop of the tallest building in the area to put in place the radio communications infrastructure I had brought with me from Canada. Although I kept in touch with my family through cyberspace, my first two years at MIT were lonely years in real life. I was studying at the cutting edge Media Lab founded by Nicholas Negroponte, but for the first two years I was the only one there who had a wearable computer. The prevailing attitude was surprisingly negative. As Negroponte told the *Boston Globe*, Steve Mann "brought with him an idea that was very much on the lunatic fringe." But, Negroponte goes on to say, that idea planted ". . . an extraordinarily interesting seed, and it grew."[3]

Wearable computing as a subject of interest is now a worldwide phenomenon. When I first arrived at MIT, however, I found the school to be somewhat less conducive an environment for the field than it is now. I was assigned to a lab over which a certain professor had substantial influence and interest. The professor expressed intense objection to my research on wearable computer inventions. The opposition was twofold, comprising both an effort to prevent me from wearing the apparatus at MIT, and an effort to prevent me from transmitting images to the MIT Web site, even from locations not on MIT property and despite the fact that the apparatus was entirely my own personal property. An extensive and intense debate ensued, during which Mitch Kapor, founder of the Electronic Frontier Foundation, intervened on my behalf. Finally, it was ruled that I could not be prevented from conducting experiments related to WearComp.

Then, in 1993, a local engineer built a wearable computer for a fellow student. Although the design did not possess the advanced capabilities of WearComp (it lacked any appreciable graphics capability or wireless communications), I was no longer the only cyborg at MIT. Still, it took some years to achieve even the small semblance of there being a group of cyborgs at MIT, thus enabling the beginnings of a sense of interconnectivity. I never succeeded in outfitting a larger community with my high-speed packet radio systems, but cellular telephones began to emerge, providing another answer to the problem. While not as fast or as reliable as my original voice, video, and data network, a certain sense of connectivity was eventually realized, with small groups interacting and experimenting with various kinds of ongoing communication links.

Despite the initial hostility I faced, once Negroponte and other faculty began describing my invention to those outside MIT, interest suddenly increased. In 1995, "wearable computing" became an officially sanctioned topic of study at MIT. By 1996, my work was attracting serious academic interest. I proposed that the Institute of Electrical and Electronics Engineers' (IEEE) conduct a conference on wearable computing. I figured such a symposium would legitimize the field, which until then had consisted in many people's minds of "Steve, that crazy guy running around with a camera on his head." The proposal was put before the Computer Society, which responded in 1996 with a surprisingly enthusiastic "yes." A great many people attended this first IEEE-sponsored symposium on wearable computing, held in Cambridge, Massachusetts in October 1997. A gala "Wearables" event the following day drew nearly three thousand people. In that same year I received my doctorate from MIT, in the very field I had initiated. This was a gratifying culmination: I had turned a childhood hobby and passion into an MIT project, the topic of a conference, and a Ph.D. dissertation.

It was at MIT that I first realized the extent to which corporate and institutional control over our lives manifests itself — particularly when we seek to challenge that control or go beyond the bounds of what has previously been permitted. In my case, I sought to develop different kinds of technologies with different kinds of uses than those currently endorsed by the corporate/government industrial complex. I was rebuffed for as long as possible, but then, suddenly, the system sought to absorb me, turn me into just another nifty product to be used as a plug-and-play entertainment accessory. I left MIT a full-fledged — though reluctant — cyborg, more determined than ever to make a place in the world both for myself and for the technologies that had become, for better or worse, an inextricable part of who I was.

ARE WE ALREADY CYBORGS?

The increasing awareness we human beings have of our own existential status as cyborg entities began as early as 1665 when virtuoso scientist Robert Hooke, inventor of, among other things, the compound microscope, wrote:

The next care to be taken, in respect to the Senses, is a supplying of their infirmities with Instruments, and as it were, the adding of artificial Organs to the natural...Glasses have highly promoted our seeing, so 'tis not improbable, but that there may be found many mechanical inventions to improve our other senses.[4]

Today, mechanical inventions to "improve the senses" pervade. Many of them don't just correct (as prescription lenses do) but actually improve above and beyond our "natural" physical capabilities. A simple example is clothing, which improves our skin's ability to retain heat and survive inclement weather. Most of us wear shoes and clothing and don't really think too much about it. However, there are still indigenous peoples in warmer climates who have not yet found the need for much clothing. Many tribes in the rain forests do not wear shoes either, since the ground there is damp and soft. So, not surprisingly, ethnographers who visited these people for the first time removed their clothing and shoes when initially approaching them. Otherwise, they would have looked like freakish alien beings. Perhaps these tribespeople would have said to those clothed anthropologists: "Hey, what planet are you from?!"

Because our evolution toward cyborgian being has been so gradual, we have hardly noticed how much we have changed. Even seemingly simple things such as shoes have evolved to the point where we have become sophisticated performance machines. Seeing aids (eyeglasses) and hearing aids (some programmable and some implantable) have become common, yet they function as true extensions of the mind and body, to the extent that many of us are already cyborgs, or may soon evolve toward that state of being. Clothing is wearable technology, yet is taken for granted. Is a wristwatch a wearable computer? It "computes" time, and displays this "computed" result to the wearer. On the hideous end of the spectrum, it was once said that a diaper is merely wearable "restroom" technology, a portable toilet making life so much easier for the cyborg infant. "There are," states the introduction to the invaluable *Cyborg Handbook*, "many actual cyborgs among us in society. Anyone with an artificial organ, limb or supplement (like a pacemaker), anyone reprogrammed to resist disease (immunized) or drugged to think/behave/feel better (psychopharmacology) is technically a cyborg."[5] Thomas Bass made a similar point when he wrote in *Wired* that "The first wearable computer was the wristwatch created by Cartier in 1904. Or was it the pocket watch, invented in 1705? Or eyeglasses, first mentioned in 1268?"[6]

Regardless of how far you want to take the "we are already cyborgs" maxim, clearly in many parts of the world the cyborg reality pervades. Where once — in the early 1980s for instance — I was regarded as freakish and bizarre, I am now understood by those who check their e-mail in the back seat of a taxi, make a phone call on the subway, or spend time during their luxury cruise staring down at a laptop. Walking the streets, I find that stares are more curious than hostile — no longer considered an unpredictable sci-fi apparition, I am now just another cyborg in possession of advanced cyborg technologies. For better or worse, I have the latest gizmo in a society of people who worship their gizmos.

However, my new-found "acceptance" in society comes, I suspect, at a hefty price that we will all end up paying. Today, "wearables" are all the rage. What is it that makes wearable technology suddenly so compelling? The proliferation of fashion shows depicting fanciful yet nonfunctional units suggest a purely aesthetic motive inspired by bogus pop culture portrayals of cyborg technology as disconnected from everyday life (the cyborg age is always coming, never here). Which is to say that cyborgs and their true implications for everyday life are being kept safely in the realm of entertainment and fantasy. At a San Francisco bar/restaurant, after a lecture series I once gave, someone almost reached out to touch me and the early live and open 6000-volt cathode-ray-tube–based system I was wearing. You see, at the time it was a California phenomenon to wear nonfunctioning electronic devices as a fashion statement, in the spirit of other personal physical/technological interventions such as scarification and body piercings.

Despite the wide-ranging technological hyperbole characteristic of the twentieth century, there remains a powerful narrative in society that tends to minimize the extent to which we are already beings highly integrated with our technology. This is the narrative of yesterday's tomorrows or tomorrow's yesterdays that one often finds when encountering wearable computing through the prism of society. Pictures of my old rigs from the 1970s and early 1980s turn up on the covers of various magazines depicting the future of computing. CEOs and presidents of companies often use these ancient images to bolster talks about what technology in the new millennium will bring. In the month or two following a Fall 1997 exhibition at MIT's List Visual Arts Center depicting the past twenty years of my wearable computer inventions, there arose a surge of outlandish looking cyberfashions: models with strange things sticking out of their heads. The rhetoric always goes something like "The year is 2030 . . ." with a brief description of what we will be wearing in the future. Cyborg technologies retain their futuristic false promise regardless of present-day truths that tell a very different story. A "smart shoe" presented in Fall 2000 by New York designer Karim Rashid at the behest of the San Francisco Museum of Modern Art shows the divide between what is happening and what we would like to pretend will happen in some mythical "future." The smart shoe, called the Schmoo, exists only as an image on a computer. The computer schematic equips the Schmoo with a biofeedback monitor, video camera, and global positioning system. Says designer Rashid, "We could do it right now, the technology exists."7 Of course, we are already doing it, and there have already been several generations of "smart" shoes not only designed but built and used in various situations. So, why are we still pretending?

The following is an interesting on-line exchange I found while visiting the "news for nerds" Web site Slashdot. It's a snippet of spontaneous conversation that conveys some sense of the grassroots debate about personal technologies as style accessories.

Posted by CmdrTaco on Monday September 25, @08:36AM from the does-this-monitor-go-with-these-shoes? dept. ucribido writes:

> Here is an interesting story regarding wearable computers and other communication accessories utilizing technology developed

by Martin Cooper, who is regarded as the "father" of the portable cell phone. The fashion show was sponsored by Charmed Technology which is a spin off of MIT's Media Lab. Check out the hot "geek" chicks sporting the latest in info-gadgetry. Apparently, the CEO of Charmed regards his company as the answer to Bill Joy's warning that technology will soon wipe out mankind if not kept in check. Find out for yourself.

Posted by decaym on Monday September 25, @08:55AM:

The technology should be sooo sexy that it'd sell even if _I_ were wearing it. If it's really good technology, then it doesn't matter what it's draped across. But, geez, pulsating lights that give off perfume? No thanks. And just how the heck does making it look neato take care of the privacy concerns? "No, no, the mauve color alone indicates privacy guard. It's the lavender you have to watch out for." Re: The technology should be sexy, not the wearers.

In this exchange, the two chat room correspondents referred to a company called Charmed Technology. Intrigued, I visited the Web site of this California-based corporation and discovered that Charmed's "vision is to incorporate the unwired Internet into fashion, lifestyle and health applications by creating inexpensive wireless mobile devices that will allow individuals to access the World Wide Web anywhere and anytime through wireless technology."[8] Their London fashion show in Fall 2000 was a breakthrough, of sorts: for the first time the antennas and LED headpieces the models wore as they walked down the runway were actually functional (at least, according to the company). But is this really progress? Charmed Technology cofounder Katrina Barillova told Reuters, "People are afraid technology will turn them into cyborgs and make them lose their privacy and humanity. But the way to prevent the cyborg thing is to make it fashionable." While it is true that we need to go beyond the retrograde pop image of the warrior cyborg, my reservations about coupling fashion with technology are not easily displaced. Many companies seek to replace one fiction with another. In morphing the horrifying ugly cyborg into the perfect runway cyborg nothing really changes: the cyborg is still a story, a style, a twenty-first-century charm bracelet, instead of one of the most important changes in technological implementation since the Industrial Revolution.

Despite interest from companies that would make vastly simplified forms of the wearable computer widely available and ubiquitous, the emphasis remains on the uniform or single-function model — smart add-ons to clothing that will allow us to fulfil our function as airplane bomber pilot or typist or wounded soldier or mass entertainment consumer that much better. As the *Reuters* article notes, "companies are racing to market with the first mobile applications combining data, communications, entertainment and transactions in a single system."9 Another way to put this, is to say that companies are in a hurry to link our ability to buy stuff and our ability to consume that stuff to personal, mobile communications networks. You can hear the song on your jean jacket radio, and then you can use your watch to find the portal where the album is for sale and have the album instantaneously shipped to your earphones. But is this merely the smart uniform in another guise? Wearable entertainment fashions fall far short of what is needed to arm/protect ourselves in the coming battle for ownership of cyborgspace. Truly "hip" outfits will incorporate designs that allow us to fulfil the promises of the information age by facilitating our burgeoning desire to shape our own cyborg destinies.

The cyborg is accepted not as a present-day incarnation of how we all are, but rather as a walking embodiment of future shock. Although we are now used to seeing portable technologies functioning in all scenarios, the actual truth of the cyborg revolution — that we are all already cyborgs — remains far from social acceptance and understanding. Fashion shows, movies, and news reports demonstrate the prevailing faddish approach to cyborg technology as just another cultural offshoot, no more important than the latest teen singing sensation. At a time when dramatic substantive changes in the way we are using technology should be receiving serious reassessment, fashion fluff and frivolous fantasy dominate our discourse — meal to feed the grindstone of the society of spectacle. In the postmodern era, science has lost its objectivity and become a media tool by which otherwise serious Ph.D.s invent science through vociferous assertion. Thus the question is no longer: What are the real scientific and theoretical issues? or Where is the real research? There is, instead, this sudden desire to jump on the wearable computing bandwagon without a clear sense of where it is going, as long as it is going somewhere at a sufficiently frenetic pace.

A colleague once told me about how Digital Equipment Corporation (DEC) named their computers PDP (those who recall entering machine instructions into a PDP8, PDP11, or the like will no doubt reminisce about these wonderful machines), and how this acronym stood for Programmable Data Processor because the marketing folks felt that the term *computer* had earned a bad connotation. You see, the term *computer* had been all the rage, and the resulting hype had created inflated expectations. Whenever the popular press and mainstream media inflate the expectations of a research field beyond what can actually be delivered, the tendency is for a backlash against the field. Therein lies the danger of science by press release, in which the needs of the individual are constantly predetermined by hypothetical exhortations that only serve to disappoint and make us crave more all at once.

Just look at the field of robotics/artificial intelligence (AI). After spending the 1970s promising such marvels as the fully functional robot assembly-line worker and robot domestic butler, the discipline failed to deliver by impressive margins. Great things were promised by researchers in this field, there was tremendous hype, and, finally, when the research failed to meet inflated expectations, there was a backlash. One rarely finds glowing articles in the press these days about the new wave of worker automatons who will clean our houses and collect our garbage. (Although

I did recently read an article joyfully reporting on what was essentially a $2000 self-operating vacuum cleaner.)

Even as popular acceptance for the full-fledged cyborg grows, wearable computing technologies are being set up for an inevitable regressive backlash similar to the one that faced AI. Although we are all already cyborgs, there will be a welling up of frustration — tempered by relief — that our populist notion of cyborg society has not (yet) been realized: Where are our Terminator-style war machines and our kind-hearted RoboCops? What has become of the dream of eternal life, in the form of either endlessly replaceable organs or brains downloaded into indestructible machines? What happened to the Six Million Dollar Man mantra — "We can do it, we can rebuild him, we have the technology"? A report on ABC News gleefully tells us that the "Bionic Man is on the horizon."10 But he really isn't; he's already here. Still, the divide between cyborg reality and the cyborg of the mythical future continues to widen. The more we interface on a daily basis with technology, the more we seem to deny and misrepresent this aspect of our lives and our world. To admit the truth is to admit that our bionics — our cyborg eyes and ears — have been with us for decades, and have failed, along with so much other technology, to create the utopia we have always thought would be the end product of human ingenuity. The future is upon us, but we still suffer all the indignities of human life. No wonder Michelle Lloyd argues, in her essay on cyborgs and pop culture, that "the cyborg, as an intimate representation of humanity's relationship to technology, has moved from a utopian figure to a dystopian one."11

HIGH-TECH FAERIE: THE POP CULTURE CYBORG

The sustained omnipresence of pop culture narratives dealing with the cyborg reveals one of the more accurate explorations of the terrain between cyborg myth and cyborg reality. In pop culture, the benevolent cyborg first turned into the evil cyborg and now, as in *RoboCop*, has undergone another metamorphosis to portray the tormented cyborg perpetually torn between a machine nature (bad) and a human nature (good). Thematically, pop culture actually represents the true ambiguities that are inherent to the cyborg age. The movies argue, correctly, that the dream of the benevolent (or dastardly) cyborg future is turning into a much more complicated, awkward, and confusing reality. A 1985 Paris exhibit called "The Inmaterials" featured displays of artificial realities and computer-assisted interactive artworks. As Jean-Francois Lyotard, the exhibit's curator, explained at the time, "We wanted . . . to indicate that the world is not evolving toward greater clarity and simplicity, but rather toward a new degree of complexity in which the individual may feel very lost but in which he can in fact become more free."12 As is so often the case, technological reality provides us with neither the ability to build new, better bodies from scratch, nor the ability to escape our bodies altogether. Rather, wearable computing represents an amalgamation — artificially enhanced "robot" bodies bound to wires, circuits, and batteries, even as our minds are set free from physical constraints: two concepts both intertwined and seemingly irreconcilable.

As a result of all these interrelated social pressures and promises, a new form of cyborg hostility is sure to arise out of the early twenty-first century cyborg-friendly media frenzy. Personal cybernetics, in solving some problems, causes other problems. In many cases, wearable technology exists to solve the problems of previous technologies, causing us to wonder where the cycle will end, if it will ever end. Despite advances, utopia seems as distant now as it was four hundred years ago.

Though pop culture may be accurate in showing our conflicting relationships with personal technology, by and large the sci-fi myth of the cyborg does more harm than good. The unrelenting pop/media technological fantasy serves to keep the human being safely out of the loop of technological change. We are the passive spectators/consumers. We have no role in development, in creation, in anything other than using the end product. The media/pop culture continuum at once ridiculously hypes the possibilities of technology, even as it presents technological innovations as abstracted and dehumanized from social and existential contexts. In the media, as in the movies, inventors and scientists become gods who grudgingly dispense technological treasures. Fragility and humanity are minimized; oddity and separateness are maximized. Thus a familiar theme in newspaper articles on my work is to inform readers that Steve Mann "walks stiffly, stares intently . . . his social skills are nonexistent." This may be true (like many computer geeks, I am not exactly a social butterfly) but the prevalence of such descriptions immediately puts my efforts in a hostile context. Why is it so necessary to start off a feature on my work by depicting me as already subhuman and freakish? An article on me in *Newsweek* starts: "Steve Mann looks at the world a little strangely."13 And? So? Do we not live in a strange-looking world? Who doesn't look at the world "a little strangely"? Never mind. *Time Magazine* began a piece on me with a slightly less hostile variation on a prevailing theme, stating that: "Steve Mann has an exotic wardrobe."14 It's a measure of the facetiousness with which many of the articles written on me have been approached that a 1998 article in the *National Enquirer* — written, naturally, without my consent but as if I had given an interview to the reporter — reads, minus the occasional exclamation point, not all that differently from the articles in leading newspapers and magazines. "Steve Mann is a walking computer — literally!"15 bleats the *Enquirer* article, which presents the material with an unadorned incredulousness that is, to tell the truth, kind of refreshing.

At any rate, the textual similarities between America's biggest news magazines and America's biggest proprietor of celebrity scandal and shock are undeniable. "Steve Mann is ____." Fill in the blank with any adjective you chose, as long as it serves to set me apart from the rest of the world. If I ever wondered why so many people are so hostile to the tangible visible incarnations of the permeating invisible features of postmodern society, I need to look no further: according to populist narratives perpetuated by the media convergence, technology is the domain of experts who, having the wisdom of mini-deities invested with all the power of the corporate state, are not — cannot — be human. Allan Newell, chair of computer science at Carnegie-Mellon University until his death in 1992, put it this way in a speech: "The aim of technology, when properly applied, is to build a land of Faerie . . . the computer [is] the technology of enchantment."16 Technology, then, is an extra-human creation and must be used in such a way as to limit everyday human understanding of technological possibilities and precepts. Technology is the mythical future, a high-tech faerie land, and those in command of technology are always abstract alien beings with powers that must be respected, feared, and patronized. As technology commentator Thomas Bass declares early on in his account of an attempt to build a wearable device to assist in gambling, "it requires strange talents to build computers."17

How the media report on my work reflects how our society approaches technology in general; our minds are flooded with false perceptions about technology and human possibility that at once leave us in the throes of cyborg envy and cyborg hostility. These false perceptions — partnered with the needs of a surveillance superhighway — have long since taken root; where technology is involved, we prefer the covert to the overt, we prefer to defer to authority than to investigate the underlying causes of our actions.

That said, most of the articles written about me are relatively accurate. The biases come in subtle gradations — not "Steve Mann is a dangerous freak" but "Steve Mann dresses weird," "Steve Mann looks weird," and "Steve Mann is more like a computer than a human being." The result epitomizes both cyborg fear and cyborg envy; wonder and whimsy (what will they think up for us to buy next!) coupled with fear and alienation (oh, that crazy inventor-scientist, don't try this at home kids, you'll end up a computer!).

Reporting on technology in the media reached a fever pitch at the end of the twentieth century. The millennium ended amid a fervour of misunderstandings about computer function, a.k.a. the Y2K paranoia, an excellent example of our anxiety and skepticism about technology, as if all along we had suspected that the technology we don't understand and have no control over would ultimately fail us. With Y2K, the notion of technology as a kind of act of nature over which we have little control was firmly embedded. It will either happen or not happen. Either way, we are in the hands of our godlike experts, who themselves barely have control over what they have wrought.

Despite attempts to portray technology as scary and dangerous and best left to the experts, the explosion of personal electronics — particularly the home computer — has facilitated a shift whereby more and more of us are learning to take an active role in using and creating technology. The number of people programming their own Web sites and their own computers is continually growing, challenging the assumption that technology is a terrain best left to the experts. At the same time, our uneasy fascination with technology as a beast no one knows how to tame or even control is also evident and prevalent. This unease is manifested in our tendency to both worship and fear the technologically confident — the high-tech business guru, the genetic engineer, and the cyborg all find themselves labelled both pariah and prophet (profit?) at the same time, often by the same people.

Over the last twenty years I've moved from being — as they used to call me at McMaster — Crazy Computer Steve, the Medusa Mann, to a new media prophet, one of the select few who can lead society to the promised land of electrical nirvana where we will all be walking computers, freed of the barbaric constraints of humanity. In the late 1990s, as in the mid 1980s, I began to notice another shift in attitude toward cyborgs. With the twentieth century coming to an end, reactions to my rig became less and less hostile — both in the everyday social sphere and in my confrontations with authority. Where authority is concerned, miniaturization and improvements to the system meant "they" increasingly did not realize that I was a fully functional cyborg computer and camera; thus I could cross borders and walk into banks and casinos without being harassed (though security at airports remains a problem). In my more casual interactions, I have found that, where ten or twenty years ago families would cross the street to get away from me (cyborg fear), today they cross the street so their kids can get a better look at me (cyborg envy). When the cyborg concept fails to live up to the promises foisted on personal technologies, a different, more skeptical, era of cyborg hostility will be upon us. This will be the precursor to a time in which society finally accepts the role of the individual in marrying new technologies to communal and personal values that enhance freedom and human sanctity.

REFLECTIONISM

In chronicling the functions of WearComp, I have discussed functions including ad filters, WearTel, and even the Vibravest. All these are functions of the WearComp system that can be grouped under the heading of what I call Diffusionism. In the Diffusionist model, the concentrated power of technology is diffused in proportion to the number of people who could have a wearable computer system at their disposal. This approach relies on serious and practical engineering solutions to the problem, where the solutions involve subversion of the problem through mass production. In other words, to cite an example, the more people who have the technology allowing them to fashion and broadcast their own television show, the less likely it is that, say, the television news will be able to act as the sole agent of information presenting only one point of view.

However, I wish to contrast Diffusionism with the other way I have approached technology's incursions into our lives: the Reflectionist approach.

In Reflectionism I rely on parody to hold a mirror up to technological society by creating a ludicrously nonsensical, yet very nearly symmetrical, construct of the current way we understand the relationship between technology and the body. In each performance piece an extreme Reflectionist scenario is devised to create a symmetry that allows society to see in the wearer an image of itself and its own hidden dependencies. The Reflectionist philosophy borrows first from the Dadaists and Surrealist art movements and then from the more politically charged Situationist movement. The Situationist movement sprang up in France in the mid-1950s as a response to increasingly alienating technological change. "Situations were designed to provoke a recognition of alienation."18 In Reflectionism, the goal is not to re-situate an image or spectacle as a kind of haunting moment that shows us how removed and alienated we are from our own society, but simply to show how the technological tools of everyday life are really being used to affect our physical and mental lives. Thus the goal is not momentary disruptions of everyday life (situations) but rather ongoing projects that constantly confront hidden biases.

I got my start as a performance artist and social critic in the burgeoning Toronto art scene of the mid-1980s. At that time, I became known as a photographic cyborg making distinctive images utilizing lightspace technology. My work was exhibited in various art galleries around that time (particularly at the now-defunct Night Gallery on Richmond Street), and I entered — and even won — photography contests.

Multimediated reality and my unique approach to photography — in which I used WearComp technology to blur the boundaries between photography, painting and computer imaging — provided me with a growing reputation as a visual artist. Gallery exhibits led to a following of people who shared (or at least appreciated) my vision. I started receiving invitations to shoot pictures for various projects, including album covers, advertisements, and even magazine pictorials. By mid-1985, I began to realize that it wasn't just the finished pictures people wanted: they also seemed to enjoy watching the process of me taking the pictures. Often I would take pictures in warehouses with large audiences. This was when I began to realize that while technology — particularly personal prostheses — can be alienating and off-putting, when put into the context of culture, the cyborg individual is much more likely to be accepted and emulated.

"PLEASE WAIT"

The manager of a large department store is summoned by a clerk in the men's suit department. He hurries over and is confronted by a man in a jacket and tie standing motionless in front of a display. Instead of a face, the man is showing a video camera, opaque safety glasses, sound-blocking ear protection, and a magnetic stripe card reader (similar to the machine that reads your bank card). On the lower part of what should be this strange spectre's face is a list of instructions on how to "use" him. The instructions inform the manager of the following:

The helmet used in a Please Wait encounter

- *I do not talk to strangers.*
- *Therefore, you must slide a government-issued ID card through the slot on my head if you want to talk to me.*
- *These SAFETY GLASSES prevent me from seeing or hearing you until you identify yourself!*
- *Until you provide positive ID, the camera and microphones on my head will not be connected to my head-mounted display set.*
- *Your time is very important to me, so please wait for my next available moment!*
- *If you would like to try to sell me a new product, press 1.*

- *If you would like to ask me to fill out a form, press 2.*
- *If you would like to show me an advertisement, press 3 and slide your credit card through my slot to purchase my attention.*
- *For quality-control and training purposes, this conversation may be recorded or monitored.*
- *If you would like to inform me that photography is not permitted on your premises, press 9 and wait for my next available moment.*

Almost inadvertently, the manager tries to see the face through the display screen, tries to make some kind of contact with this creature so rudely imposed between him and the wares for sale. The manager looks for eyes, but the apparatus completely covers his gaze. The manager puts a hand on the creature's shoulder, but gets no response. Nothing the manager does gets a reaction. Bewildered, the manager wants to walk away. But how can he walk away? This is, after all, his store, his responsibility. The manager feels drawn toward this mute creature — so out of place in the mall, and yet, somehow, not all that unfamiliar; there's something about the figure, the language of corporatese, the ominous lack of human connection, and, finally, the vague welling of frustration that boils up inside the manager at his failure to get an explanation, a human response, a recognition that his time has been occupied, his energies disrupted. Reluctantly, the manager steps away, heads back to his desk to call security. The manager looks behind him as he leaves, to see if the joke is over, if the man will now take off his mask. He does not. The manager returns to his office, shaken, perplexed, no longer in the mood to make the company money.

"Please Wait," like all of my Reflectionist pieces, assumes a built in obsolescence. The technological mummy should not be seen as a practical device that might have widespread use (one for every mall!), but rather as an interventionist piece meant to eliminate the need for its own existence. The goal is to propel society in such a direction that there would come a time when the reflectionist intervention would hopefully no longer be needed. Which is to say that these pieces look forward to a time when we have reached a more open and mature understanding of the dangers of blindly allowing technologies that we aren't permitted to understand to dominate our lives (even as we refuse to acknowledge the extent to which technology changes not just appearance and ability but, more substantively, being).

As a cyborg, I am, essentially, "performing everyday life," a process that, as art history professor and "happening" pioneer Allan Kaprow writes, "is bound to create some curious kinds of awareness."[19] Awareness is exactly the state I hope to cause in those observing my interventions. Thus, I coined the term *Reflectionism* because of the mirror-like symmetry that is its end goal and because the goal is also to induce thought ("reflection") through the contemplation of this mirror. Reflectionism allows society to confront itself and see its own absurdity.

"Please Wait" is just one of several Reflectionist experiments I have conducted and purposely taken to the extreme in order to (1) illustrate a point and (2) experience reactions and observations first hand. An early 1995 article in the *Boston Globe* commenting on the Reflectionist experiments called me "part performance artist, part computer geek, and part vigilante." This, I think, accurately describes the contradictions and possibilities of these kinds of endeavours. As much as I consider the interventions a form of obnoxious entertainment — the cyborg version of the prank phone call — I don't propose and undertake them for the purpose of being randomly annoying. They have a methodology and a greater purpose; their goal is to embody the Humanistic Intelligence philosophy through a Reflectionist approach to the issue of cyborg technology in everyday society. "Please Wait" functions as a visual filter to allow the wearer to exclude the voice and appearance of any stranger who refuses to identify himself or herself. As a result, the overall tendency of exclusion and filtering through technology at the auspices of the corporate is explored or, as I prefer to think of it, reflected back so we can see what it really looks like. How many times have individuals been asked to show their ID, enter their credit card number, and then wait on hold or in the holding room for some indeterminate amount of time for some indeterminate reason? Why are we so passive, so willing to be told what to do, particularly where technological issues are concerned?

Reflectionism is, in many ways, more complicated than the Diffusionist approach to technology, in which the individual is empowered through the use of mechanisms and techniques that can "defuse" technological power. In Reflectionism, the goal is to reveal the trappings of technological power as they are currently employed in our society. Why would I want to do this? Because it is easier to oppose and understand current uses of technology if we can see them for what they are — not the human/machine looping interfaces put in place to help and protect us but, all too often, impositions of technology designed to control and limit us. One might come to Reflectionism the same way the Surrealists came to what was once a stodgy and controlling art world — when Marcel Duchamp attempted to submit a urinal to an art show in 1917, he set off a flurry of repercussions and reconsiderations that still resonate in considering the role and practice of art. I aim to do the same for what is now the new terrain limiting our cultural expression — technology and the quasi-public spaces it creates and causes us to live in, including the television set, the Internet, the highway, the mall, the office building, all designed to control and monitor us without our consent.

The Australian-born performance artist Stelarc has made a career out of off-putting interventions. For instance, his "Event for Amplified Body, Laser Eyes and Third Hand" featured a protruding third hand activated by his abdominal and thigh muscles. He has also suspended himself above the streets of New York from skewers hooked through his skin. I do not share Stelarc's opinion that the human body is becoming obsolete, but I do share his desire to create a spectacle that is really a mirror forcing us to take another glance at what we really look like. Another interesting artist working with technology is Canadian David Rokeby, a self-educated computer tinkerer whose art depends as much on his video camera and his computer as it does on what he may or may not do on stage. When he dances, the computer and the camera work in tandem with his movements, creating the effect of a highly choreographed piece, though the work is actually spontaneous. Perhaps the greatest difference between my work and these other technologically-inspired creators is that, where possible, I prefer to address these issues at the everyday points of human contact such as the mall and on the street, rather then in specific performance situations. "Science and technology . . . dictate the languages in which we speak and think," argues the novelist J.G. Ballard. "Either we use those languages, or we remain mute."[20] To use those languages, first we have to recognize that they are being whispered all around us, their sound as pervasive as the passing of cars and the gentle whirr of the computer's fan.

People often ask me: "Doesn't the WearComp invention get in the way of ordinary face-to-face social interaction?" As an answer, I like to refer them to the "Please Wait" intervention, which I "performed" several times in the early 1990s (although by and large the piece was more about the interaction between me and mall security rather than the shoppers, who tended to ignore me or watch from a safe distance). "Please Wait" is a way of asking those critical of cyborg hardware what exactly "ordinary" social interaction is in a time when so many of our daily interactions with those around us have become militarized and corporatized. Our interactions are as much about identity cards, filling out forms, programming the VCR or TiVo, roving the Web for information, and pressing the right buttons on the Touch-Tone phone as they are about reaffirming relationships, making and meeting friends, and genuine human contact.

The truth is, technology is already in place in our everyday lives in such a manner that it comes between us and others, us and our own physicality — allowing us, causing us, and forcing us to rely on techno-logically imposed systems of social and self-interaction. This kind of cor-porate-mediated social interaction is in ample evidence in the "Please Wait" project. Here, the apparatus completely covers the eyes. When individuals attempt to make eye contact with me, the wearer, they instead make contact with a wearable bureaucratic organizational "corporate body" enshrouding the otherwise vulnerable individual behind a techno-cratic infrastructure. You can't see me; you can only see my "corporate" persona as mediated by the kinds of technologies that guide our everyday interactions, often without us even realizing how cyborgian we've become. "Please Wait" is about the cyborg age, an age that has already begun. Now is the time to stop gawking at all the electronic devices that have forever changed our lives. This perspective of wonderment (or longing for the past) simply prevents us from getting to a deeper understanding of the way technology is either imposed on us or by us. We are all already cyborgs. That much, though many might not think of it as such, is a given. The challenge is to discover what kind of cyborgs we are: voiceless, passive cyborgs cowed into blindly responding to corporate authority? Or proac-tive cyborgs who know how to harness and use technology for the purpose of individual and community sanctity and interaction?

"MY MANAGER"

Recently, I began to wear my older rigs from ten or twenty years ago in public areas. By wearing the same bulky, obtrusive versions of WearComp I wore twenty years ago in similar settings, I was able to gauge changes in society's acceptance of human/machine interaction. For example, walking down the popular and crowded Yonge Street in downtown Toronto in the late 1990s was vastly different from walking down the same street in the 1980s. This time, people barely gave me a second look, let alone moved away from me or stopped in their tracks. Despite the fact that I was wearing one of many old rigs (still fully functional), rather than one of my sleek, new, virtually undetectable systems, I was barely noticed. From that, I concluded that society's attitudes really have changed significantly.

I have also been experimenting by wearing my fifteen-year-old rig into a department store — a store that, in fact, ejected me fifteen years ago. Returning to the store, I am now able to create the kind of dialogue that forces a grudging acceptance of my right to be a cyborg. When I wear obtrusive versions of WearComp/WearCam inside various department stores, these bulbous objects very clearly show me attached to a camera. When paranoid department store security guards accost me and demand to know what I'm up to, I tell them I am wearing "personal safety devices for reducing crime." Their reactions to various forms of the apparatus have been most remarkable. On one occasion, I told a department store employee that, for example, if someone were to attack me with a gun or knife, it would record the incident and transmit video to various remote sites around the world. He was, literally, unable to respond. The rhetoric of the corporate had been turned back on him. If the store could photograph me for the same purpose, he could hardly say my approach was illegitimate. By taking charge of the situation, by employing corporate rhetoric for personal ends, I could overtly take pictures in their establishment, while telling them that I was doing so, even though such behaviour was prohibited. If I had entered a store with a hand-held video camera as opposed to a device that was presented to them as a machine "for purposes of personal safety and reducing crime," I would have been instantly barred from recording images.

My visits to department stores wearing early embodiments of WearComp are, generally, minor disruptions of business as usual. Another performance project, which I called "My Manager," took my desire to expose and explore the mentality of passivity in the face of technology to more dramatic levels.

In "My Manager," participants, via the Internet, are allowed to take over — to direct — my movements and activities. They become managers and remotely contribute to the creation of a documentary video in an environment under totalitarian surveillance, a quasi-public area where any form of personal imaging is, of course, prohibited.

In "My Manager," I am metaphorically merely a puppet on a string (to be precise, a puppet on a wireless data connection). "My Manager" explores issues of agency, freewill, surveillance and accountability, and prods us to think about the dangers of localized agency in a networked world. By receiving electric shocks from a body-worn computer, wirelessly connected to the Internet, the body is controlled by a "board of directors" who monitor remotely by way of a tap into the right eye of the body. Thus the human body becomes a corporate body, responsive to its "board (of directors)" rather than to its brain. This "board over brain" performance momentarily allows the body to escape from the moral implications implicit in free everyday action. In particular, the body is compelled to take pictures, and therefore becomes a mere computer peripheral and functionary, its right eye becoming an involuntary element of a surveillance society. I might, for example — by the use of remotely controlled electric shocks — be made to dutifully march through an establishment, go over to the stationery department, select a pencil for purchase, and march past the magazine rack without stopping to browse, because I am not permitted by "my manager" to look at magazines. In this example, I have been sent on an errand to purchase a pencil for a higher and unquestionable authority. When challenged by the department store's clerks or security guards as to the purpose of the cameras I am wearing, I indicate that I am wearing a company uniform and that my manager requires me to wear the apparatus (the uniform) so she can ensure that I do not stop and read magazines while I am performing errands on company time. Sometimes I remark: "I trust you, and I know you would never falsely accuse me of shoplifting, but my manager is really paranoid, and she thinks shopkeepers are out to get her employees by falsely accusing them of shoplifting."

Just as representatives of an organization absolve themselves of responsibility for their activities and, of course, their surveillance systems by blaming their actions on managers or others higher up the official hierarchy, I absolve myself of responsibility for taking pictures of these representatives without their permission because it is the remote manager(s) together with the thousands of viewers on the World Wide Web who are taking the pictures.

The subjects of the pictures — for example, department store managers who had previously stated that the use of video surveillance was beyond their control — either implicate themselves in their own accusations by showing fear in the face of a camera or acknowledge the undesirable state of affairs that can arise from cameras that function as an extension of a higher and unquestionable authority.

If their response is one of fear and paranoia, I hand them a form entitled RFD (Request for Deletion), which they may use to request that their pictures be deleted from my manager's database (I inform them that the images have already been transmitted to my manager and cannot be deleted by me). The form asks them for their name and social security/insurance number and asks why they would like to have their images deleted. The form also requests that they sign a section certifying that the reason is not one of concealing criminal activity, such as hiding the fact that their fire exits are illegally chained shut.

It is my hope that the department store attendant/representative sees himself/herself in the bureaucratic "mirror" I have created. "My Manager" forces attendants/maintainers/supporters of the video surveillance superhighway, with all of its rhetoric and bureaucracy, to realize or admit for a brief instant that they are puppets and to confront the reality of what their blind obedience leads to.

REJECTING THE REFLECTION

Needless to say, there have been some interesting reactions to my Reflectionist interventions. These reactions are quite revealing in what they say about the way we use technology in our everyday lives. It is notable that the more overt the wearable apparatus and, in particular, the camera, the more immediately hostile the reaction is to the performance interven-

Here I am in a "Maybe Camera" shirt buying products under the watchful eye of a surveillance camera. See a close-up of the shirt on page 251.

tion. If you tell people "this is a hidden camera and I'm taking pictures of you," they will not necessarily react with hostility. However, if you pull out a video camera, the hostility will be immediate. Once, in a dispute at an airport with an attendant who refused to identity himself to me, I pulled out a regular camera and took a picture of him. He jumped over the counter and slugged me. The irony, of course, is that, equipped with a wearable broadcast studio, I was secretly capturing video of him all along. I took the picture simply to show him that I, too, had recourse to the structure that empowers us to authenticate inappropriate behaviour — I, too, could evoke the fearsome spectre of procedure and managerial observation.

If I wear a sign stating that I am filming everything in front of me, but no camera is visible, I will very often be completely ignored, even in totalitarian environments. For instance, eight of us wore the "Maybe Cameras" (one was actually recording) into Casino Niagara, and nobody complained, even though our white shirts stated in noticeable black letters that video recording may be transmitted. However, when I was accompanied by a film crew and tried to shoot footage in the casino, the move to eject us came instantaneously. Similarly, if I have a large camera mounted on my head, I will invariably be harassed, even when I demonstrate that the camera is disconnected. Ironically, when the picture-taking act is hidden or not overt, it is treated as less of a threat — as if what we don't know about what the technology around us is doing cannot hurt us.

Another fascinating pattern I've perceived has to do with the factor of externalization. The more my interventions are attributed to an external source — such as "My Manager" which "requires me" to take pictures or have certain ludicrous forms signed — the less likely it is I'll be blamed for my actions. If I have a camera mounted on my head that takes flash pictures every ten seconds and I claim I am powerless to stop the pictures because my boss requires that mechanism, I may even gain sympathy from those confronting me. The more I claim that I'm bound by regulations, the more accepting is the otherwise hostile reaction. The implication of this is clear: as I discussed earlier, technology and the technological process allow us to escape the human gaze, the "I," and replace it with the mechanistic "eye." Once this is permitted, as history has shown, atrocities and terror are easier to orchestrate under the guise of science and progress "ordered" by "superiors" but carried out by the general populace.

My Reflectionist experiments are startling and frightening. They portray a world in which we are already far more subjugated and controlled than anyone wants to believe. In the 1960s, Stanley Milgram performed an infamous experiment in which students were instructed to deliver continuous electric shocks to a fellow student volunteer. Despite obvious evidence that the volunteer was in pain — screams of agony, for instance — the students all mechanically continued with the shock process, blithely following the authority of the figure leading the experiment and surrendering their autonomy to the processes of technology. (In the end, the screaming volunteer turned out to be an actor.) This experiment stunned many at the time, and still raises debate today: Was it ethical? Was it right? Is this something we really want to know about human nature? My interventions raise similar issues: How far will we go in blindly following an authority that appears to have the full weight of technological authority behind it?

So, what do you think? Do these projects come across as pointless spectacles? Hopefully you will think that this kind of spectacle has relevance — that if more people engaged in the kind of Reflectionist interventions I describe above, there would be a greater understanding of the way we can and must turn the tables on a technology that has forced us into the role of cyborg slaves. Reflectionism, similar to a movement such as Situationism, is more than just abstraction and hypothetical dissent — it is the deliberate act of dissent occurring in the very places of everyday life one wishes to change. If you want to challenge art practice, go to the gallery. If you want to challenge our relationship to technology, go to where that relationship asserts itself — in the mall and other pseudo-public spaces that mark the shifting boundaries of personal and communal existence.

I don't use the Reflectionist idea just as a way to engage in dramatic conflicts via the contrivance of pre-planned art experiments. I also turn everyday moments into scenes of Reflectionist drama. And, oddly enough, because of my WearComp gear and my slightly off-putting demeanour, I have found that where in other cases my claims would have been ignored and dismissed (perhaps with the assistance of the police or private security), the wearable system functions as a kind of superhero costume; I become the technologically powerful, and thus I am validated; I am the electronic unknown who must be taken seriously.

I have encountered not just governmental and corporate but also philosophical objection to the Reflectionist approach. I remember taking part in a panel discussion during which I described some of my Reflectionist experiments. The audience's reaction to my work surprised me. The audience primarily consisted of young students whose political inclinations veered toward the left, yet they seemed shocked that I would spend my time harassing "the worker." They accused me of simply inconveniencing the day-to-day lives of those who have little or no power to alter their situation. All I accomplish, they said, is to cause the day of the junior manager or salesperson or security guard to be that much more unpleasant. I find this to be a very reductive way of looking at social interventions. Can one ever stage a protest or engage in any activity not sanctioned by the corporate world without causing momentary unpleasantness for those who are being paid to "do their job"? (Security guards are just doing their job, as are members of the police force, the secret service, the army, etc.) Furthermore, should we excuse the actions of those on the front lines of the surveillance highway just because they, too, have to earn a living?

Though critics of the Reflectionist pieces argue that they are not effective if they simply target "low-level" workers as opposed to top management and shareholders, I don't agree. Such criticism assumes that individual "workers" are powerless, incapable of effecting change or even just changing his or her mind and approaching an issue from a new perspective. I believe that if we are going to make changes to the way we employ and understand cyborg technologies, those changes are going to come from the ground level, the result of a grassroots welling of disgust.

In Reflectionism, all of society is confronted because we are all part of the process that allows our humanistic information to be stolen. It is true that the relatively innocuous manager might not need the additional stress I bring to his or her life when I install myself in the lobby of the store muted and blind. It is also true that the innocuous shopper does not need the stress of an environment in which unseen authorities are licensed to collect personal information and otherwise violate our humanistic space, for the purposes of maximized profits and efficiency. In some cases, authority and even surveillance may be necessary, put in place for the good of the collective whole. But in a rapidly changing electronic society that has, so far, primarily served the purpose of authoritarian structures at the expense of individual and community needs, we have not yet determined exactly where the line is drawn, what will and will not be permissible, and how much of our personal space must be violated to maintain a democratic state or any other form of communal living.

Reflectionism holds up the mirror and asks the question: Do you like what you see? If you don't — and most don't — then you'll know that other approaches by which we integrate society and technology must be considered. When Reflectionism is successful, we smash painfully into the mirror it has held up to us (society). At first it appears as an idiot or a drunk, driving on the wrong side of the road, until we realize it is a mirror image of ourselves. Collision with the mirror, it is hoped, will reveal truths otherwise hidden from us. What we see is not the detached, grotesque cyborg entity in its tangled mess of circuits and wiring, but rather the idyllic society we have built that says, "Please wait while I steal your time, your life, and your soul."

CYBERNETIC PHOTOGRAPHY —
THE BEAUTY OF BEING A CYBORG

Being a cyborg can be beautiful. There is the preconception that what one sees through EyeTap will be at best fake, at worst distorted and frightening. This isn't the case. The cyborg has as much potential to see beauty as anyone else, perhaps even more. It is true, however, to say that the cyborg version of beauty may not exactly correspond to our traditional conception of the term. Indeed, it might be argued that the cyborg, whose mediated view is only a slightly more dramatic version of the mediated reality we all live in (what could be more fake than the mall, than TV?) sees in the vast plains of artificiality that construct our ever-expanding cities, suburbs, and interior communal cyborg spaces, a truth and hope that might otherwise be unapparent. In a world where every-thing is false, everything is a fabrication, the cyborg (yet another con-struction) is uniquely positioned to portray and explore what can now be considered beautiful by reconstructing the entire idea of what beauty is. O.B. Hardison, Jr., in *Disappearing Through the Skylight*, his prescient book on culture and technology, eloquently captures this sense of aes-thetic and cultural creation in flux:

> A horizon of invisibility cuts across the geography of modern culture. Those who have passed through it cannot put their experience into familiar words and images because the lan-guages they have inherited are inadequate to the new worlds they inhabit. They therefore express themselves in metaphors, paradoxes, contradictions, and abstractions rather than lan-guages that "mean" in the traditional way.[21]

Last year, I shot a series of still-life portraits at Niagara Falls. Where bet-ter than the honeymoon capital of the world to illustrate the dramatic nexus of artificiality and nature, the optic terrain of the coming cyborg age that confronts us in our day-to-day existence? The premise of the series was this: I put a sleek computer video display on a stand. The monitor showed the view of an adjacent camera pointed at, in this case, a sunset sky hanging over the Falls. I took a picture of the entire scene — sunset over the Falls, camera, screen, using the personal imaging technique I've been developing since the 1980s, first called lightspace and, in more recent years, called dusting (more on dusting in the next section). The "Falls" series of images begins with the sunset sky and the Falls in the back-ground. In the foreground is the wooden easel on which you would expect to see a pastoral watercolour. Instead, the monitor displays the back-ground in miniature. This miniaturization of the background is obviously the view of the video camera adjacent to the easel and monitor. I am out

Image from the Easel series I shot in Niagara Falls using the dusting technique.

of the camera, though the slight blurring of light and the unlikely vibrancy of the purple and blue background make it clear that the picture is quite different from our normal visual perception of reality. Nevertheless, the scene is beautiful; the elements form a whole that speaks to the truth of a cyborg world in which we are at once alienated from and cling to those experiences that can be considered "real." What is real, after all? The image on the monitor? The background sunset as expressed by my dusting technique? Here, natural and artificial collude and complement each other. No one thing looks out of place. The easel series is an argument about the assumptions we make concerning such things as natural beauty, though they make little sense in the cyborg age. Doesn't it depend on what lens you look through? If I simply took a picture, would the scene be any less natural? If I took a picture of the scene on the monitor, would the Niagara sunset be any more real or beautiful? "In truth," comments

Image from the Easel series shot in Niagara Falls.

the introduction to a special issue of *Scientific American* titled "Your Bionic Future," "America is extremely uncomfortable with nature; hence its culturally sophisticated preference for the fake and nonnatural . . . any dumb cow can make whipped cream, but it takes a chemical factory to make Cool Whip."[22] A cyborg perspective allows one to see beauty in surprising moments of incongruity — the sun setting over the heart-shaped motels and all-you-can-eat buffets (newlywed discount!). The water flowing over the Falls powers both imaginations and electric turbines, regardless of how you want to look at it.

The original motivation for the invention of the wearable computer was to mediate reality, to experience the world around me in different ways. I discovered early on that experience of this kind is as much a matter of an aesthetic terrain as it is an intellectual or technological one. Currently, artistic endeavours are not considered a particularly potent means of reflecting how new technologies may affect society. This attitude toward the arts retards our ability as a culture to grapple with technological change in a meaningful way. The scientist, artist, and New York University lecturer Natalie Jeremijenko puts it this way: "The art world is a very prissy little thing over in the corner, while the major forces are being determined by technoscience."[23]

WearComp closes the gap between art and technoscience, requiring the user to respond creatively to the world — shaping it, changing it, and exploring it in different ways. New vistas for exploring and understanding the way we now mediate our physical space on a daily basis are opened up. The view through the EyeTap is essentially an honest one: it demands that we accept artificiality as a given, something not to rebel against but to explore and even occasionally to revel in. WearComp photography is a way to celebrate the fake as real, the supposedly unnatural as actually very much part of a natural world fashioned out of human intervention and creation. I want to break down the dichotomies that prevent us from using and understanding technology for social and communal goals. This doesn't have to be in the form of elaborate, complicated projects. It can be something as simple as it is natural. For instance, I was the photographer at my own wedding. Why not? How better to remember one of the most important events in one's life than through one's own perspective? The results — quirky, funny, moving — suggest that a personal relationship with technology does not necessarily require a distancing from humanity; rather, the opposite can be the case.

DUSTING

Early on, I created a wearable photographic lighting studio and the lightspace technique to facilitate the imaging process I would eventually call dusting. Dusting is the evolution of lightspace, essentially a more refined version of the cyborg photography technique that connects mind, eye and camera, altering and enhancing light, giving images an otherworldly depth and contrast. Dusting came out of my desire to create a new kind of visual art characterized by a hybrid form of picture — a combination of a painting, a photograph, and a computer graphics rendering. In dusting, I literally dust light across an image, my eyes acting as both paintbrush and camera. The intention of dusting, besides simply capturing the world in front of me in a photograph, is to explore the way the cyborg sees the world — at once artificial and natural, real and false. "Photomontage," comments critic Jennifer Gonzalez, "has served as a particularly appropriate medium for the visual exploration of cyborgs. . . . Photographs seduce the viewer into an imaginary space of visually believable events, objects, and characters. . . . The discrete elements are familiar, though the total result is a new conceptual and ontological domain."24

A central theme of my early days of wearable computing was lighting, illumination, and, in particular, electronic flash. This use of electronic flash is integral to dusting, essentially a process of painting with light vectors in which the flash acted as a kind of visual free verse poetry, sweep ing light poems that turned familiar scenes into otherworldly expressions of the cyborg reality, at once futuristic and yet somehow old-fashioned, like a hi-fi set and a disco ball pulled out of the dusty rec room and placed in some Silicon Valley office building. Indeed, there is an inherent element of nostalgia to the dusting technique. After all, by "flash" I don't mean "macromedia" or "compact flash memory," but, rather, the soon-to-be outmoded idea of a light source that comes on briefly yet brilliantly. A flash tube is a gas-filled tube, usually filled with xenon gas, to which a high voltage is applied via electrodes at opposite ends while an even higher trigger voltage is applied. When working on a dusting project I generally run it from a backpack-worn 4000-volt power supply, with external capacitors carried separately. Preferably the pack is powered by a chainsaw motor running a small generator, rather than by a battery. I mount the lamp in a seventy-five-centimetre highly polished reflector with a mirror-like finish. There are two handles on the reflector, with a keyer on the right handle and a cursor control device (predecessor of the mouse) on the left handle. With this system I can walk around in a large city, illuminate tall sky-scrapers, and "paint" the entire city with light vectors.

Throughout the 1980s I took numerous pictures for hair salons, musicians, and other arts groups, and found myself creating a "cyberfashion" movement with wearable computers. I was commissioned to do a hair fashion shoot for Umbrella Hair, a Toronto salon. A large number of people gathered to watch me make these cybernetic photographs. Music was playing and the lights were dimmed. Since I worked in a darkened environment, they could not see me but for the glow of various elements of my WearComp apparatus and then the sudden bursts of light that froze the individual light vectors therein. As for myself, I couldn't see anything but the glow of lit cigarettes moving in the dark.

There was a sense of alienation in these performances, and I began to find cyberfashion and cyberperformance to be somewhat uninteresting realms — they were surface mediums attuned to the values of a spectacle society in which we are trained to watch, not do. (I'll leave the performances to Stelarc, who, along similar lines, has been known to bounce laser beams off mirrored contact lenses, "drawing" with the beams that emanate from his eyes.) I had never intended wearable computers to be art in and of themselves; rather, the intent had been to explore the WearComp system's capacity to represent a distinct sense of being by way of a new process of imaging.

Despite drawing away from cyborg performance art, I haven't abandoned the dusting system of cyborg photography. Having served as one of the earliest functional applications for the wearable computer, I have returned to it time and time again both as an outlet for my own desire to convey some sense of what it is to live as a cyborg and as a Reflectionist project that causes us to question our own alliance to the increasingly meaningless dichotomies of natural versus artificial.

Out of all the photography work I've done, one photo shoot in particular has stuck with me as particularly relevant to the project of wearable computing overall, while also best embodying my own personal fascinations. This project occurred in my days as a Ph.D. student at MIT, when I was given the opportunity to take pictures in the lab where the electronic flash was invented. Since wearable computing has evolved over time into a wearable photographic system for the production of the visual arts, including a complete wearable photographic and television production studio, I felt it was particularly appropriate to use the WearComp dusting electronic flash system to capture the essence of the lab.

The series of photos was eventually titled *Microseconds and Years*. They were made as a group of light vector photographic paintings in the laboratories of Dr. Harold Edgerton. Edgerton was the inventor of the electronic flash, a key figure in the area of high-speed photography, and the author of the famous book *Stopping Time* (a groundbreaking book of pictures of events that otherwise occurred too quickly for the naked eye to see). Edgerton taught at MIT for almost forty years, and he had, among other accomplishments, a long association with the underwater explorer Jacques Cousteau, who collaborated with Edgerton on many stunning *National Geographic* photo shoots.

The images I produced were done approximately three years after Dr. Edgerton's death and just prior to the renovation and modernization of the space (installation of computers and digital imaging software, etc). Thus there was in the series not just a sense of nostalgia for a past age, but also a sense of imminent and inevitable change. As I worked to capture the lab's essence as best I knew how, I was reminded of my somewhat odd but nevertheless genuine affection for those old flash tubes — devices that were made to freeze time — covered in the dust of years gone by. I would often catch

myself just standing in the lab, watching the light of the setting sun swing across the bench and fall over the faded writing on the boxes labelled "microflash parts new," "microflash parts old," etc.

Images from the Microseconds and Years series shot at Dr. Harold Edgerton's studio on the MIT campus.

Here was a place where the passage of time was dramatically evident, but also a place where the goal of the project was to make time stand still. The artifacts of "stopped time" were all around me, ranging from scattered playing cards that

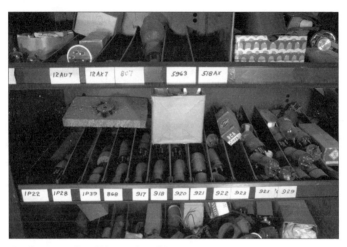

Another image from Edgerton's studio.

had been shot in half by dusty old bullets lying about the lab, to glass tubes and high-voltage capacitors. These objects were visible through the dusty veil of past years, enhanced by the narrow shafts of sunlight streaming through cracks in the decaying roof. By using the wearable lighting studio (including the wearable high-voltage supplies of my early rigs), I was able to bring a sense of life to the old tubes, to make them glow for possibly the last time. As I worked, I realized that at last I had found a project that fused all my fascinations. Electronic flash, wearable computing, and electricity itself were all elements of my own childhood as a hobbyist tinkerer. In returning to Edgerton's lab to use WearComp to chronicle the dying moments of the electronic flash, I was affirming my own struggle to create and invent, my desire to merge the fake and alien with the natural and familiar (and in the process portray the cyborg life, full of curiosity and desire but also, sadly, hostility).

The golden days of the electronic flash are over. With the death of Edgerton, and the more recent death of Wyckoff, Edgerton's long-time assistant, who invented extended response (XR) film, we have come to the end of an era. Perhaps we might even argue that the golden age of film itself is over, as we drift toward digital image capture media. Soon the beautiful "soft ceiling" compressive response of film may be forgotten. Already gone are the days of cathode ray tubes and my 6000-volt eyeglasses, the surprisingly dreamy world I chose to live in more than twenty years ago. My favourite images from the *Microseconds and Years* photo shoot were those photos that subtly evoked the fuzzy, grainy flash photography of yesteryear. In one picture, stacks of weathered cardboard boxes labelled "microflash," and "elapsed time camera and flash" dominate the foreground. In the top right corner is a kernel of popping light, a subtle tribute to a place time has passed by. In another image, visibly dusty cameras and voltmeter are juxtaposed with a sign that warns "do not touch this set up high voltage." Floating suggestively is a flare of blue exploding light, a tribute to the enduring potency of this ageless — and yet soon to be forgotten — early era of personal imaging.

For too long, my cyborg existence has been a lonely one. The *Microseconds and Years* project addressed my own solitary nature, even as it allowed me to pay homage to the work of one of my most admired inventor heroes. In the process of shooting Edgerton's lab, I sought to portray the "natural" essence of invention and technology. Like forests and mountains, the inventive life is measured in terms of thousands of years. And yet, much can be done (and undone) in the span of a lifetime. My life as a cyborg embodies contradictions and realities with which we as a society are just beginning to struggle. My work as a photographer and Reflectionist performer is about a beginning as much as it is an homage to an ending.

SHOOTING BACK

privacy in the cyborg age

4

WEARABLE WIRELESS WEBCAM

■■■■■ or two years, from 1994 to 1996, I continuously broadcast what
■■■ I saw in my everyday life to the World Wide Web. I transmitted
images through my WearComp system, which allowed me to send and
receive full-motion wireless video constantly, often reaching thirty
frames per second both ways simultaneously. Early on in the course of
the experiment, thirty thousand people a day were visiting my life, seeing what I was seeing.

By 1995, the Wearable Wireless WebCam project was getting a fair
bit of attention from media and other interested parties. "Cool Site of the
Day," at the time the world's most popular portal, linked to my site on
February 22, 1995. Visitors who followed the Cool Site link that evening
found a headline that read: "A Hot Fire Concludes Cool Site of the Day."

Images from a fire on MIT's east campus as they were broadcast to the Internet via Wearable Wireless WebCam.

The text on my site, accompanied by photos, went as follows: "Most of that day was quite boring; a typical day in the life of an MIT student, walking to the lab, looking at the computer screen, buying a slice of pizza from the food trucks, etc. Toward the end of the day (around 10 p.m. to midnight) there was a fire in East Campus, and those on the World Wide Web had a chance to see news as it happened."

Faced with today's barrage of Internet broadcasts, one might assume that my experiment was just another variation on the theme of on-line exhibitionism. However, I was broadcasting before the phenomenon of the on-line life. As the unplanned broadcast of the fire at MIT demonstrated, my goal was not simply to show that one could use the Internet to entertain in novel ways. This first ever attempt at an on-line broadcast of everyday life was started, not as a further extension of generic, passive entertainment, but as a cultural and technological experiment meant to extend the communicative capacity of the cyborg. In this version of the on-line broadcast, instead of sending images of the subject (myself), as with the many static Web cameras that would later go on line, I sent images of what I saw: what I was looking at as filtered through the camera lenses of my WearComp sunglasses. The fact that I wasn't broadcasting pictures of myself, but rather of what I was seeing, was significantly different from the experiments and broadcasts that were to follow. My explorations allowed me to explore the coming shared medium of cyborg-space, while confronting one of the most challenging aspects of a wired society: our right to privacy and solitude on the cusp of the cyborg age.

My experiences as a cyborg existing in mediated reality live on the Internet proved to be a turning point for me. Looking back, this was hardly surprising, given the radical nature of the Web experiment, its extended duration, and the resultant frenzy of interest in what "crazy Steve" was doing. At that point I realized the extent to which my vision of wearable technology — so different from the vision of wearable computers that continues to predominate — was a clear challenge to the way things are done in the industrial complex: Control over broadcast communication was subverted. Traditional lines of ownership, celebrity, privacy, and personality were crossed. On the one hand, the effect of the experiment was to habituate myself to the speed and interconnectivity of the mediated existence. That is to say, I was hooked. At the same time, the experiment was perceived by many as a stunt — an attention-seeking campaign not unlike the many variations on the on-line life that followed my own.

A PERSONAL BROADCAST MEDIUM

When I conducted my on-line experiment, I immediately perceived that new terrain was being explored, terrain that could not easily be dismissed as mere passive entertainment. The perception I had was underscored by the number of objections I faced concerning the project. These included, ironically, the rights group Privacy International advising me that I was crossing boundaries into dangerous territory, and a member of the MIT faculty warning that the institute was in danger of being sued by some unwilling participant caught on camera.

Others were more supportive, particularly a fellow student and friend I met at MIT, who urged me to conduct the experiment as I saw fit, regardless of objections. This friend was inspired by my attempts to create a dialogue concerning the relationship between privacy, surveillance, and videography. At the time, my friend was working as a student in a lab involved in creating a "smart room," and he described to me a feeling of being constantly watched. His sense of surveillance reflected his mounting unease concerning the nature of the smart room project. He encouraged me to pursue the Wearable Wireless WebCam project, seeing it as another direction from which to approach the issue of potentially intrusive observation. Sadly, my friend committed suicide in the midst of the WebCam project. With his passing, I lost a valuable ally who — though working on a project of ubiquitous surveillance — was becoming increasingly concerned with the kind of world such spaces would entail.

The collapsed "space" of the World Wide Web when used as a personal broadcast medium challenges society to rethink the differences between private and public. Not only can detailed private moments be willingly exposed in a surveillance-like way (that is nevertheless under the control of the individual), but such exposure contradicts our very understanding of what "entertainment" might consist of. In the past, we assumed that the entertainer and the person behind the persona of the entertainer were two different things. Today, we are gradually coming to understand that acting is not necessary. You can entertain just by being yourself. The celebrity's arrest for drunk driving is as entertaining as the celebrity's latest blockbuster. Persona and person merge, leaving us trapped in a topsy-turvy territory of real fakes and false truths. We deliberately violate our own privacy, for the very sake of blurring the space between our private selves and our potential mass projections as celebrities. Is this collapse indicative of a new way by which we will understand each other, a new kind of on-line existence that will be a precursor to cyborg life in the millennium? If it is, its solipsism and obsessive individualism certainly gives one pause. Has culture hopelessly intertwined with technology turned us into our own celebrity clowns, each citizen clamouring to sacrifice privacy for a chance to be part of the joke? Perhaps it has, but at the same time one can imagine a positive transformation in this legacy. The solipsistic pseudo-interactivity of the 1990s may yet give way to a cyborg era of genuine creative freedom in which we are at once plugged in to millions of lives around the world while maintaining our identity and our right to our own physical and mental space. This will be a cyborgspace where we can participate in the entertainment confluence without becoming subsumed by it. Thus the move from, say, television to Web sites, suggests an ironic truism that governs and confounds our changing understanding of what privacy is: In the cyborg era we often choose to deliberately violate our own privacy, often as a way to enhance our lives by exploring our notions of connectivity and autonomy. At the same time, as the gulf that exists between my project and the ensuing proliferation of voyeur Web sites suggests, we still have a long way to go toward figuring out what will be permissible and acceptable in a cyborg society.

JenniCam versus MannCam

Some time after the Wearable Wireless WebCam project began, Pennsylvania art student Jennifer Ringley caused a sensation in 1995 when she became an early Internet celebrity for using stationary Web cameras to project images of her home twenty-four hours a day to the Internet. Called JenniCam, at the height of its popularity in 1997 the site garnered an unbelievable twenty million visits per day. In her wake any number of would-be celebrities have followed suit, posting everything from the mundane to the sensational on Web sites both widely promoted and totally obscure. There have also been an explosion of text-based public e-diaries, with Web sites hosting hundreds of thousands of diaries designed for the reader to casually visit and comment on. Critic Earl Miller, writing about the nature of WebCam broadcasts, argues "that the private space visible on the World Wide Web is not the private space of real life."[1] However, in my experience, the difference between "real life" space and cyberspace is rapidly collapsing. Where does Jenni end and JenniCam begin? The very fact that we have to ask this question suggests a serious transformation in the nature of entertainment, individuality, and, ultimately, reality.

In the mid-1990s, I found myself, oddly enough, on a talk show sharing the stage with none other than Jennifer Ringley. At the time, I thought there was very little connection between JenniCam and my own WebCam experiment. However, as the show progressed, it became clear to me that I was the only one present who saw important and significant differences between the two on-line ventures. Despite our being lumped together as on-line pioneers, the yawning chasm between SteveMannCam and JenniCam represents the gulf between our understanding of what privacy is and how privacy actually functions in today's interconnected society.

In my WebCam experiment I was in control of the picture. The watcher wasn't treated to a voyeuristic experience at my expense. If the experiment could be said to be violating anyone, it was perhaps those with whom I was interacting as I went about my life — the unwitting "actors" appearing in my movie. (Thus the objection of the privacy group.) Nevertheless, at first glance the output of the experiment on the Web could easily seem like a variation on television (which, in the end, is what JenniCam proved to be). As in television, in any Wearable Wireless WebCam experiment the viewer can be accused of replacing active time in their own lives with passive time submerged in someone else's (real or imagined) life. And yet, on my "channel," the absence of a central subject or character constantly challenges the viewer. The question is not will Jenni take off her top (or a host of other puerile issues), but why are Steve Mann's activities more interesting than my own? The tables are turned in my experiment: the watcher cannot rely on objectifying the subject of the spectacle, turning the subject into a stand-in for one's own less eventful life. A (subjectless) life on the Web implicitly demands of the viewer: Why are you watching this? In refusing to provide a real subject, the story is left characterless, and viewers are forced to admit that they have been the subject all along, whether they are watching Steve Mann's hand raise a spoonful of cereal to his mouth or watching Jenni hunched over the breakfast table sipping coffee.

The idea of questioning the illusion of hypnotic mass entertainment by presenting an entertaining illusion was further enhanced by the connective element of my project. In conducting the experiment in WearComp gear, I was able to offer the would-be voyeur ongoing real-time interactivity. The viewer could see what I was seeing, and then send me an e-mail commenting on my view or recommending a course of action. The viewer could also e-mail Jenni, but that email would not function as a comment on the moment, would not serve to install the viewer in the action, but would instead serve to further emphasize the viewer's role as a passive spectator. My real-time communications capability meant that viewers recognized a person I was talking to as a friend and asked me to say hello. I had viewers jokingly chastise me for ogling cleavage.

All this activity and possibility serves to complicate the standard relationship of the viewer as a passive empty shell whose existence is as an object sublimated by the more compelling subject on screen. In my scheme, the viewer, too, becomes a player, and is genuinely drawn into an interactive position, further emphasizing the watcher's own identity and calling into question what the overall goal of this "watching" activity might be. Why are you watching me go about my life? Isn't your life more interesting to you? You want to talk to your friend? Call him up. Why do it through me?

WATCHING THE WATCHER

The distinction between watcher and watched is an uneasy one in our society. In many circumstances in our lives, we are both watching and watched, at once part of the entertainment (or some might say surveillance) continuum even as we stand outside it. The crowd watching the game is, in many ways, the game itself. The camera roves, picking out the outrageous fans and turning them into momentary celebrities (is there any other kind?), just as the camera pans the field in search of the next big play. It is by now a pat and meaningless but undeniable truism to say that the camera penetrates and changes everyday life. By continuously wearing the apparatus of my WearComp invention while transmitting wirelessly a visual signal to the World Wide Web, and simultaneously inviting others to interact in a form of two-way communication, I was confronting a world that, in many ways, horrifies me. I was challenging and trying to understand the way we allow our mental space to be consistently invaded and corroded. At the same time, I was also searching for a framework by which I might begin to build the foundations for establishing how a cyborg community lived out largely on-line might function, a community in which we are all at once installed in the action and yet free to engage as passive spectators. It's true that in allowing so many people into my head to see what I see I was whittling away a little of myself, giving myself up for free, confronting what I most fear by actually enacting it — the equivalent of the man who fears heights volunteering for a high-wire act. But how could I do otherwise? I am responsible, at least in some small part, for raising the ante of surveillance society by putting in motion fundamental changes in our relationship to technology. Soon, we'll all be looking at each other through the lens of a camera, each individual their own observation and anti-observation station, Spy Vs. Spy taken to its ridiculous conclusion as we are "empowered" by wearable computers containing wearable cameras that insist we become part of the new aesthetic of observed life — a life in which nothing is private, nothing is protected, nothing is shocking or outside the experience of entertainment.

How did I feel, knowing that thousands of people were watching a continuously updated picture of what I was looking at? In becoming what

I most feared, was I not simply providing more entertainment fodder for the "system"? At a certain point, I could just forget that I was broadcasting. Jennifer Ringley puts it this way: "Essentially, the cam has been there long enough that now I ignore it."[2] In other words, what would have seemed impossible is easily achieved: you can be perpetually monitored/monitoring and still go about your "real" and "normal" life. At times, when I forgot I was broadcasting, I would get an e-mail from a person I didn't know on the other side of the world commenting on the "action" that would jar me back into "reality." Gradually, I realized that the knowledge of myself as an entertainment conduit was affecting certain of my mannerisms. I changed my way of walking so that I was always conscious of framing the shot, ensuring that I was moving down the centre of corridors and sidewalks in order to provide a cinematographic perspective. I was, essentially, optimizing my gaze to give the viewer the best possible view of the "scene." Even on those rare occasions when I wasn't wired (when I went swimming or took a shower) I persisted in this behaviour, unwilling or perhaps unable to imagine the unconnected life. I became all too conscious of my role as a camera, as a conduit, and when I did momentarily forget myself, all it took was an e-mail, which could come at any moment, to prod me back into (cyborg) reality. Clearly, even unconsciously, my private existence had become a tool, to be used and exploited for my unseen audience. Like Jenni, I was optimizing some aspect of my private life. Unlike Jenni, the central object of my exploitation wasn't my physical presence, it was my interior, my mental unconscious, a terrain arguably more valuable than the exterior. Jenni used her body. I used my mind. Jenni's performance was largely traditional — she became a surface celebrity and her fame was not all that different from, say, any cast member of *Survivor* or *Gilligan's Island*. My own experiment proved to be of a different ilk. In forming a true community of watchers and users, players and audience, I changed the paradigms of entertainment by challenging the viewer to consider where they began and where SteveMannCam ended. The questions I raised in doing what I did are ones that will reoccur repeatedly as we enter the cyborg age. These are the ever-present dilemmas of the post-human future already upon us — we ignore them at our own peril.

THE PRIVATE PUBLIC CYBORG

Many people would strongly oppose a government-installed camera in their homes, offices, or labs. A camera that would be connected to the police department to ensure there was no illegal activity happening on the property would be considered invasive. Yet my experiments in live Web broadcasting began what would become an entire movement of people who willingly subject their lives to anyone's scrutiny (including, though not expressly, agents of state authority). Today, WebCams in private spaces (Jenni's house) and in work-stations and workplaces are all the rage, installed not by employer overlords or interloping security forces but by the employees themselves. (One of many examples is the Rome Lab WebCam, which allows anyone to look into one of the Rome Lab computer rooms at any time.)

Though we have a growing number of spaces that any employer, government official, police officer, or the like, can look into without needing permission from a judicial authority, many people — including myself — find it far more acceptable to make the video available to everyone in the whole wide world than to have a video line secretly go to some hypothetical "Big Brother" entity. In the cyborg epoch, we seek to capitalize and trade on our own private lives, even as we jealously guard the notion of privacy. "So peculiar are recent notions of public and private," writes Edward Rothstein in the *New York Times*, "that at the same time the private realm wants to lose itself in a feast of celebrity and exhibitionism, there is also a widespread fear that privacy needs vigilant protection."[3]

Thus we find that the same people who protest against illegal strip search-es are the ones who also fight for the right to go about nude or topless. What they're fighting for is not greater or lesser exposure, but rather, con-trol over their own chosen degree of exposure at any given time. Similarly, the same people who complain about employers spying on their e-mail are also likely the ones who fight for the right to publicly post their own writ-ings (perhaps the very same writings spied upon) to news-groups, the Web, and anywhere else they think they can find an audience.

This contradiction became increasingly evident to me throughout the two-year "show" I provided to the world. In broadcasting live to the Web, I created three records — my own, that of the watcher, and the public shared record that exists in perpetuity in cyborgspace. These records, themselves a form of surveillance, might also be said to consist of a kind of protection against surveillance and its misuses. Thus our willingness to install and operate what amounts to surveillance cameras on ourselves relies in part on our understanding that any accusations that might arise as the result of our actions are going to occur in public and in the present. For the on-line cyborg, response occurs right away, rather than years later in the form of an accumulation of secret dossiers. Similarly, if someone watching what I was doing wished to use my actions against me, I would know where the material came from, and would have my own record of that material. This, then, is the ultimate contradiction of cyborg autono-my: faced with ubiquitous surveillance, our only (il)logical response is: more surveillance.

Have deliberate privacy violations become the benevolent counterpart to totalitarian surveillance? WebCams of any capacity function not unlike casual snapshots. I don't usually mind when friends or relatives take my picture. I don't even care when someone shows me a magazine in which my picture appears completely without my consent or knowledge. (As was the case with the *National Enquirer* article on me.) Someone snaps a pic-ture of me in front of a computer terminal and publishes it in a magazine, but I don't feel wronged. A visitor to my lab once pointed out a picture of me on one of the bulletin boards at the university. It is quite common within our research group for people to take pictures at parties and other social events and post them on bulletin boards (on their office doors, behind glass in the hallways, and, more likely these days, on their home pages). In a sense, research groups, workplaces, or the like, operate much like extended families with regard to the picture-taking process — it's part of getting to know one another and commemorating everyday life, and no harm is meant. That said, I've always felt that surveillance cameras take a bigger bite out of our soul than Dad's Super-8 movie camera, or a co-worker's Instamatic, even though pictures taken by family and friends will probably be considered repeatedly over the years, whereas surveillance footage is likely to go unseen for as long as it exists. Unlike Big Brother's repository of Video That Nobody Ever Looks At, old home movies and family photo albums are constantly being thrust upon any and all new visitors who will tolerate them. Similarly, I continue to show selected footage from my two-year WebCam broadcast on various Web sites, and I edited some of the more provocative material into a quasi-documentary (more on that later). I feel okay with everyday picture-taking (and even everyday WebCam taking), but am uncomfortable about the video surveillance cameras that seem, these days, to be everywhere, rising over our city streets on high poles, looming over our neighbourhood stores, banks, schools, and parks.

This dilemma, the conflict between our desire for privacy and our desire to violate our own privacy (for our own protection, for profit, for entertainment) can be found in other aspects of the privacy debate. We often hear from our governments that "they" are concerned about the proliferation of surveillance techniques that corporations use to extract marketing information. The government rhetoric holds that we must get away from allowing institutions to accumulate knowledge of individuals by enacting various laws to safeguard our privacy. Yet, within these same governments, there is the tendency to accumulate greater and greater banks of data about us, whether it's the FBI collecting every e-mail ever sent via a particular server, or the Canadian government holding elaborate files on the lives and health problems of low-income citizens on welfare. Similarly, we often respond with outrage to the latest violation, even as we repeatedly indicate preference for "entertainment" that at least seems to involve privacy violations and/or exhibitionism. We indicate our approval by religiously watching (and trying out for) reality TV shows such as *Temptation Island*, by posting our intimate thoughts on public e-diary sites, by clamouring to offer our opinion to a multitude of talk shows, court shows, and sporting events, and by making home recordings of all aspects of our lives from the perverse to the mundane (in many cases for the express purpose of sending these tapes in for potential broadcast to an audience of millions). All the while, we bemoan our loss of privacy and demand that the government safeguard our rights to an unobserved, unrecorded life!

GAS LEAK: SMELLING THE NEW PRIVACY

Contradiction and general confusion is the rule when applying privacy to the emerging cyborg society in which we already live. There is, first of all, a blurring of the distinction between involuntary surveillance and voluntary public "exhibitionism." Surveillance is done to us without our consent. It violates our privacy utterly and completely. Public exhibitionism occurs when we choose to violate our own privacy, when we make the deliberate decision to put our lives into cyborgspace for reasons that range from for-profit schemes to a simple desire to establish a new sense of connectivity and inclusion in an age of mass communication. The blurring results from the recognition that privacy is not always what we most desire, despite our heated demands that our privacy be maintained in the face of frightening technological change. We quite often deliberately violate our own privacy, as I did with my experiment in Web broadcasting. Furthermore, when I conducted my experiment, I filmed and broadcasted many people who became unknowing participants in my ongoing cyborg movie. Thus, I, too, became a violator, and not just one of the many whose privacy is systematically violated. (However, just as few can resist the allure of appearing on the nightly news, I suspect that the bulk of those who appeared on my Web site would not have objected — indeed, surprisingly few objections were registered in the course of the two-year experiment.)

It seems necessary to break down the very concept of what privacy is, so we can understand how the cyborg future will allow for a complicated nexus of voluntary and involuntary — good and bad — privacy "violations." One way to do this might be to compare privacy to natural gas. Think of lost privacy, a leak of personal information, as a natural gas leak. Natural gas is particularly dangerous because it has no smell of its own. It smells bad because the gas company has added foul-smelling gases to the mixture so we will know when there is a natural gas leak. When we complain about the targeted junk mail we receive because someone has discovered personal information about us, it is like complaining about the bad smell from our gas stove, rather than complaining about the fact that our stove is leaking. That our stove has a leak (for example, that our private information is leaking out) is a problem that cannot be addressed by simply making the gas we put in our stove smell like roses. Complaining about targeted marketing (such as junk mail with your name on it) is equivalent to discovering that our stove has a gas leak and then asking the gas company to improve the smell of their gas so that it will stop bothering us, instead of fixing the leak. When we ask for legislation limiting the use of leaked private information, we are simply asking for the smell to stop — while the leak continues.

Many traditional privacy advocates are asking the government to pass laws that are equivalent to improving the smell of natural gas. These laws will not fix the problem. In fact, these laws could reduce the incentive to fix the problem at its source, which would involve tracking down and repairing the leaks to our personal information. The fact is, many people make good use of the "bad smell" of junk mail for diagnostic purposes, in order to trace the source of a privacy leak. They typically do this by using a different middle initial for each service they sign up for. Such initiatives turn the tables on the organizations by allowing individuals to follow the database trail by tracking information embedded in their names or addresses (for example, deliberately misspelling a street name or inserting additional characters into an address field). Ironically, we are better off knowing that our names are on various lists, our personal details are being traded for profit, than we are not realizing that privacy violations are happening daily at our expense.

Similarly, we are better off knowing that we are or could be filmed in certain spaces than we are pretending that surveillance does not exist. Simply banishing the signs of privacy invasion results in allowing us a pseudo-privacy, a false sense of security that leaves us even more vulnerable. In Foucault's discussion of punishment's evolution, he basically charts the emergence of today's surveillance society. He argues that, with the origin of the concept of prison in the nineteenth century, a new concept around power and society emerged. In particular, Foucault describes Jeremy Bentham's design of the panopticon prison in which the prisoner is isolated and perpetually observed (though the inmates cannot see their observers and are never sure exactly when, if ever, they are actually under surveillance). Foucault argues that society has been changed dramatically by the emergence of the panopticon. As he writes:

> Side by side with the major technology of the telescope, the lens and the light beam . . . there were the minor techniques of multiple and intersecting observations, of eyes that must see without being seen; using techniques of subjection and methods of exploitation, an obscure art of light and the visible was secretly preparing a new knowledge of man.[4]

This "new knowledge" would be the beginning of secret police, hidden dossiers, massive data banks, and, of course, hidden cameras. As the idea behind the panopticon spread outside the prison walls, we all gradually became inmates who required secret obscivation for our own good. Foucault concludes:

> Hence the major effect of the Panopticon: to induce in the inmate a state of conscious and permanent visibility that assures the automatic functioning of power. So to arrange things that the surveillance is permanent in its effects, even if it is discontinuous in its action the inmates should be caught up in a power situation of which they are themselves the bearers.[5]

Today, Foucault's words seem not like cultural theory, but prophecy. The panopticon extends the power of itself, and we, the possibly observed, prefer to pretend that we retain our autonomy and privacy, in the face of all evidence to the contrary. As a result, we crave the "pseudo-privacy" of pretend anonymity — we ask for the right to not have to smell the leak, but refuse to acknowledge how much our actions are bounded together with a surveillance state. So it is that the only way to break out of the surveillance system is to negate its secretive power over us by destroying the surveillance monopoly. The "self-surveillance" I and others have practised (allowing others to see us) builds a sense of community that subverts the panopticon gaze. In this way, the very concept of exhibitionism itself challenges the panopticon vision of surveilled isolation.

In the age of the wearable camera, in the age when we all clamour for the right to film and broadcast and otherwise participate in a cyborgspace known as the media, which has heretofore been closed to us, we must adjust our conflicted reactions, accepting that the cyborg age will also be the age in which "privacy" becomes something we trade on — for profit, for excitement, for communication and commerce, and even as a reminder that, in today's world, we are always on camera. Still, we struggle to maintain the essential vestiges of our dignity and solitude. Is the leak more acceptable if we can "smell" the leaking information? Public dissemination helps to close the feedback loop and keep us aware of the effect the camera has, and of how the world sees us through the camera. While at first glance people often express concern about the dissemination of personal information, one could also argue that this very dissemination enhances privacy, because it brings the violations of privacy to light. As I've suggested, junk mail and annoying phone calls may very well be a good thing (or at least a necessary evil) because they continually remind us how much of our personal information is known by other entities. In the same way, when I broadcasted what I was seeing, I was essentially confirming what we already know: that the right to live a private — which is to say unrecorded — life in public has already been lost. Scott McNealy, chief executive of Sun Microsystems, famously summed up the issue this way: "You already have zero privacy. Get used to it."[6]

SOLITARY CYBORG (THE RIGHT TO BE LEFT ALONE)

We are being recorded, all the time, every time. How should we respond to a surveillance society? We can deny all knowledge of what is happening, or we can equip ourselves mentally and technologically with the tools we need to respond to an ever-expanding surveillance network. In disseminating our own private information on our own terms, we do not just assert our right to a place in the entertainment cyborgspace continuum, we also raise the awareness of surveillance by no longer continuing to deny the fact of ongoing systematic privacy violations. We become what we hate and even fear. But in doing so, are we conquering our fear and channelling our anxiety into possibility?

My own WebCam allows me to be in control of how my "life" is acquired and disseminated through an on-line signal. This is true of all

WebCams, even purposely trashy ones like JenniCam. However, the experience of watching what Steve Mann watches was also a critical one. It asked you why you would want to bother watching, and to consider the implications for a future where we are all, at once content producers and consumers. I enacted the WearCam scenario because I believed — and still maintain — that an inevitable move forward into a cyborgspace consisting (at least partially) of perpetual voyeurism is preferable to society's current, parallel, less publicized move into a shrouded space of panopticon perpetually secret surveillance.

People who are being watched by a camera have a right not only to know that they are being watched, but also to know what others are seeing. They have a right not only to see the camera, but also to view the signal it produces. The cyborg future will not solve the problem of privacy violation, but it can at least level the playing field. Surveillance cameras do not allow us the right to participate in our own cultural obsession — surveillance of ourselves — but WebCams do, because they allow us to see ourselves on the World Wide Web and perceive exactly how we appear to others, as well as how others react to our appearance and actions. Thus, one incentive for deciding to participate in the cyborgspace entertainment confluence through the Internet is that of control. If you have a voice in the information continuum of disembodied cyborgspace (a.k.a. the media), you are probably more in control of how you will be perceived than if you simply allowed yourself to be either a passive watcher or a passive (perhaps ignorant) player in someone else's movie.

I am arguing, then, that privacy as we understand it has already been irretrievably lost. Rather than lament this loss and long for the way things were before the dime-sized video camera, we must find a way — both conceptually and actually — to move forward into the cyborg era. To that end, I would further hold that the difference between dissemination and acquisition of private information suggests we must begin to distinguish between acceptable and unacceptable privacy violations. We must also start to separate the notion of our right to privacy (which we can and may even wish to deliberately violate) and our right to solitude (which should be inalienable and constant).

I prefer to define privacy in such a way that it is very clearly and precisely distinguished from solitude. I therefore define privacy as that which may be violated by input devices (measurement instruments/sensors such as cameras, microphones, etc.), while I define solitude as that which may be violated by output devices (video displays, loudspeakers, mass mailings, random phone calls, etc.). My definition of privacy differs from the commonly used "right to be left alone" definition that expands privacy to include solitude. This "right to be left alone" definition conflates two very distinct concepts, thereby blurring the crucial distinction between privacy (as I define it) and solitude in the cyborg age.

The distinction between privacy and solitude is obvious when we ask: In the age of the wearable computer, will it be possible to retain one's solitude and still live in some form of communal (voyeuristic) cyborgspace? When I post what I see every day on the Web, I am deliberately violating my own privacy. When I send an e-mail, I am knowingly violating my own privacy and sometimes the solitude of the recipient. However, in living in symbiosis with WearComp I increase my solitude, insomuch as I can control the kind of information to which I am open. I can control what I see and hear, preventing unwanted solicitations from penetrating my mental space. If I am taping/broadcasting, I am potentially disrupting the privacy of others (depending on what/who I am looking at, and depending on the extent to which I advertise that I am broadcasting our interactions), though, again, I am respecting the solitude of others in that I am not invading their space with an output they cannot ignore. A wearable computer such as WearComp — which allows the wearer to filter out unwanted invasions while facilitating broadcasts — provides mechanisms that will change the nature of privacy from something to be closely guarded to something understood more in terms of sharing thoughts and experiences, while at the same time ensuring mechanisms by which we can preserve our solitude, which is to say our right to be free of inbound violations of our mental and physical space. Again, we need to distinguish between secretive violation of privacy by institutions, and the communal sharing of perspectives. In making the distinction between deliberate uses of personal information to form shared communities and those who secretly steal our personal information, we are groping toward an answer to the complicated problem of how we must navigate and marry the conflict between our desire to participate in a communal cyborgspace and preserve our solitude. As our sense of the concept of privacy undergoes substantive changes in the age of the cyborg, our solitude — our right to be in our own mental and physical space — becomes increasingly more important.

The chance of attaining a ban on hidden free-standing surveillance cameras is nonexistent. More likely, it will be the video-cyborgs (the photoborgs?) who will find their rights restricted, as the surveillance infrastructure is confronted by the fragmented ubiquity of the camera. Still, we cling to our right to insert ourselves into the cyborgspace swirl. Our metaphorical presence there is a way to suggest that what we want out of the new ever-shrinking wearable technologies is the right to violate our own privacy for the sake of entering the larger feedback loop of the media/cyborgspace. We want a way out of what critics have noted is the "social isolation" that surveillance cameras at first seem to compensate for, but actually intensify. However, we also want to maintain our right to decide when and how we will be invaded. We want to be able to turn off the camera, whether the camera is pointing at us or we are watching through its gaze. Such a theoretical position — that we must be free to violate our own privacy, but that our right to solitude should be inalienable — unfortunately opens a Pandora's box of problems around what happens when we deliberately violate the privacy of others (even if their solitude is preserved). This will become an increasingly contentious issue as the number of photoborgs proliferate. As so-called "reality-based" entertainment and on-line voyeurism continue to merge with everyday (cyborg) life, the problem becomes even more extenuated. Thus our greatest challenge in the cyborg age remains preserving solitude and some new definition of privacy where ubiquitous surveillance is invisible and we are constantly connected to a cyborgspace/media in which our communal space is both enhanced and subject to invasion by an ongoing proliferation of logos, slogans, and catchy jingles. My experience as an on-line photoborg has convinced me that, in the very near future, we will face unprecedented violations of both our privacy and our solitude. This will be an inevitable — though not necessarily catastrophic — aspect of the cyborg age. The struggle to find some way to balance the needs and desires of deliberate exposure with the right to be free of unwanted invasion is just beginning.

NAKED IN THE HAPPY HOUSE

As I see it, technology has built the house in which we all live. The house is continually being extended and remodelled. More and more of human life takes place within its walls, so that today there is hardly any human activity that does not occur within this house. All are affected by the design of the house, by the division of its space, by the location of its doors and walls. Compared to people in earlier times, we rarely have a chance to live outside this house.

— Ursula Franklin, *The Real World of Technology*, Massey Lecture Series, 1989.[7]

In many ways, we are already too late. The project of rethinking and upholding cyborg versions of privacy and solitude — elements crucial to human freedom in the age of the wearable computer — has foundered as technologies proceed in advance of conceptual and practical frameworks necessary to prevent abuses. New technologies developed without moral frameworks are lurching ahead, ill-conceived Frankensteins that may soon turn on their creators. These technologies also impose totalitarian structures on creators and users alike — whether they were intended or not. In building the house, technology has destroyed much of the natural habitat outside the house, in effect, forcing all of us into the house. Therefore, technology has an obligation to allow displaced people into its house, even if those people do not agree to the rules of the house.

When I look at the pace of technological change, particularly in the realm of wearable technologies, I become increasingly uncomfortable with the very idea of a cyborg future — certainly a strange development for someone who has been wearing computers for more than twenty years. In my encounters with the recent waves of wearable technologies designed to "simplify" our lives, I often feel profoundly ill at ease.

Take, for example, the first time I wore one of the new all-in-one "computer" chips we keep hearing about. (This is the wearable version of the "smart card" concept various governments and corporations occasionally threaten to impose on us, with your identification, your bank and credit cards, and your "cash," all on one chip.) Ironically, the following incident occurred just after I gave the keynote address at the International Conference on Wearable Computing (ICWC99) in Stuttgart, Germany. Stuttgart is known for its mineral baths, pools and spas, and there happened to be one such place (Schwaben Quellen, German for Swabia Source, near the source of the mineral water) not far from the conference site. I decided to take advantage of its proximity and bathe in the healing waters.

As part of the bath entry procedure, I was given a device resembling a wristwatch and told to press the watch against the control console, which would display my locker number. At that time, a record would also be made of my entry time and attendance, which turned out to be

June 12, 14:05–17:19. When I pressed my wristband against the console, the number 369 was displayed. I also heard a loud click down the hall to my right, and when I looked down the hall I saw that a green LED on one of the lockers had lit up. It turned out to be locker 369, and it was the only locker that wasn't locked. After I tested the locker a couple of times (walking back to the control console to press my wrist against it and unlock my locker again), I was confident that nobody else, except of course the owners of the establishment, could likely open it. I would have felt better with my own combination lock, but I nevertheless changed into my bathing suit and put my clothing — including WearComp, which would have never survived the steam rooms — into locker 369. As usual, I felt "naked" without my WearComp system.

After closing my locker and making sure that it locked, I went down the hallway and stepped into a bathing (pool and spa) area. There was an official-looking information desk, and behind it a large room full of control consoles and flashing lights. A staff member at the information desk yelled at me as I walked past the desk toward the pools and spas. He was speaking German and I didn't understand him so I kept walking. He emerged from behind the information desk and came running after me, still yelling in German. I didn't understand him, but he began to grab onto my bathing suit and pull at it.

I thought that perhaps he was upset because my bathing suit was not of the kind that most people ordinarily wear. I was wearing a black unisex triathlon suit, sort of like shorts and a tank top in one piece (I wear this kind of bathing suit because it covers the shaved points of contact on my chest where electrodes normally meet my body). Although it looked a little like the bathing suit my grandfather used to wear (roughly like the 1913 product of Speedo Knitting Mills except of modern fabric and design) it certainly wasn't street clothing. Finally the staff member found someone who spoke both English and German, and it was explained to me that the custom is to be completely naked.

Immediately, I noticed that the only clothed people in the complex were the staff. I returned to the locker room and removed my bathing suit, so that I was now totally naked except for the smart watch I had been issued. I then decided to participate in a sauna session that was just starting. The door to the sauna was propped open, and people accumulated inside. Then the attendant brought two large wooden buckets full of crushed ice into the sauna, put a sign on the door, and closed the door. Inside were thirteen men and women (naked), not including the director of the session (clothed). She heaped the ice on the sauna heaters using a large wooden ladle. This produced a tremendous burst of hot steam along with the sizzling sound of sublimating ice. Then she swung a large towel around in the air above us, directing the steam downward. She repeated this activity three times. She spoke in German the whole time, but later I found out she spoke English very well. It was easy to tell when she was finished for the day because she started to undress (presumably finishing her role as staff member). I asked her about bathing attire (or the lack thereof), and she told me that bathing suits would become sweaty in the sauna, and the sweat would not be easily removed in the showers that bathers were supposed to use prior to entering the various pools. However, the bathers didn't seem to be using the showers, and I didn't totally believe her story.

Since most bathing suits don't conceal very much of the body, I don't think there's much difference between being totally naked and almost naked, but for the fact that almost every bathing suit has some kind of pocket. Often the pocket is inside the waistband and although small, is large enough to hold a few coins and a key or two. I began to think, half jokingly, that the notion of requiring total nakedness is just a conspiracy of the chip manufacturers: the rationale behind the chip is that the steam rooms require nakedness, which prevents us from carrying locks for our lockers and money for drinks, and thus requires us to have smart watches that can replace these items. In this model, you can be conveniently naked, and — almost as a by-product — conveniently observed and charged to the exact second. Simply pass your right hand over the scanner and you will be identified instantaneously and processed automatically wherever you are. When I went upstairs to the bar to buy a drink, I instinctively reached for the coins in my pocket. But there were no coins, because there was no pocket. There was no pocket because there were no clothes. To buy a drink, you simply press your wrist-worn "wearable computer" against the conveniently located countertop interface.

There is no cash register, and therefore there is no cash register tape, printout, or any other receipts. No paper at all. Nothing that the individual might use to keep their own record or even make a personal note. Why would we want a receipt anyway, since we had no pockets to keep them in? The history of my visit to the spa, time and attendance, purchases, etc., was entirely in the domain of an outside entity. I had no personal record, up to this point. I wondered how disputes might be resolved, for example, if the computer network somehow decided I owed more money than I thought I did. I would never know until I left this idyllic world, since there was no way to view any of the information inside that chip on my wrist. I had visions of revisions — visions of the Ministry of Truth maintaining a historical account of where I was and how many glasses of orange juice I had that day, and the exact microsecond at which each was purchased. As Orwell once said, "Control the past and you control the future." The past record of what I had consumed was soon to become the debt I would pay in the near future.

Schwaben Quellen is a relatively big water park. It's sufficiently vast and expansive to feel like it can go on forever, especially with all the trees and artificial rock formations. In fact, it's easy to get lost in the park; trying to remember where the exit is, and finding your way out, takes a few minutes — a few minutes of extra time ticking away at a cost of DM 3 per half-hour. As I stepped back into the "reality" of laser light shining into my eyes, the comfortable warmth of my computational clothing, and the sixth and seventh senses of the "real" world I have come to know and love, I felt somehow relieved that the cost of getting away from reality for approximately two hours was only DM 32, plus a little extra for drinks. I guess they decided not to alter the past, at least not too much anyway. What will the future bring? A swim-up bar? Swim-up blackjack? (Both of these "luxuries" are already available today, on the charge-it-to-my-room principle.) Perhaps in some domed city, with a tropical climate (real or artificial), we will all be able to drink, gamble, and frolic with reckless abandon, without ever having to come into contact with cold hard cash. And to do so, we'll be asked (not forced) to wear a computer we have no control over. In most cases, we'll simply choose to do what seems to be expected of us, in order to receive the benefits, or what we perceive to be the benefits, of becoming similar to electronically tagged animals at feedlots. What could be easier than running around naked and pressing your wrist against the counter every time you want something? No need to worry about program source code, makefiles, and optimizing compilers. Just put absolute trust in your water park owner, your casino operator, your insurance company, and your bank.

Here, again, the "smart" model that takes care of your needs is touted as superior to other ways in which you may interact/integrate with technology on an everyday basis. But easy does not always mean good for you. Drugs are not hard to use, nor do they require you to learn how they work, their principle of operation, or any of the details of their user interface. Like drug use, the future of wearable computers could feel good, comfortable, and easy. It could also be addictive. With so much profit to be made, how could anyone oppose it? Perhaps government and industry will work together to make the world comfortable and easy — "safe and calm if you sing along."

CEILING DOMES OF WINE-DARK OPACITY

What if you don't want to sing along and allow your daily life to become part of a giant government/corporate improvement scheme in which wearable technology underpins a surveillance infrastructure? Professor and social critic Margaret Morse warns that

> Cyberspace is not merely space as a scene where things could happen, it is also the artificial intelligence or agency that puts the virtual scene in place. . . . As a consequence the virtual environment that surrounds the visitor can appear to be something "live" or inanimate, that sees us without being seen. One implication is that cyberspace has the potential to be the most powerful and effective means of surveillance and social control, not merely of the user in cyberspace, but of the external material world, yet invented.[8]

We are already being recorded as never before, all without our consent. A landmark 1995 article in *Wired* by Phil Patton underscored the ubiquitous nature of video surveillance, and also touched on its darker side — hidden cameras. Patton refers to "glass ceiling domes of wine-dark opacity."[9] These smoked glass or plastic domes are a surveillance smokescreen, installed in an attempt to hide their contents. However, I've occasionally seen them opened up for repair. Inside is yet another layer of secrecy: an opaque matte-black shroud that prevents light from passing through the dark cover, leaving the camera cloaked in darkness. Why are the designers of these systems (and those who buy them) so paranoid? What are they trying to hide? Once, when taking a picture of a "ceiling dome of wine-dark opacity" (at the MIT bookstore, double-shooting, that is, looking through the viewfinder of an ordinary camera using my eyeglass-based Wearable Wireless WebCam, so that my viewing audience could experience vicariously the process of taking a picture with an ordinary camera), the store manager instantly appeared out of nowhere, telling me that I was not allowed to take pictures. I asked her why, and she said it was store policy. I asked her if the store policy was available in written form anywhere, and

she could not provide me with any such policy. Thinking on my feet about one of the research projects I was working on at the time (to make a 3-D computer-aided design model of the university campus), I asked the manager about taking measurements in the store, to which she said special permission would be required. After

In response to the ubiquity of opaque ceiling domes, my students and I created our own line of opaque dome fashions.

talking about this for a few minutes, it became apparent that I would need to get written permission from head office just to stand in one corner of the store and count the ceiling tiles (to make a note of the dimensions of the store in units of ceiling tiles). To what purpose was her all-consuming paranoia?

In addition to the by-now-pervasive "ceiling domes of wine-dark opacity," there are the partially silvered domes, the dark windows, and the partially silvered mirrors. Patton makes reference to the fact that "many department stores use video cameras behind one-way mirrors in changing rooms." There are ongoing reports concerning hidden cameras in change rooms, washrooms, and employee locker rooms. As if that wasn't bad enough, the recent proliferation of one-way mirrors or dark windows in the back of many toilet stalls, used in conjunction with automatic flush toilets and faucets, must raise some questions as to their potential misuse by employers and other organizations. The management of a prominent hotel chain — accused of using surveillance cameras in employee change rooms — justified their practices by claiming that they suspected drug use.

Another dome fashion.

Whether we're using an intelligent automatic teller machine, or an intelligent automatic flush toilet, we're seen through the glass, darkly. In the coming decades, with the proliferation of ever-smaller technologies — particularly, though not limited to, cameras — we will have to reconsider seriously what our rights are in terms of when and where we should be observed. "For many years," reports an article on shrinking gadgets, "technology of all sorts — electronic and otherwise — was big and frightening. Soon enough it will be too small to see, and therefore scary in another way."[10] Already, we rarely know when and how we are being recorded. Only if we do something wrong will we see our accuser (in court). Yet, I believe we have a right to know how and when information about us is accumulated, processed, and used. Should we simply place absolute trust in authority? It's hard to place absolute trust in organizations that don't trust us. There are some serious issues here that go far beyond getting off a mailing list or having a driver's license number that is different than your social security number. These are, after all, just attempts to shore up the notion of a privacy — a pseudo-privacy — that seems ever more fragile. Coming from the showers in a

University of Toronto locker room, I find myself face to face with a pair of lenses above a urinal. I do not know what is behind the metal plate, so securely fastened with tamper-proof screws. Machine vision has become a little too omnipresent.

AUTOMATIC RECOGNITION

The perceived "success" of video cameras in banks has led to their use in department stores, first at the cash register and then throughout the store, monitoring the general activities of shoppers. "Success" there has led to governments using ubiquitous surveillance throughout entire cities to monitor the general activities of citizens. In Baltimore, throughout the downtown area, the government installed two hundred cameras as part of an experiment that, if "successful," would lead to other cities becoming similarly equipped. Britain already has around 200,000 video surveillance cameras monitoring streets and shopping centres. The use of hidden cameras by both businesses and governments is increasing dramatically. Meanwhile, another form of visual surveillance and environmental intelligence is becoming popular: Automatic Face Recognition:

> A computer system being installed at welfare offices will compare each applicant's face to a database of thousands of other recipients' faces . . . exposing fraud faster and more efficiently than other methods such as fingerprinting. . . . Viisage Technology, in Acton, bought the rights . . . and produced the fraud-detection system for the welfare department. Under its $112,500 state contract, Viisage will provide facial-recognition and fingerprinting services to welfare offices in Springfield and Lawrence as part of a six-month pilot program.[11]

Companies are integrating Automatic Face Recognition technology with the surveillance infrastructure so that cameras, for instance, can be programmed to notice if someone is lingering in one spot too long or to recognize a reappearing face. It all culminates in secret mass searches, such as the Tampa, Florida police using Face Recognition software to compare all 72,000 people attending Super Bowl XXXV to a database of wanted criminals. Although there is significant resistance to Automatic Face Recognition, the vast majority of us willingly submit to invasions of privacy as long as they appear to enhance the comfort and safety of our lives.

One minor example is television set top-boxes, designed for deployment in people's homes, with built-in devices that allow the cable TV company to track what people watch and when. These are willingly accepted by many, with the numbers growing as pay-per-use and individualized digital satellite technologies become available in the home.

In the workplace, possible future innovations include pressure-based imaging sensors inside office chairs that provide a so-called "butt print" in real-time video. The stated goal of the smart chair project is "to build a smart chair by making it aware of the user's activities (posture, movement, and sitting habits.)"12 Mark Weiser, head of Xerox Parc's Ubiquitous Computing Project, pursued the ultimate "interactive" office in which, as Mark Stefik puts it in his book *The Internet Edge*, "individuals would carry small badges linked through infrared beams to let the Net keep track of where they were."13

Just as frightening is a synthetic aperture camera capable of seeing through clothing, with applications such as "securing buildings from employee theft" or allowing "police to covertly monitor crowds for weapons." Although proponents envision recorded images "being viewed only by same-sex security officers," the situation raises the question: Would a security guard be willing to pose naked with a promise that images would only be viewed by a same-sex citizen?

Meanwhile, researchers at British Telecommunications are working on a computer chip that, once implanted in the brain, can record (and even transmit) memories. "A micromemory chip implanted in the human brain, implanted for the whole of a lifetime, meant to record the whole of a lifetime,"[14] is how the invention is described. However, the attractive notion of recording your life as you live it has a dark side. Here's a posting to an on-line discussion group I came across, originating from the University of Texas Southwestern Medical Center at Dallas: ". . . a more mobile . . . device would allow for criminal's movements to be tracked even when they're on parole instead of just under house arrest. The implant approach would be the ultimate, allowing us to track criminals after they're paroled . . . Ethics shmethics, I can see a real benefit to tracking . . . and no downside."[15]

Why not match all this activity to the "smart" house or office that will "constantly watch" us and "try to be helpful at all times"? Such help could include a camera in the bedroom so that as soon as the occupant wakes up, the coffee starts brewing. There could also be a camera in the shower, perhaps to trigger the toaster, or perhaps to scan the skin for developing abnormalities. Smart spaces, along with implantable chips, could eradicate human freedom, no matter what rhetorical hoops we jump through in order to redefine privacy and solitude to make sense of shifting priorities in the "information" age.

Though not all of these developments reside strictly in the domain of the wearable computer, many of their underpinnings depend on the smart clothing concept and are certainly influenced and encouraged by the arrival of various wearable technologies:

CELEBRATION, FLA.—(BUSINESS WIRE)—March 17, 1999—Dallas Semiconductor (NYSE:DS—news) jointly announced that Celebration School, a K-12 innovative public school in Celebration, Florida, has issued students small, wearable computers that will grant access to buildings, classrooms, computers and

Web pages. The 'key' to Celebration School is a Java™ computer chip armoured in a small stainless steel case . . . the student will press to gain access to a building or a specific classroom door . . . conditional access to a Web page from any computer on the intranet at school or from home using the Internet. Michael Bolan, vice president of product development at Dallas Semiconductor, said, "Of course students use computers, but they haven't been able to wear them until now. Each student is issued an iButton that can be worn according to the individual's preference — on a ring, a key fob, a dog tag, or a watch. . . . The authentication server controls all access privileges to the networked doors, computers and Web pages. . . . Class attendance can be automatically captured by the networked classroom door. The doorknob has an embedded Java computer that . . . forwards the time and attendance record to the server."[16]

As at the German spa, the principle of for-your-own-good "smart" badges and watches is now being applied to schools. Again, these are devices over which the wearer does not have control. They are programmed, controlled, tracked, etc., by remote means. They violate the principle of existentiality, and they violate the humanistic notion that wearable technology should allow us to control how we choose to use our own privacy. The ownership of the humanistic property (the data trail showing where a person has gone, what they ate for lunch in the school cafeteria, etc.) is of great interest to large corporations. Thus, not surprisingly ". . . the school is a partnership between the Walt Disney Company, Stetson University and the Osceola, Florida school district."[17] Perhaps in time schools and corporations will complete their merger, offering their students a quasi-education and including on the mandatory smart card such services as the teen-targeted M2Card, which provides bonus shopping points for "purchases or consumer information." I wonder how the functionality of these devices differs significantly from that which would be obtained by issuing prison uniforms each bearing a number: ". . . a computer chip contained in a small, durable stainless steel case about the size of a dime. The Java-Powered iButton has a unique identity: a 64-bit registration number engraved in the silicon. And best of all, it runs Java. Each student will be issued [one]." The central issue here is ownership of space, versus use of space. Prisoners, for example, are often allowed personal effects (such as family photos) in their cells, but the defining characteristic is that they do not have personal space that is inaccessible to the guards. The computer chip described above facilitates guarding even as it allows for some recording of personal data by the individual — personal data that are wholly available to the issuer, a.k.a. the guards. Of course, the device also acts as a tracking and surveillance mechanism: "Door access authorization is managed by operator defined time schedules and door combinations. Audit trail data can be viewed in multiple real-time filtered views or with a history based query . . . can support access for almost unlimited doors and individuals and keeps a complete audit trail of who entered and when."

We often place infinite, or near infinite, trust in government officials and large corporations as the keepers of our personal information. However, even if the value of this information is small on an individual basis, the market for it is sufficiently lucrative that there will be theft through bribery, corruption of officials, or other means:

A small New Hampshire company that wants to build a national database of driver's license photographs received nearly $1.5 million in federal funds and technical assistance from the U.S. Secret Service last year. . . . These details about Image Data's development add fuel to an intense privacy debate that was touched off last month by reports that the Nashua, N.H., company recently bought more than 22 million drivers' images in South Carolina, Florida and Colorado. As the company lobbied to gain access to motor vehicle files, officials apparently told few people about its ties to the Secret Service or the money it received from Congress . . . [18]

The Canadian government held a massive database on millions of low-income citizens with information including education, marital status, income tax, employment, ethnic origin, disabilities, and social assistance history. When the press marshalled a public outcry, the database was claimed to have been destroyed. On-line companies who promise not to sell the personal information they collect do just that when they fall on hard times, reports *The Globe and Mail* in an article entitled "E-tailer Shakeout Punctures Privacy." The British government has passed a law that gives "authorities . . . broad powers to intercept and decode e-mail messages."[19] The FBI has developed Carnivore, "which, once installed on the network of an Internet Service Provider, can troll through millions of e-mail messages and home in on the electronic correspondence of suspects."[20] All this brings to mind the dissenting opinion of famed American Supreme Court Justice Louis D. Brandeis who, objecting to a 1928 decision to allow wiretapping without a warrant, wrote: "The progress of science in furnishing the government with the means of espionage is not likely to stop with wiretapping. Ways may someday be developed by which the government, without removing papers from secret drawers, can reproduce them in court, by which it will be enabled to expose to a jury the most intimate occurrences of the home."[21]

Is this the post-human future? "Those who desire to give up Freedom in order to gain Security, will not have, nor do they deserve, either one," warned Thomas Jefferson. "There is no place for the privacy factor when public safety is concerned,"[22] rebuts John Fitzgerald, a U.S. postal service supervisor. It's not hard to imagine getting cheaper insurance rates if one is willing to wear a monitoring device. One could be provided with a device that would track its location at all times, and also monitor and record various bodily functions. The value of the humanistic property the corporation could simultaneously collect with such an apparatus (where you go, what you buy, etc.) could easily offset the moderate cost, such that wearable computers might be provided free of charge to anyone wanting one. Initially, the program would be voluntary, of course. However, as more and more daily activities are set up to facilitate integration with the wearable system, people will find themselves passively "required" to have a wearable computer to live a "normal" life just as, today, we are "required" to have a bank account and a credit card and a driver's licence in order to do things in society such as buy a car or rent an apartment or get a job. Someday soon it will seem abnormal not to have a wearable computer provided by an insurance company to keep track of your health and whereabouts for your own safety, even as the insurance company sells information about where you go, what you do, and what you buy to the highest bidder. Once a "smart" card becomes familiar, even inconvenient, how about a programmable, implantable tattoo featuring a computer chip with readout visible through the skin? Science fiction? It's already been patented. As a reporter for the *Toronto Star* noted in an article titled "The Little Brothers are Watching You": "Big Brother is not going to appear one day, announce himself and take over by force. He will come in by stealth, bit by bit, in the guise of small and reasonable intrusions."[23] The Critical Arts Ensemble puts it in more bombastic terms: "Extreme body invasion as socially accepted practice is a key step in cyborg development." The arrival of the wearable computer is inevitable. However, with its onset, must we also say goodbye to our right to live an even partially unobserved life?

PERSONALIZE YOUR VIDEO:
WEARCOMP VERSUS HANDYCAM

As more and more of us enter into a cyborg existence, we will harness personal technologies in new and unexpected ways. I believe that the only way to successfully challenge ubiquitous surveillance and its "safe and happy in the happy house" smart card counterpart is to use the machine against itself, to turn the tables. I've already discussed WearComp's potential uses for journalists, filmmakers, photographers, etc. My own experiment with the device as a way to further the project of inserting our lives into the milieu of the media (a popular enough project, if you consider how many e-zines/personal/quasi-public Web sites and e-diaries there are now) suggests further "practical" applications for its use as a tool in providing fair access to the mass media. At the same time, my Wearable Wireless WebCam project was undeniably an act of performance in the spirit of the Reflectionist interventions described earlier in this book. In confronting viewers with their own addiction to watching someone else's life, I hoped to challenge and reassess our shared societal obsession with voyeurism and privacy invasion.

But in making that challenge, I also came to realize other, perhaps more immediate and practical, everyday applications for the widespread use of wearable technology. Diffusionism, you may recall, is my attempt to answer the problems that technology creates in society with more technology, battling the machine with the machine. In addition to the practical methods already discussed — WearComp as a potential broadcasting tool, as an ad-exclusion filter — in the case of privacy and solitude, Diffusionism has several roles to play.

Perhaps the most potent Diffusionist strategy for challenging the concentrations of power endemic to the age of surveillance is the subversion of the totalitarian nature of surveillance through a proliferation of wearable and "maybe" cameras.[24] As Foucault has noted, it is not essential that the guard in the tower be watching a particular prisoner, or even that there be a guard in the tower; it is only necessary that the prisoner not know whether there is a guard watching in the tower. "The perfection of power should tend to render its actual exercise unnecessary," he states.[25] Similarly, to subvert panopticon ubiquitous surveillance, it would not be essential that the guard be watched at all times, but just that there be a possibility that the guard could be observed by a "prisoner" at some time. In the coming cyborg age, it will be increasingly difficult to ascertain who is wearing and broadcasting at any given time. Just as human rights violations in Yugoslavia and abuses of authority such as the Rodney King incident in Los Angeles have been uncovered in recent years largely due to the spread of portable video cameras, the wearable WebCam ups the ante, turning the tables on those who would have us constantly monitored by applying a similar constraint. Those in authority tempted to break the law will have to be aware that there is very little in the public sphere that will happen free from the prying eyes of a potentially public broadcast. At the same time, anyone who commits a criminal act against another individual will be aware that their visage could be not just recorded, but instantly transmitted to a remote location they are unable to destroy.

Of course, it will not be feasible to equip every citizen with a potentially broadcasting wearable camera. Will the underprivileged be left out of this potential new safety system? Not necessarily. In the same way that many residences claim to have alarm systems that are not actually installed, and similar to the man who installs a fake cellular antenna on his car, we can imagine a proliferation of nonfunctioning "maybe" cameras. Is the camera on the computer I'm wearing actually broadcasting? Well, do you feel lucky?

That someone — anyone — might be equipped with a hidden WebCam would, I believe, be a strong disincentive for those tempted to abuse authority. As frightening as it may be to imagine, certainly, this kind of proliferation would be more of a catalyst for change than the camcorder has proven to be. The WearComp system addresses the flaws of the camcorder as a means of empowering individuals to turn the tables on a surveillance infrastructure. There are a number of weaknesses to camcorder technologies including inconvenience, obtrusiveness, destructibility of the evidence (for example, lack of wireless transmission to offsite backup), and the inability of the camcorder operator to conceal its intended use.

A camcorder's use requires an active role. Despite names like HandyCam, it does require thought and effort to pull it out and begin recording with it, whereas its Big Brother equivalent (the surveillance camera on the lamppost or ceiling) requires zero effort to engage — it is always on. I know from experience that pulling out a camcorder attracts considerable attention — often resulting in attempts to confiscate or destroy the machine. Holding a camcorder up to the eye shows intent to take a picture, whereas an EyeTap device is incidental (it's not clear whether the picture taking act is deliberate, or incidental, such as when the wearer simply forgets to turn the rig off.) This brings us to the second weakness of the camcorder: local storage. WearCam sends the images over the Internet, so they can be backed up in one or more remote locations, in various countries around the world. Basically, WearCam can instantaneously produce an indestructible visual record. I won't go as far as saying that such a record would be a "record of fact." We know that images can be electronically altered. William Mitchell's book *Reconfigured Eye* gives a thorough account of the multiple visual truths possible in the digital era. However, multiple independent accounts will bring us closer to truth than the account of one omnipotent entity. In fact, we can learn quite a bit by comparing multiple independent accounts of an event. We may compare them and, if they differ, we may scrutinize them thoroughly in the areas in which they differ. In particular, a party falsifying and manipulating images will no doubt overlook some subtle kinematic constraints on object motion, or perhaps there will be an accidental glint of a clock face in a mirror somewhere, or perhaps the pixels won't quite dance in exactly the right way.

If camera images can no longer be used as a record of truth, they can be used to augment our memory. I can relive my Christmas vacation by scrolling through my WearCam flashback image sequence, even if it is severely downsampled (showing me only one of every hundred frames or so). The lowest resolution video brings it all back to my mind, even if the images are barely discernible. The distributed nature of the WearCam visual memory prosthetic's data would make it less subject to a totalitarian control than traditional HandyCams, which can easily be confiscated and destroyed. The ubiquitous use of WearCams will tip the balance a little toward the centre — toward a little bit of fairness on the surveillance superhighway. While the taxi drivers, law enforcement officers, shopkeepers, and government officials will continue to have surveillance, now the passengers, suspects, shoppers, and citizens will be able to keep their own memory of the event, putting everyone on a fair and equal footing.

Once one of my images is distributed via the World Wide Web, it is further beyond the destructive powers of department store security guards and the like, as I no longer know how many copies of the transmitted pictures might have been made. Evidence that might, for example, show that a department store has illegally chained shut its fire exits is not only beyond the store's ability to seize or destroy, but is also within easy reach of the fire marshall, who, following my directions via cellular phone from the department store, need only have a standard desktop computer with Web browser to see first-hand what my call pertains to. WearCam on the Web thus extends this "personal safety" infrastructure and further deters abuses: on one hand, I have collected the indestructible evidence of hostile actions, and on the other, friends, relatives, even strangers, may be watching, in real time, at any given moment.

This process is a form of "personal documentary" or "personal video diary." Wearable Wireless WebCam challenges the "editing" tradition of cinematography by transmitting, in real time, life as it happens, from the perspective of the surveilled. Although other technologies, such as desktop computers, can help us protect our privacy with programs such as Pretty Good Privacy (PGP), the Achilles heel of these systems is the space between us and them. It is generally far easier for an attacker to compromise the link between us and the computer (perhaps through a so-called Trojan Horse or other planted virus) than it is to compromise the link between our computer and other computers. So wearable computing can be used to create a new level of personal privacy because it is almost always worn, and therefore less likely to fall prey to covert attacks upon the hardware itself.

My WearComp invention formed the basis on which I built a prosthetic camera that was worn rather than carried and could be operated with both hands free. In this sense, the video-recording/transmission functionality of the apparatus appeared incidental rather than intentional. When I wore the WearCam into an establishment, I did not give the impression that my purpose was to record video, partly because the apparatus was less visible than a traditional camera, but more importantly because the apparatus did not have the appearance of intentionality. In this way, the apparatus provided a mirror-like symmetry between myself and those placing me under surveillance (for example, a mall's security guards): The apparatus provided a means of taking pictures of representatives of establishments that place customers under surveillance, in such a way that those representatives could not determine whether such pictures were being taken (just as we never know whether a department store surveillance camera is actually capturing an image of us at any given time).

SHOOTING BACK

The fact that I, as an individual, had the technology to replicate long-standing forms of institutional surveillance both frightened and encouraged me. It also gave me an idea for what would prove to be my longest and most daunting Reflectionist experiment: During the two years of my Wearable Wireless WebCam project, I shot a lengthy documentary on the subject of hidden cameras, systemic surveillance, and the individual's right to confront that surveillance with their own monitoring. Since in some sense I am already a camera, I do not need to carry a camera to make a documentary, but in *ShootingBack*, I did anyway. This second camera, an ordinary hand-held video camera, which I carried in a satchel, served as a prop with which to confront members of organizations that place us under surveillance. I focussed primarily on the retail world, a world of inviting stores that beckon you in to see their wares, record your every move, and usually prohibit customers from taking pictures. I attempted to draw attention to this phenomenon of unreciprocated video surveillance in *ShootingBack*, compiled from video transmitted to the Internet from several different countries during the course of the WebCam experiment. Whenever I found myself in a store or some other establishment with electronic eyes perusing the customers, I asked management why they were taking pictures of me without my permission. They would typically ask me why I was so paranoid and tell

Scenes from the anti-surveillance documentary *ShootingBack*.

me that only criminals are afraid of cameras. Of course, I was covertly recording this response using my own hidden EyeTap video camera. Then I would pull an ordinary camcorder out of my satchel and give them a chance to define themselves. (The camcorder was simply a prop, as the virtual EyeTap video camera had been capturing and transmitting the video to my Web site.)

Oddly enough, the same people who claimed that only criminals were afraid of cameras had an instantly paranoid (and sometimes violent) reaction to my camcorder. At a gas station in Toronto the attendants physically prevented me from leaving and demanded the film from my camera. I calmly explained to them that, in fact, there was no film and that if they wished to have my footage of the gas station deleted they would have to talk to my system manager, who was unavailable at the moment. This agitated the employees even further, and I was physically assaulted and unlawfully detained by the employees and the manager. What did this group have to hide? Probably nothing. Theirs was simply an extreme reaction to the very idea that they — agents of the corporate — should be asked to undergo the same scrutiny as the customer. Who was I to take pictures of them?

ShootingBack was, I

Scenes from the anti-surveillance documentary *ShootingBack*.

believe, the first documentary to be transmitted in real time to the World Wide Web, as it was shot. Again, *ShootingBack* was both performance art and a practical solution to ubiquitous surveillance. What better way to actively confront the way we are being filmed by the infrastructure than to pull out a camera and make a record of those who are filming us? WearComp devices will make this practice not just pragmatic but ubiquitous. We can and we must turn the tables on those who would watch us. The more possible and actual cameras there are available to those capable of on-line broadcasting, the more likely it will be that *we* are watching *them*, to the detriment of *their* ability to watch *us*. Sandy Stone writes of the "conflict between the technologies of government by which societies have traditionally kept order and the multiple fragmenting entities that political 'citizens' are actually becoming."[26] In exponentially reclaiming surveillance as the right of the individual, we devalue surveillance as an authoritarian tool (something that everyone can do is hardly as frightening as something that only large institutions can do) even as we explore the effect on society of the cyborg's new-found ability to fragment the monolithic technologies of media and surveillance.

A LEVEL PLAYING FIELD

In almost any society, you can rank observation in decreasing order of acceptability and perceived fairness as follows:

- Government looking at people.
- Establishments looking at people.
- Establishments looking at establishments or people looking at people.
- People looking at establishments.
- People looking at government.

Obviously, I am hoping that something similar to WearComp will be used to level that playing field. Why should it be more acceptable for the government or a store to spy on us than for us to spy on them? From my perspective, surveillance is actually desirable when aimed at Big Brother (and possibly also at Big Business). It would seem logical that organizations capable of wrongdoing should be placed under a degree of surveillance proportional to their gain over the individual. The potential damage to society of a large and unaccountable organization operating above the law is far greater than the damage an individual might inflict by stealing a loaf of bread. Thus it is possible that society would do well to place certain large organizations under greater scrutiny than a shopper at the local convenience store or someone walking down a public sidewalk. I call this public scrutiny of establishments/governments "sousveillance" (the opposite of surveillance). Surveillance is French for "watch over" (authority watching from above), whereas what I propose is an "inverse surveillance," whereby we keep watch on those in high places.

Should we be afraid of an EyeTap device wirelessly connected to a computer network? Perhaps the question makes better sense this way: Who should be afraid of the wearable camera transmitting live to the Internet? True, such a contraption does reduce our privacy, slightly or dramatically, depending on what we perceive to be our current ability to live an unobserved life. Any way you look at it, it's one more camera in a world already full of cameras. However, given a choice between hidden cameras in my workplace and cameras mounted on people in my workplace, I'd choose the latter.

Even at this budding stage of the cyborg age, we must accept that we are being watched or recorded when we are in public spaces. In many ways, our rhetorical discourse on preserving our pseudo-privacy has obscured the issue of how we can fight to counteract ubiquitous surveillance: Certainly, the answer is not to lobby our government to make privacy leaks even less noticeable (taking the stink out of the gas). We must instead shift our priorities and, in some way, cut our losses. We are better off assuming that in the public sphere we are always being recorded than we are insisting that we shouldn't have to be confronted with the evidence of those who sell our personal information to the highest bidder. (Let the gas leak, we say, only don't let us have to keep smelling it.) So, yes, I advocate proliferation — let the leak continue, let the smell get so thick that none of us, even those in the cloistered offices of power, can stand it.

In "performing" the Wearable Wireless WebCam experiment, I was perpetually mystified by the number of people who wanted to spend time watching me go about my daily activities. Similarly, Laura Lee, a thirty-eight-year-old Toronto resident whose day job consists of going about her condo scantily clad for the benefit of her Web subscribers, has commented that she "can't believe there are so many people who'll pay to watch me waxing the floor."[27] I wonder whether, in observing "regular" individuals going about their "regular" lives, we hope to catch some glimpse of ourselves. If so, experiments such as my broadcast cannot help but add to the pacifying entertainment illusion. I invite people to subsume their lives in mine, providing yet another ersatz experience that stands in for "real" life. But perhaps we should also consider the issue in this way: What happens when the on-line videographic life becomes more "real" than so-called "ordinary" life?

The WebCam experience reaffirms the mass media "system" by recording and broadcasting people without their knowledge and adding to the sense of a technological infrastructure we are powerless to confront. At the same time, it challenges the illusion of a safe, homogenized world in which only criminals fear surveillance technology and only professional entertainers appear on our screens. How do we reconcile these conflicting paradigms? Do we want into the illusion, or out of it? I, like many others, want the best of both worlds. I want freedom from illusion, and freedom to create my own illusions.

toward community

5

CYBORG TELEVISION STATION

I n the spring of 2000, a group of my students joined me in "broad-casting" live the events of a protest in Toronto staged by a group called Ontario Coalition Against Poverty (OCAP). As it turned out, nobody from the Ontario government wished to acknowledge the protest being undertaken on the lawn out-side Queen's Park, its legisla-ture. The protesters became agitated and, with a massive police presence acting as a cat-alyst, a degree of violence ensued. We, along with the journalists and various televi-sions crews, ran for cover. However, unlike the reporters,

Image from the 2000 OCAP protest in Toronto as transmitted live to the Internet through my student James Fung's EyeTap.

my students and I were still broadcasting, capturing almost by accident the entire event. Whatever we saw before us was captured and sent instantly in real time to the World Wide Web, without our conscious thought or effort. Wearing devices that tapped into our eyes and transmitted what we saw, my students and I could not do anything but act as instantaneous recorders. For teaching purposes, some of the EyeTaps were built oversize and placed on the outside of glasses, or on the bright yellow engineering hard hats that engineers traditionally wear on construction sites. As a result, many of the devices were more obvious than the models of WearComp I use, and their presence probably had a mitigating effect on both police and protestor behaviour. More importantly, our perspective on the event was captured and transmitted to remote locations, and the official, typical response to the protest as put forward in the media — that a dangerous bunch of radicals threatened to storm the legislature for no apparent reason — was countered by our poignant images of police massing and moving in on the primarily peaceful protestors. The images of the police preparing to rush the crowd are frightening, but perhaps more

ominous was the relative absence of those images from the local news. Other recorded moments were too fragmented and personal for the media, and yet, they, too, spoke to the

More images from the OCAP protest as transmitted.

events of that day: a lone protestor throwing a brick through a window of the legislature; an observer witnessing the police response to the protest and spontaneously breaking into a satiric fascist salute; several police officers surrounding a young girl writing with chalk on the sidewalk.

We live in a time of media concentration, consolidation and, most dangerously, what media executives proudly describe as convergence. This latter term is the process by which media conglomerates acquire media networks in all the various formats so that they own and recycle content through their grand interconnected network of television, print, film, and World Wide Web. The results of this convergence are twofold. On the one hand, information that the network (increasingly in the hands of fewer and fewer multinational players) does not deem appropriate simply disappears. Opposing points of view are downplayed and distorted in favour of opinions that shore up a system of mindless consumption — whether of movies, junk food or technological tidbits. On the other hand, the prevalence of an interconnected media where news and entertainment merge into one seamless, endless flow of prepackaged content has become, as a *New York Times* reporter put it, "a kind of constant alternative consciousness in which we are all forced to dwell."[1]

I evoke the *doppelgänger* reality of media only to suggest that one of the emerging problems of the twentieth century and its legacy of mass communication is that large percentages of the population are permitted little or no access to the media web. Too many of us are forced dwellers, passive, suppressed, living like the famous figures trapped in Plato's cave who spend their lives staring at the enticing glow — desperately clinging to their version of a reality that only serves to maintain their confinement. WearComp represents a solution to this legacy of suppressed creativity and confining imagination in an age where ever-fewer sources of information seem to reach us, even as the conduits of information grow exponentially. What my students and I undertook in deciding to "cover" the OCAP protest was an experiment in media diversification. This is the process by which we merge our cyborg narratives with the demands of a growing cyberspace that we should, and one day will, be able to interact with and control. Facilitating the individual's creation and broadcast of their own narratives and perspectives is an important aspect of wearable computing technology. With this ability the Internet will become a true (cyber)space where, as Kalle Lasn, editor of the anti-consumption magazine *Adbusters* puts it, "people . . . tell their stories to the whole world."[2]

What my students and I did — and continue to do — is something far more important than just providing "home movies" and "alternative" images for viewing on the Internet. We are also engaging in a process of cultural reclamation, where the individual is put back into the loop of information production and dispensation. In *All Together Now*, an examination of what happens when each household of a suburban community is given access to high-tech connectivity, Paul Hoffert describes this transition. He writes that "the old mass media framework was predominantly a framework of few to many . . . The new connectivity, on the other hand, is essentially symmetric and configurable: one to one, one to many, few to many, and so on. It is also interactive, so we can supply information as well as receive it."[3]

With an ever-increasing number of media-empowered cyborgs able to act as their own videographers, news-gatherers, filmmakers, and publishers, the corporate convergence will be only one version of an increasingly permeable shared reality. WearComp creates a possibility that choice can proliferate. In such an environment, those content providers that maintain an autocratic grip on what kinds of news, music, books, and television shows we have access to will be challenged. Choice will proliferate and ideas around what is and is not permissible to enter the media convergence will be irrelevant. Don't like what's on TV? Make your own show tonight, and send out a million e-mails to alert the cyborg community of your broadcast. Disagree with the version of the protest the one-sided nightly news is putting forward? Set up your own Internet broadcast to address the issue. Since WearComp specifically causes your eye to function as a camera, it is a system that implicitly recognizes the increasing importance of individual voices (or sights/sites) in a world where pretested, focus-grouped replaceable entertainment product is permitted to saturate the mental environment — pushing out much of our ability to use new technologies to chronicle our own lives and communities. In Neil Gaiman's sci-fi comic *Miracleman*, an android Andy Warhol copy exuberantly pronounces: "I don't need a tape recorder any more — I am a tape recorder."[4] In the near future, we will all be tape recorders, and video recorders too. One cannot enter the cyborg world without learning a lesson in how images are framed and presented — a lesson that will be, ultimately, about freeing cultural discourses from the power brokers by making culture the business of "amateurs" who can tell their own stories from their own point of view. This is not to say that our cultural discourse will lack sophistication or that no one will continue to make their living as a writer or painter or director. Rather, the point is that devices such as WearComp can and will make a variety of different kinds of cultural narratives possible — professional artists will no longer feel that they must conform to the strategies of mass-marketed cultural product, and non-professional creators will no longer feel that the media and their vortex of proliferating narratives are the exclusive terrain of experts. A greater variety of narratives that allows for both professional and non-professional cultural expression can be fostered by wearable computing devices linked to the Internet, particularly since the desire to create culture on an independent basis is hampered, not by a lack of creative energy, but by the expense involved and the monopoly that "professional" dispensers of cultural product maintain on systems of mass distribution. Once this outmoded system is abandoned, a new kind of convergence will be possible, this one a convergence of social interaction with a media owned, operated, and facilitated by an infinite number of interrelated (cyborg) communities.

THE MEDIA AS CYBORGSPACE

What may sound like a radical pronouncement is mediated by the fact that the onset of mass media has always been the terrain of cyborgs. Here we have a non-physical space — an "alternative consciousness" in which, nonetheless, real lives and communities situate themselves. The question is, then, which lives, which communities, will be able to "be" in this mediaspace, known today as cyberspace but perhaps in the future to be known as cyborgspace? There have been those who have sought to turn cyborgspace into a tool for human empowerment and cultural discourse, but the more prevalent approach has been to turn this emerging cyborgspace into a tool for market outreach that converts the intrinsic desires of the human being into a system in which our stories are the tools of our subjugation, our very lives reduced to shimmering images of commodities we must acquire. (A line from Michael Jordan's *Space Jam*, quoted in Naomi Klein's *No Logo*, comes to mind: "Michael, it's show time. Get your Hanes on, lace up your Nikes, grab your Wheaties and Gatorade and we'll pick up a Big Mac on the way!")[5]

Radio, television, and now the Internet, each has promised new levels of individual and community participation. The first two mediums have failed to deliver on the promise. With the Internet — our emerging "cyborgspace" — we again have the opportunity to insert individuals into the mass media feedback loop. This opportunity is countered at every turn by multinationals that essentially see the Internet as one more medium to sell the ads they attach to their exclusionary entertainment product. The merger of Time-Warner (international purveyor of generic magazines, books, movies and music) with America Online is the largest, most egregious example of what could happen to cyborgspace. However, despite predictions by the new company's CEO that the merger will bring about the world's biggest company with a market value of $1 trillion, so far the merger, like the many attempts to do big business on the Web, hasn't made money, and critics are skeptical.

The truth is, the Internet is designed to serve an entirely different kind of synergy: the synergy between the individual and the community. Since the invention of the various mass communication apparatuses, potent countermovements have emerged to challenge and co-opt corporate domination of media/cyborg space. Amateur ("pirate") radio, 'zines (independently published not-for-profit magazines), and a multitude of Web broadcasts and small press publishers represent our burgeoning need to inject our lives into the "alternative consciousness" that mass media represents. On the Internet — the closest we've yet come to a truly democratic, "free" medium of cultural expression equally available to all — independent sites proliferate, ranging in subject matter from independent reviews of movies and indie videos to scholarly debate, "reverse engineering" (scientific analysis of how commercial products and programs work), criticism of commercial establishments, collections of amateur nudity, alternative news, and on-line public diaries. These sites represent our need and desire to reclaim the media, to inject our own voices and dialogues into it, to create a circle of participation rather than straight lines of ownership and top-down dissemination. E-diaries are particularly interesting — and will become more so as cyborg technologies that permit constant Internet access proliferate. Here we have millions of people publicly posting the details of their lives on the Internet. This is truly the foundation of a new kind of communication — an interactive, accessible hive of activity where the boundaries between public and private, of entertainment and reality, finally break down. The myriad voices demanding to enter cyborgspace on their own terms tell us that narrative, which is at the core of what the French thinker Michel de Certeau calls "the practice of everyday life," is no longer simply the means by which we are entertained, but rather the way we convey and understand our being. In today's cyborgspace convergence, narrative isn't a substitute for experience: it *is* experience. Thus, the project of cyborgspace is moving forward, propelled by technological innovations that allow us to present our own versions of events and access an audience with relative ease. In 1999, an estimated 2.5 million WebCams were purchased. These stationary cameras broadcasting to the Internet showing everything from three marijuana plants sunning in pots on an Amsterdam balcony (a site titled "Watch Them Grow"), to a coffeepot, to views of highways around the world, to people shopping for furniture in a Texas store, to people going about their personal lives in their own homes. They are just the beginning of what the cyborg revolution promises.

YOU WILL BE ASSIMILATED: CYBORG U.

In September 1998, I taught the world's first course on personal cybernetics (how to integrate the wearable computer and the human being). Flyers advertising the course were posted around the University of Toronto campus. The course attracted approximately twenty electrical engineering graduate students who explored the theory, philosophy, and practice of wearable computers and used the machines to produce collaborative digital visual art.

In this course, I not only taught students about WearComp and its functions, but also how to learn by "being at one with the machine." My intention here was both instructional and exploratory. The students had the opportunity to become some of the world's first cyborgs, thus creating the sort of community I had envisioned since my early days at McMaster University. More importantly, the students were also exposed to skills and approaches to technological innovation that they could not learn through any other means. Thus, I justified my own excitement at establishing a community of cyborgs by assuring myself that educative principles were also being applied. Looking back, it was a fairly audacious manoeuvre on my part: the students had the opportunity to, in some sense, become me, so that they could, hopefully, become more themselves, empowered by the communal spirit of the wearable computer to explore their own free-spirited sense of individuality.

The core of this experiment was really an expansion of the limited applications of the Vicarious Soliloquy and WearTel models to the classroom. It did not take much of a leap to realize that if I could deliver a speech and have the audience "become" me, I could teach a class in the same way. The question became, then, how could I go beyond mere facilitation and into true communication? How could I improve on the limitations of the Vicarious Soliloquy so that the students would realize that the cyborg experience incorporates both the values of the solitary skeptical Luddite and the values of an interpersonal and connective community?

The major differences between the classroom and the speaking engagement are the length of time available and the number of participants. In a classroom, enrolment is limited, and there is enough time to equip the students with wearable computers and help them explore the technology. Over many months, the students moved from being exposed to technologies such as the Vicarious Soliloquy to taking control of the experience — by becoming a new entity: student and machine, cyborg in training. Here, the philosophical principle of humanistic intelligence would be applied to this new cyborg technology with the hope of finding a new way to educate. I was, essentially, searching for a way to expand and understand what the process of "becoming" through personal communication technology actually entails. I turned to education, because it is the learning process that best embodies the flux of change and becoming at which the Vicarious Soliloquy and WearTel hint. I agree with Paul Hoffert when he argues that "on-line learning will form the core of all education and training within a few decades."[6] I also agree with his assertion that this shift is not necessarily preferable, but at a time of ever-growing, increasingly impersonal classes it is at least partially a solution to the problem of providing "individual" instruction on a mass scale. As Hoffert notes: "Most students today do not mind the mediated experience of learning on-line, since they rarely have the one-on-one relationship with a lecturer they prefer." I tend to agree with Hoffert's argument that some kind of virtual learning could work better than the current system in which lectures are delivered by professors encumbered by huge classes and an education system that relies on standardized exams for evaluation. So the question becomes not, Should we have on-line classrooms? but, What form will those on-line classrooms take? Can we move away from a static model of education where we first show (lecture), then have the students do (in the form of tests or practicums)? Can we use new technological innovations such as wearable computers to have the students learn not by doing but by being?

The notion of student cyborgs, cyborgs in training, has a rather ominous tone to it. The image is of free spirits who arrive feisty and full of will and leave the classroom as drones pacified and taught to perform their newly acquired functions. Such an image is, in some odd way, the reverse of the challenge the educator faces today. Today, the student quite often arrives in the classroom passive and docile, a product of a fast-food childhood and too many Saturday nights at the movies. They arrive expecting to be hand fed information and, of course, entertained. The question is: What happens to them in the classroom? Are they taught the analytic skills they need to begin to look around them, challenge assumptions, and demand answers that reflect their new-found experience? Or are they shown videos and Web sites and taught pre-packaged lessons designed to reflect the values of a society that depends on our acquiescence and silence?

THE INTERACTIVE HIGH-TECH MEDIUM KNOWN AS THE CHALKBOARD

My approach to cybernetic existential education is in many ways as much of a move backward to older technologies as it is a move forward to newer technologies. I seek to return to a time when the classroom was a place for free-ranging learning, not just another territory to encounter the domineering values of corporate entertainment (although it is true that such a time might not ever have been — like democracy, it is an ideal that may very well never have been put into practice). Regardless, the student cyborg technique of teaching relies on what I think of as the somewhat idealistic age-old concept of the interactive teaching experience.

Consider it this way: The chalkboard (and likewise, the blank sheet beneath the document camera or overhead projector) is a very interactive medium, far more interactive than any multimedia CD-ROM spectacle. When I, or any other professor, work through each equation on the chalkboard, my mind is following along in the development of the derivation, and therefore it is at one with those of the students, who are also trying to follow along. This is a truly interactive process in which all those in the classroom are drawn into the same space. Indeed, one might even say that the chalk-wielding educator is an example of humanistic intelligence at work, in that there is a system of information-sharing that includes all present in the loop. When it comes time for a student to ask a question, the professor can answer the question intelligently because of the shared mind-space, and the fact that the mind of the professor is in roughly the same state (notwithstanding a few years of additional experience) as the students. As a result, the professors who use chalk are cyborgs, while the ones who play pre-recorded multimedia spectacles are often somewhat less than cyborgs. In fact, the interactive media now infiltrating our schools at all levels — from kindergarten to university — offer just the opposite of genuine cyborg interaction. Films, videos, PowerPoint presentations, most of them have to do with passivity — knowledge passed down in the most rote, unimaginative way possible, a way that does not encourage questioning, articulate minds but rather fosters classrooms of slack-jawed TV watchers. How strange that chalk is more cyborgian than so-called "interactive" multimedia. Ironically, what I think of sarcastically as "the spectacular research society," together with the so-called "cost saving" measures of replacing knowledgeable in-person instructors with video lectures augmented by multimedia kiosks, may very well end up doing a disservice to students as opposed to preparing them for the much-touted "knowledge" economy. Similarly, the utopian promise to bring cyberspace first to all schools in North America and then to institutions across the globe, is a dubious goal. Far better to send out a cadre of committed teachers, each one equipped with nothing but a thick chunk of chalk. One purpose of my invention is to bring people together and facilitate new forms of communication and interaction. Thus it is not surprising that I like to use low-technology media such as chalk (or pen and paper) within the context of technology that facilitates true communication. We should consider that the chalkboard or the document camera allows the presenter to write directly on the medium with a compelling fluidity that far exceeds the cumbersome mouse cursor or graphics tablet of a software drawing package. The classroom is not a place for projected pie charts on pretty pastel backgrounds.

LEARN BY BEING

There have been other attempts to explore the ways in which technology may change the learning process for the better. A first step in the evolution of learning has been the shift from the standard lecture to the Constructionist Learning model. Constructionist Learning is all the rage at my alma mater MIT, which recently used a $42 million donation to erect a new centre devoted to the Constructionist Learning research effort. Constructionist Learning is, loosely speaking, "learning by doing." As the MIT Epistemology and Learning Group Web site says: "Constructionism suggests that learners are particularly likely to create new ideas when they are actively engaged in making external artifacts that they can reflect upon and share with others."[7] As much as this method makes intuitive sense, there seem to be considerable limitations to this kind of hands-on approach. For instance, how does one approach the building blocks of human thought, which include not just mathematics and concrete experiment but also philosophy, literature, and the abstract concepts that buttress all aspects of scientific inquiry? The Constructionist model may work with young children (especially when supplied with everything from programmable glowing beads to "smart" Lego), but I fear that it will lead to the abandonment of abstract study, and an increased emphasis on practical problem-solving skills that attempt to mirror the challenges of rote employment. (Too many schools are already cutting back their "unprofitable" humanities departments in favour of business schools and corporate-financed laboratories.)

My own approach to teaching through the WearComp system does not reject the Constructionist Learning model. Rather, what I am proposing is to go beyond "learn by doing" to something I call Existential Education (ExistEd) or "learn by being." ExistEd follows naturally in the evolution from traditional learning by rote, to Constructionist Learning and onward. We have already recognized the value of "hands-on" approaches such as computer laboratories, exploratory experiments, etc. Existential Education takes this notion of self-exploration a step further by encouraging the student to become one with the very subject about which he or she is trying to learn. By working in close synergy with the machine, the cyborg entity learns about the computer from an existential viewpoint in which the computer functions as a true extension of mind and body. Just as we learn to walk and run, and learn to operate our own hands and feet, students learn how to operate the apparatus of the WearComp invention. As a result, a different view of technology is adopted, one that is as much about creativity and love of knowledge (analogous to the infant's love of new-found language) as it is about circuits and batteries and learning a trade.

Critics may argue that such a system, similar to the system of Constructionist Learning, can only be applied to hands-on skills. However, the unique capabilities of the wearable computer challenge that argument. Existential education returns the learning process to the individual, but it also requires abstract skills that speak to the community: storytelling, the development of narratives — aspects of the philosophical abstraction we understand to be culture. As our experience broadcasting the OCAP protest indicates, being a cyborg is greatly enhanced by the development of a photographic mindset. The operation of the camera and new skills of cinematography and videography become natural modes — ideas around media, culture, and community are introduced into a dialogue that, at first, seemed to be about the nuts and bolts of constructing and using a wearable computer.

So, what happened in my 1998 classroom experiment? By becoming at one with the machine, the students, in effect, became the machine. In this way, they learned by "being" the computer, and discovered the existential principles of self-empowerment and self-exploration. I believe that one of the most enlightening discoveries arising from the creation of a "community of cyborgs" was that students took a personal interest in computing, once they had a collective shared "space" (mediated cyborgspace) of their own. In particular, when students felt that they owned their own hardware/software/space (as opposed to licensing it — that is, asking permission to run software — as in the Microsoft model) usage of the computer entered into ordinary facets of day-to-day living. Students communicated with each other in the course of their everyday activities and built new and interesting devices to connect to the computer that went beyond what was required in the classroom setting. Some of my students, having long since finished the requirements of the personal cybernetics course, continue to incorporate WearComp into everyday life, joining me as cyborg pioneers and applying their own experiences and innovations to what is gradually becoming not just a shared project but a collective transformation in being. Where students had previously dutifully done their lab work dragging their feet, in my course they approached the subject with excitement and passion — a far cry from the grudging duty of memorizing course material for a final exam.

Many of my students are now in the process of building WearComp systems of their own. Some have already completed their systems and have experienced the videographic cyborg world for themselves. These students have done so, not as a requirement for any course, but on their own volition. Though none of them wear the system continually as I do, they have nonetheless described to me the way their perspective and world view have changed. Students have told me that putting on their own wearable computer system has been a major event in their lives. One of my most enterprising students, James Fung, has had several experiences that mirror my own observations on cyborg life. He has told me of wearing WearComp on a trip to attend a conference in Italy, and becoming embroiled in difficulties in customs (an experience I am all too familiar with). James has worn the system long enough to begin to use it in innovative ways that one could not have anticipated (which is exactly what one might anticipate). On that same trip to Italy to attend a conference, his luggage went missing. When he later cited a conversation with a particular airline representative, and was asked who exactly he had been talking to, he was able to e-mail the airline a picture of the employee he had dealt with — even though that employee had refused to provide a name. Recently, James described to me a weekend camping trip. When night fell, while sitting around the campfire, it was asked if anyone knew any ghost stories. James did an Internet search in his right EyeTap, and began to tell the group a ghost story (reading out of his EyeTap). Most impressively, James has also developed a new program for WearComp, what he has dubbed the Musically Mediated Reality Visualization Project. This is a program that, when running, alters the wearer's visual reality in time to music playing in the MP3 format. As James writes in his report on the program, "MRV takes a video stream and alters it in time with the music." This is not the kind of research that changes the world, but it is the kind of research that integrates the human being and the computer in the search for new ways to explore cultural expression and visual perception. Quite simply, it is an example of the learn-by-being model, and an example of the way we can use technology to assert our own cultural and community identity in an anonymous digital world. I have no doubt that James will continue to assert new potentialities for the wearable computer — soon, I'll be learning as much from my students as they do from me.

Clearly the experiment has been a tremendous success, one that I believe could and should be replicated in other contexts, and also one that I found personally inspiring. What I discovered is that in an ExistEd framework of learning, students acquired a greater understanding of the world around them and explored many more avenues of pursuit than is typically the case in a traditional "learn-by-lecture," or even a Constructionist "learn-by-doing" course. The tremendous desire to learn, even among student "observers" who don't receive course credit, suggests to me that the apathy and disaffection constantly attributed to younger generations belongs not to the young but to the system that the young face.

Here, at last, the practical applications that the Vicarious Soliloquy methodology suggests take root. In being and doing at the same time, students were introduced to their own innate desire to transform themselves. They at once implicitly understood the need for approaches to technology that are not reductive (for example, rejecting the pencil just because it doesn't come with a battery), and also discovered that computer connection does not necessarily compromise humanity or individuality. Would it be fair to say that ExistEd is a new concept for education? Perhaps we should simply say that it is a very old concept in education, one that relies on the idea that education awakens the individual's passionate quest for knowledge. New or old, I believe that this concept should be expanded as an important tool in understanding and shaping the coming cyborg age.

PERSONAL IMAGING: RECLAIMING THE STORY IN
CYBORGSPACE

I don't like to watch television or see movies. I prefer my own construc-
tions of reality. In the course I teach at the University of Toronto (I continue to teach ECE1766 today) I try to instill in my students a similar desire
to interface with reality in ways more proactive than pre-packaged. This
was a course that not only introduced students to the wearable computer
and its applications, but also required the students to engage in the specific project of exploring ways in which the WearComp system allows
them — even forces them — to manufacture and interject their own narratives into society. It's no accident that I focussed the world's first course
on becoming a cyborg specifically on personal narratives and their impact
on the media of film, video, and photography. What I call Personal
Imaging will be one of the most far-reaching and important aspects of the
coming wearable cybernetics revolution.

Personal Imaging is the branch of personal cybernetic systems that
deals with the construction of realities. It is a camera-based computational framework in which the camera behaves as a true extension of the mind
and body, after a period of long-term adaptation. Examples of ways that
Personal Imaging manifests itself are the Wearable Wireless WebCam
project and the subsequent documentary *ShootingBack*, as well as the live
Webcasting of the OCAP protest. In Personal Imaging, the computer
becomes a device that allows the wearer to augment, diminish, or otherwise alter his or her visual perception of reality. Moreover, it allows the
wearer to permit others to alter the user's visual perception of reality,
thereby becoming a communication device. Within the classroom setting
I sought to underscore one of the primary assets of Personal Imaging: the
way it allows us to create and disseminate our own perspectives and seeks
to negate the need for the imaging specialist intermediary. To put it simply, the cybernetic field of Personal Imaging will allow us to reassert the

primacy of the individual creative spirit over and above the generic content currently found in the media (that vast network of cyborg space disseminating cultural information, including television, newspapers and magazines, music, books, the Internet, and movies). In giving ever-greater numbers of individuals the opportunity to produce and propagate their own version of events and selves — just as my class did when we did a live Webcast of the protest — Personal Imaging completely changes the paradigms that restrict individual creativity. In his book *Virtual States*, Australian Jerry Everard comments on how important it is for individuals to take responsibility for and have control over what they communicate about themselves and their community:

> For if individuals are identified by and through their signifying practices — their language, their actions — and if these actions are meaningful only insofar as they identify boundaries between Self and Other, then individuals, as a philosophical imperative, must take responsibility for their own actions. Indeed, individuals must take responsibility for their own being, their very identity as a member of this or that community.[8]

The first step in this reclamation process is to make the shift to a photographic mindset. When I asked the students in my course at University of Toronto to focus their attention particularly on Personal Imaging, what I was really asking them to do was to assert their own perceptions by realizing the art and humanness in the processes of everyday life. In essence, the students were given the opportunity to explore a networked multimediated videographic reality. Here — as in all things involving the EyeTap technology — the eye itself becomes a camera; thus, in sending everyday experiences to the World Wide Web, students found themselves developing a cinematographic awareness. The students had the opportunity to wear the apparatus continuously, so that a photographic awareness developed over time, as opposed to the traditional notion of only looking through the camera viewfinder while shooting or preparing to shoot. By giving students the ability to wear the devices over an extended time period, they were able to internalize the mapping from 3-D to 2-D and the laws of projective geometry. Each student had the opportunity to "make a movie," viewed in real time by their friends and relatives. In this way, without even being aware of the learning process, the students learned far more about cinematography than if they had taken traditional "learn-by-doing" photo and film courses.

By becoming a camera, the student truly learns what a camera is. The successful photoborg learns to shoot high-quality documentary video without conscious thought or effort. In the process, this fosters new approaches to media and personal narrative. The photoborg no longer feels shut out of the process of culture, an amateur observer in a world of anointed experts who convince us that we are not smart, beautiful, or interesting enough to tell our own stories. This is the significant difference between teaching individuals to become photoborgs as opposed to courses that teach an "expertise" in photography, journalism, or filmmaking. A photoborg integrates media creation into daily life. This is not a specialist privileged position, but the right of individuals to create and assert their own narratives on a daily basis. As futurist scholar Scott Bukatman argues in *Terminal Identity*, "The body must somehow be inserted into this newly revealed plane and granted the mobility and embodied presence which is the next step toward control." A photoborg has taken several large steps "toward control."[9] A photoborg does not shape, glamourize, and homogenize other people's stories into "expert"-sized bits. A photoborg translates everyday reality into meaningful, uncensored, unabridged moments.

Personal Imaging has many far-reaching implications. The most obvious of them is simply that the idea of constant filming and ongoing personal narratives begins a process whereby ordinary citizens are empowered to gather and broadcast their own information and perspective. Kurt Vonnegut has written that "We are not born with an imagination. It has to be developed by teachers, parents . . . But now there are professionally produced shows with great actors, very convincing sets, sound, music. And now, there's the information superhighway."[10] His disgust for the notion of teaching through pre-packaged entertainment experiences is clear. But what if we all could be drivers — not passengers — on the information superhighway? Sadly for Mr. Vonnegut, we are not likely to dismantle the Internet, or take television off the air. Rather than lament all forms of passive entertainment, the challenge is to assert our ability to interact in a meaningful way with a variety of cyborgspace media. When my students joined me in "observing" the OCAP protest, we were experimenting with ways that new technologies might suggest new kinds of learning and being. We were essentially asking: What would happen if parents bought their kids video cameras instead of videos?

VIRTUAL REALITY: AN INCOMPLETE PROJECT

If we hesitate to embrace the ubiquity of cyborgspace, if we are reluctant to envision a learn-by-being education process in which our children learn to "be" the camera, perhaps this reluctance can be located in the previous decade's approach to "enhanced" realities, particularly Virtual Reality. Virtual Reality (VR) was supposed to create a place where imaginary spaces could be embodied, where, in essence, our dreams could become real. However, from the outset, there was a sense of a technology displaced by its own proclamations. The VR end product — individual fantasies realized through the fantasy of a fantasy machine — seemed to emerge fully formed from the minds of basement-dwelling science fiction readers. Which is to say that the concept appeared to be frivolous, impractical, and inapplicable to the bigger project of life. After all, wouldn't it just be pretend, a silly game that, similar to television, was a sign not of progression but of society's degradation into delusion and narcissism? It didn't take long for VR to be thought of as just another entertainment medium (one that had not yet, and perhaps never would, reach its potential).

Why couldn't we think of Virtual Reality as an empowering progression? Here was a technology that could, at last, marry our desire for thrill-seeking extreme adventure to our need for safety and controllable environments. VR sought to insert the human being into a nonexistent space that could, nevertheless, function as the physical counterpart to the parallel media universe of entertainment. On the surface, it seemed like the natural evolution of the entertainment package. So, why the failure? Why the lack of sustained scientific and corporate interest?

Is it that VR, like the wearable computer truly integrated into the cybernetic loop, potentially offers too much power to the consumer? After all, a shared common reality isn't to be taken for granted; it's something to be defended through ceaseless public relations campaigns ever dedicated to fostering a positive marketing environment. Thus, VR in its ultimate embodiment would be going too far. It would fragment an entertainment consensus that has, as its central function, the goal of selling stuff to us. The mass media have always been about imbuing the passive "watcher" with desire for the trappings and products of status. With an accessible VR system, we may not be limited to fulfilling our desires and needs through proxy purchases of fancy cars and glitzy jewels. An open-ended virtual reality system in which we could be and have and do anything we chose (even temporarily) would transcend the scheme by which all desires are packaged into commodities that, although they don't quite fit the bill, seem at the time of purchase to come close enough.

Tellingly, in its current incarnation, VR spaces are game spaces enclosed within padded railings. The players are protected from falling. They are so cut off from tangible existence they are in danger of hurting themselves on the physical aspects of the "real world" they can no longer see. The player is supposed to replace one reality with another, but the actual world lingers like a bad hangover. Far from replacing reality, VR, like television, deliberately underscores its primacy by maintaining the power of the institution over the individual. VR, in its embodiment as an entertainment medium, stops short of providing us with the fulfilment of desires, allowing us instead to simply stand at the portal of desire looking in. Today, Virtual Reality permits us the chimera of our own imagination, while underscoring the fact that there remains one singular reality of money, status, and position (ultimate attainment in the "real" world) of which our collective fantasy should consist. Similar to movies, television, and computer games, VR never quite dares to stand in for our product world. Instead, it entices us with the unattainable, then disappears without ever trying to live up to its promise.

Having reached its nadir as an entertainment device of limited utility, in recent years Virtual Reality has quietly fallen off the map in terms of interest (both popular and academic) and funding for research and development. An article discussing the University of Washington's Human Interface Technology lab, charts what is now a fairly typical progression: "The HIT Lab originally focussed on virtual reality, and its work received much publicity in the early 1990s. But over time, the lab's research has shifted from head-mounted simulation to various interface venues, notably voice recognition, gestural interfaces, augmented reality, wearable computers and digital entertainment."[11] The decline of interest where VR is concerned seems to relate to a growing sense that further advances do not necessarily serve the corporate interest. If there are to be any innovations in the field of VR, it will be in making VR more like television (smaller, cheaper, and used as a delivery mechanism for pre-programmed entertainment). Beyond that, there is very little interest in completing the VR project — it's fine as it is, a kind of voyeuristic entertainment form forever trapped between the spectacle of our (implanted) desires and the real world perpetually for sale. As the Critical Arts Ensemble notes:

> VR functions as a technology that is out on the horizon, promising that one day members of the public will be empowered by rendering capabilities which will allow them to create multisensual experiences to satisfy their own particular desires . . . Unfortunately, most technology is being designed for precisely the opposite purpose from that of a wish machine, that is, to make possible better control of the material world and its population.[12]

AUGMENTED REALITY: ENHANCING THE "REAL"

The truth in the Critical Arts Ensemble's paranoid screed can be found in Virtual Reality's younger brother, Augmented Reality (AR). Instead of replacing reality with fantasy, as in the Virtual Reality scenario, the updated corporate/institutional strategy has been to make reality "better," which is to say "augmented" or imbued with increased functionality geared toward specific tasks. "Real" reality is improved when our functionality as workers and consumers is improved. AR does what VR cannot do — it acts as a serviceable marriage of the real and the virtual, better fulfilling the overall corporate project of "control of the material world and its population."

A typical AR apparatus consists of a video display with partially transparent visor, on which computer-generated information is overlaid. This allows the mechanic to call up a diagram of the plane's engine, the bureaucrat to refer to the correct form, the lawyer to pull up the right precedent. It offers something similar to the view through the Terminator's gaze, which shows both the picture of the real world and the information needed to get the job done. AR, although not as well rooted in the popular consciousness as VR, is currently widely used in specific applications: helicopter pilots often use a see-through visor that superimposes virtual objects over one eye, and the F18 fighter jet, for example, has a beamsplitter just inside the windshield that serves as a head-up display (HUD), projecting a virtual image that provides the pilot with important information.

I have already discussed the increasingly corporate/military direction of wearable research and development, even within the context of supposedly "pure" university research. Clearly, the AR concept plays a large role in fine-tuning these developments, as in, for instance, the U.S. military's development of the cyborg soldier. AR is growing in use and popularity even as VR recedes. (VR is a desert oasis illusion we will die of thirst searching for, while AR provides just enough water to keep us alive and wandering.) Like VR, AR is an adjunct that seeks to reinforce the way the world is, and even the way we think about how the world could or should be; both AR and VR offer the potential for heightened entertainments and increased ability to enhance one's skills on the job, and these are not innovations without import. At the same time, both AR and VR are attempts to modify reality without challenging the fundamental underpinnings of a central predetermined way to live in and think about the world. As Margaret Morse despairingly notes, "virtual spaces that simply aim toward realism of fit or appearance with a physical landscape may then risk merely serving the instrumental or hegemonic purposes of military and business interests in an information society."[13] Though innovation and improvement are the corporate buzzwords of the new millennium, true potentials in modifying reality remain unexplored by the business sector.

HISTORY OF REALITY MODIFICATION

All my life, I've sought to have control over my reality. In my early years, this control was about keeping things out, creating boundaries between myself and aspects of the outside environment I thought of as hostile. Just as one might ride the subway with a Walkman covering one's ears while keeping one's eyes locked on a paperback book, I was similarly temporarily enclosing my senses, seeking to filter out some of the more oppressive aspects of the world. It was only when I realized how much better it would be if I could alter or challenge aspects of reality that infuriate me — as opposed to completely blocking out my senses and leaving me with little or no input — that I began to understand the true potential of a wearable system that could also function as a reality shaper. As I continued to explore the boundaries between the self and the outside world, I realized that the process of reality modification is not concerned with erecting boundaries between oneself and the world, but rather with breaking down boundaries so that multiple realities can be better constructed, shared, and accessed. However, to break down realities and reveal them for what they are — the conventions we agree to share, conventions that can also be altered and manipulated — there must be a way to sustain altered individual and shared group realities. This was the beginning of the WearComp system, which, you'll recall, was first and foremost a system of personal imaging allowing me to "paint" light, at once changing my view of the world around me and capturing that view in photographs.

Reality and mediation could hardly be said to have begun with WearComp. To find the kernels of promise reality modification suggests, we have to look both ahead and behind us. In an 1896 paper, George Stratton reported on experiments in which he wore eyeglasses that inverted his visual field of view. Stratton argued that since the image on the retina was inverted, it seemed reasonable to examine the effect of presenting the retina with an "upright image." His "upside-down" glasses consisted of two lenses of equal focal length, spaced two focal lengths, so that rays of light entering from the top would emerge from the bottom, and vice versa. Upon first wearing the glasses, Stratton reported seeing the world upside down, but after an adaptation period of several days was able to function normally while wearing the glasses. Stratton became, then, the first person who sought to change his daily reality through technological mediation that would, essentially, allow him to live in two worlds at once (his own upside-down world and the "real" world we all share).

Stratton essentially showed us how the optical "transformation" could also be a more substantive change in daily life that would eventually seem "natural" to the wearer/user. This was important, since the premise of VR and AR remains that augmentation or shifts in reality must supplant or at the very least transpose one kind of reality with another in a way that is necessarily "unnatural." In AR and VR there is very little sense that we can, should, or would ever want to have the ability to reconfigure reality according to our own specifications. AR and VR rely on the concept that there is a central reality that can only be temporarily changed. Anything else would be too confusing, dangerous, weird, and unnatural — and who would provide the handrails? Stratton's experiment suggested something different; quite simply, he showed us that you can turn your own reality upside-down and still live in the "real" world. Individuals can alter their reality without necessarily falling into fantasy, confusion, and even madness. This, perhaps, is what long-time LSD exponent Timothy Leary meant when he turned his attention to technology, commenting that "Computers are the most subversive thing I've ever done . . . People need some way to activate, boot up, and change disks in their minds."14

Since Stratton's landmark experiment, certain kinds of prolonged reality augmentations have crept into our everyday lives. Prescription lenses, 3-D movie glasses, and the view through the camera/camcorder all provide different kinds of experiences in which reality is mediated.

However, the actual ongoing electronic mediation of reality has been slow in coming. In 1968 Ivan Sutherland described a head-mounted display with half-silvered mirrors so that the wearer could see a virtual world superimposed on reality. Sutherland's work, like most AR and VR experiments we see today, was characterized by its tethered nature. Because the wearer was attached to a workstation that was generally powered from an AC outlet, the apparatus was confined to a lab or other fixed location. Sutherland prefigured the way that reality modification experiments would move from being freewheeling experiments in how reality might be altered to applied projects with uses primarily in the workplace or in designated entertainment facilities (after work and on weekends). Since Sutherland, and contrary to Stratton's legacy, little or no effort has been made for AR or VR to meet the humanistic criterion of wearablity and existentiality.

Recently, Professor Stuart Anstis of UC San Diego wore special video goggles that inverted brightness so that he functioned in a negative world where blacks were whites, and vice versa. During the experiment he observed that he was unable to recognize faces in a negated environment, as a result forcing him to rely on other ways of interacting with the world around him. His negation experiment bore a similarity to Stratton's inversion experiment, but the important difference is that Anstis experienced his mediated visual world through a video signal. In some sense, both the regular eyeglasses that people commonly wear and the special glasses researchers have used in prism adaptation experiments are reality mediators, but it appears that Anstis was one of the early explorers of an electronically mediated world.

MEDIATED REALITY

With WearComp, I moved from a temporarily "changed" reality to a sustained "altered" reality. In searching for ways to communicate and understand how the wearable computer alters daily life, I came to realize that what I was undergoing was a reality alteration unlike either Virtual Reality or Augmented Reality. This was about reality sharing, reality intervention, more than it was about temporary reality "improvement" (for who besides myself should have the right to declare my reality improved?).

I called this process of reality intervention Mediated Reality (MR). Mediated Reality is not as presumptuous a term as Augmented Reality. Not all mediated environments are improved or better; they are simply different. In admitting this, we must also admit that reality is a kind of perspective, and perspective is infinitely varied and possible. With that point in mind, we can say that Mediated Reality differs from typical AR in many respects: The general spirit of MR, like typical AR, includes overlaying virtual objects on "real life," but also includes the desire to take away, alter, or more generally visually "mediate" real objects in everyday life. Thus MR affords the apparatus the ability to augment, diminish, or otherwise alter our perceptions. Typically, an AR apparatus is tethered to a computer workstation that is connected to an AC outlet, or constrains the user to some other specific site (such as a work cell, helicopter cockpit, or the like). In contrast, since its inception, MR has been built into a wearable computer infrastructure that is a wireless (untethered) apparatus worn over the eyes which, in real time, computationally reconfigures reality by adding to or diminishing it according to the user's specifications. This mediation of reality may be thought of as a filtering operation applied to reality and then a combining operation to insert overlays. Equivalently, the addition of computer-generated material may be regarded as arising from this filtering operation itself. Essentially, MR is a collection of various means and apparatuses that facilitate the augmenting, diminishing, or altering of the visual perception of reality in the context of ordinary day-to-day living.

One might be tempted to argue that Mediated Reality and Augmented Reality are the same idea, with the difference largely being a matter of degrees of intensity. However, such an argument misses the point of MR, which is not about enhancement or augmentation but about individual control. Indeed, one of the most important things that MR does is allow the elimination of information. Mediated Reality is as much a blocking system as it is an augmentation system. MR is a freewheeling interface between the individual and his or her world. MR has the potential to be existential, fully mobile, and incorruptible except by its own user. It will allow us to censor unwanted interruptions from our mental space such as billboard advertisements, thereby ensuring our solitude. It will permit us to control what we see, what we hear, and even what and how we speak and act.

MR IN EVERYDAY LIFE

What can you do with Mediated Reality? Obviously, you can read e-mail and search the Web as you walk and talk. Beyond that, you can, as I've discussed earlier, filter out advertisements, send visual reminders to yourself, and change the visual landscape to suit your activity or your mood. An example of a way I use MR in my everyday life would be a relatively simple adjustment of backgrounds. I have found colour-reduced reality mediation to be quite useful. When I am comfortably seated on an airplane or commuter train and wish to read text on my screen (say, to check my e-mail), I like to "tone down" my surroundings so they assume a lesser role. However, I do not wish to be blind to my surroundings, like someone who is reading a newspaper (newspapers can easily end up covering most of a person's visual field). This form of reality mediation allows me to focus primarily on the virtual world, which might, for example, comprise e-mail, a computer source file, and other miscellaneous work running in emacs19 (a Linux application) with colourful text, where the text colours are chosen so that no black, white, or grey text (text colours that would get "lost" in the new reality) is used. My experience is like reading a newspaper printed in brightly coloured text on a transparent material, behind which the world moves about in black-and-white. I am aware of the world behind my "newspaper," but it does not detract from my ability to read the "paper."

Even without any direct visual interventions, such as graphics over-lays, mediated realities can be interesting and useful. Colour blinding might be useful to an artist trying to study relationships between light and shade, MR can also alter (enhance or diminish) tonal range, allowing artists to manipulate contrast and colour. MR could (in principle) be used to syn-thesize the effect of ordinary eyeglasses, but with a computer-controlled prescription that would modify itself according to automatically scheduled eye tests on the user.

Another application is the ability to change one's capacity for percep-tion. Instead of a fixed delay of the video signal, I experimented by apply-ing a repeating freeze-frame effect to it (with the cameras' own shutters set to 1/10,000 second). With this video I found that nearly periodic patterns would appear to freeze at certain speeds. While looking out the window of a car, periodic railings that were normally a complete blur would snap into sharp focus. Slight differences in each strut of the railing would create interesting patterns that would dance about, revealing irregularities in the structure. Looking out at another car, travelling at approximately the same speed as me, I could read the writing on the tires and easily count the number of bolts on the wheel rims. Looking at airplanes, I could count the number of blades on the spinning propellers, and, depending on the sam-pling rate, the blades would appear to rotate slowly backward or forward, in much the same way as objects do under the "stopped-time" strobo-scopic (flash) lights of Harold Edgerton. By adjusting the processing parameters, I could see many things that escape normal vision.

Another application of computer-mediated reality is to create, for each user of the apparatus, a different possible interpretation of the same visual reality. Since the apparatus shares the same first-person perspec-tive as the user (and, in fact, the apparatus is what enables the user to see at all), the apparatus of course provides the processing system (WearComp) with a view of how the user is interacting with the world. In this way, each user may build his or her own user interface within the real world. For example, one user may decide to have the computer automatically run a telephone directory program whenever it "sees" the user pick up a telephone. This example is similar to hypertext, in the sense that picking up the telephone is like clicking on it with a mouse as if it were in an HTML document. "Clicking" on real objects is done by simply touching them. Outlining objects with the fingertip is another example of a reality-user interface. With MR, each individual user can organize his or her world the same way we organize the function and appearance of our desktop computers.

MR technology can cause inanimate objects to suddenly come to life as nodes on a virtual computer network. For example, while walking past an old building, the building may come to life with hyperlinks on its surface, even though the building is not wired for network connections in any way. These hyperlinks are merely a shared imagined reality that wearers of the technology simultaneously experience. When entering a grocery store, a milk carton may come to life, with a unique message from a spouse, reminding the wearer to pick up some milk on the way home from work. Thus Mediated Reality is not merely about a computer screen inside eye-glasses, but rather about enabling what is, in effect, a shared telepathic experience connecting multiple individuals together in a collective con-sciousness. Such a process gives new meaning to famed cyberpunk writer William Gibson's pronouncement that "everyone who works with com-puters seems to develop an intuitive faith that there's some kind of actual space behind the screen."[15] This kind of "personal imaging" also provides some new ways for individuals to interact and communicate through the use of shared environment maps that may be used in the context of "paint-ing by looking" — building environment maps by looking around. When these are transmitted to a Web page or the like, others can remotely expe-rience the space (for example, navigate around in the environment map) in much the same manner as one navigates around in a QuickTime, VR, or other environment map, except that it is in real time (being navigated while it is still being created). Shared environment maps will help us allow others not only to experience our points of view vicariously, but also to mediate our perceptions of reality. Such mediation may range from simple annotation of objects in our "reality stream" to complete alteration of our perception of reality.

In my daily life, I make no distinction between cyber-space and real space. Sometimes, I accidentally walk into walls. Other times, I use real walls as virtual scrap paper, trying out equations on an expansive white surface. In a Mediated Reality framework, I can effectively create a new kind of window manager, with what I see layered but separately visible in tiles. For example, while waiting in a lounge or other waiting area, a user might define walls around the lounge as various windows. In this way, screen real estate is essentially infinite. Although not all screens are visible at any one time, portions of them become visible when they are looked at through the WearComp glasses. Others waiting in the lounge would not be able to see them, unless they were wearing a similar system and the user had permitted them access to these windows (as when two users are planning on the same calendar space).

There are no specific boundaries in this form of windows manager. If a user runs out of space in the lounge, he or she can walk out into the hall and create more windows on the walls of the hallway leading into the lounge. I have found that it is easier to remember where all the windows are when they are associated with the real world. Part of this ease of memory comes from having to walk around the space or at least turn one's head around in the space. Real and virtual territories become one and the same. This windows manager also provides a means of making the back of the head "transparent" in a sense, so that one can see windows in the front as right side up and windows behind as upside down. This scheme simply obeys the laws of projective geometry. Rear-view windows may be turned on and off, since they are distracting, but they are useful for quick navigation around a room.

Of course, much of the process of reality mediation is far less complex. We are talking, but you are also in cyborgspace, looking for the title of that book you were going to recommend to me, or checking the score of the hockey game and the update of the hockey pool. Objects may light up and call attention to themselves, so that messages sent to you are delivered when you "touch" them. You are at once walking down the street and following an on-line map. In my own life, I do this naturally now, fusing worlds, at home in both an ever-expanding interior and the physical plane we all share. This is the nature of Mediated Reality, which, in turn, is the practical embodiment of a cyborg existence. Manfred Clynes uses the example of a person riding a bicycle to describe this sort of synergism where, after sufficient adaptation time, conscious effort is no longer needed to use the machine. He refers to this state as cyborgian. Long-term adaptation to a Mediated Reality state is, I believe, an essential characteristic of the cyborg.

THE PROCESS OF TRANSFORMATION

In her essay "Envisioning Cyborg Bodies," Jennifer Gonzalez argues that the cyborg contains "in its fundamental structure the multiple fears and desires of a culture caught in the process of transformation."[16] Nowhere is this more clear than in the transition from "imaginary" spaces to "enhanced" spaces to "mediated" spaces. Though the analogy is not perfect, the process is similar to the shift from radio to television to the World Wide Web. The move can be described as a transition from an invisible fantasy world to an enhanced seemingly "real" fantasy world and finally to a world that is both real and fantasy and yet neither of those things, all at once. The "process of transformation" Gonzalez explores is the way in which we can no longer ignore the existence and the importance of non-physical spaces and realities. The cyborg equipped with a Mediated

Reality system exists in several planes at once. However, this is also true for those of us who will never wear a computer system or mediate their reality. Television, the World Wide Web, radio, and even good old-fashioned books teleport our senses to imaginary planes that, nevertheless, enter the individual's and the community's realities. Isn't that, after all, why we need such interventions as reality mediation in the first place? (In this context, one could think of censorship as a kind of Mediated Reality.) MR allows us to intervene and assert control of a nebulous swirl of possibilities. An increasingly multiple and permeable reality demands an ever more fluctuating way to interact with that reality. Fear, desire, and hope push us forward into a world of half-reals that none of us can ignore, and few fully understand.

As a cyborg, I live in two worlds, and the perpetual challenge is to bridge those worlds. In conversation, I often appear distracted. It's true: I am distracted. I am drawn to the whirling interior of cyberspace, which moves and morphs and changes much faster than physical space. When I am wearing WearComp in my day-to-day social interactions in public, people often complain of a loss of eye contact with me. Jokingly, I have considered the possibility of constructing glasses that would generate a holo-video of my eyes. That way, if I was otherwise occupied during the course of a boring meeting, I could still present others with the illusion of wide open eyes dancing in attentive saccades.

Using my reality mediator, I repeated classic experiments like those of Stratton and Anstis (living in an upside-down or negated world), as well as some new experiments, such as learning to live in a world rotated ninety degrees and changing my ability to perceive detail. In the process of experimentation, I observed that visual filters that differed slightly from the "normal" way of seeing things (such as rotation by a few degrees) left a more lasting impression on me when I removed my apparatus. Which is to say that subtle shifts took me longer to re-adjust from when I switched back to a regular visual field than did more dramatic changes in the visual field, such as seeing everything upside down. The visual filters close to common patterns tended to leave me with an after-effect (I'd consistently reach too high after taking off the system when the images had been translated down slightly, or reach too far "clockwise" after removing a program that had been rotating images a few degrees counter-clockwise). Visual filters far from the standard (such as reversal or upside-down mappings) did not leave me with an opposite after-effect: I would not see the world as being upside-down upon removing upside-down glasses.

I came to think of this phenomenon as analogous to learning a second language (either a natural language or a computer language). When the second language is similar to the one we already know, we make more mistakes while switching back and forth than when the two languages are distinct. When two (or more) adaptation spaces were distinct, as, for example, in the case of the identity map and the rotation operation, I could sustain a dual adaptation space and switch back and forth between the identity operator and the "rotate ninety degrees" operator without one causing lasting after-effects in the other.

This leads me to speculate that the way we see the world is, to a great extent, simply a question of learned experience. We can teach our brains to "see" in other ways, and there is nothing inherently strange or unnatural about doing so. It is a matter of learning and adjustment that, as with the study of another language, is as much about immersion in the environment as it is about abstract consideration of the laws of grammar. After wearing my apparatus for an extended period of time, I eventually adapted to almost any visual field alteration I chose.

When wearing the WearComp Mediated Reality system, I subsume the visual reconfiguration induced by the apparatus into my brain, so that the apparatus and I act as a single unit. Despite the flickering of my eyes, I am not torn between worlds. I live — as one entity — in both worlds.

MIND BATTLE: INSIDE CYBORGSPACE

Clearly, Mediated Reality is a big step in the way we live our lives. It will change our relationship to every aspect of the world around us. Its underlying premise is that of technology as a dominating presence, the cybernetic loop swirling in an ever-expanding orbit and creating a gravity none of us can elude. MR is also an inversion of everything we understand to be true about technology, which no longer comes to us in the forms of laser guns, rocket ships, and walls of flickering giant television screens, but is instead secretive and possessive, invisible and invincible as it slips into the nooks and crannies of our minds. In *Terminal Identity*, Scott Bukatman argues that "the rhetoric of expansion and outward exploration has been superseded by one dominated by the inward spirals of orbital circulation — in cybernetic terms, the feedback loop."[17] Noted California pop commentator Greil Marcus describes a similar turn inward into consciousness in his ode to punk history, *Lipstick Traces*:

> Having satisfied the needs of the body, capitalism as spectacle turned to the desires of the soul. It turned upon individual men and women, seized their subjective emotions an experiences, changed those once evanescent phenomena into objective, replicable commodities, placed them on the market, set their prices and sold them back to those who had, once, brought emotions and experiences out of themselves for people who, as prisoners of the spectacle, could now find such things only on the market.[18]

The progression into our minds by the vertiginous swirl of media space is undeniable. We are being drawn into the feedback loop, regardless of how you wish to conceptualize the world we must all make our way through (call it cyberspace, cyborgspace, the media, or Virtual, Augmented, or

Mediated Reality). Mediated Reality is necessary because to fully live in an expanding extended cyborgspace that is having an ever-increasing effect on our "real" lives, we need to have the right tools: tools that work within the paradigms of wearability and existentiality; tools that, if nothing else, counter the trends toward consolidation and repression that technology and cybernetics also inevitably represent.

It may seem contrary to intuition that freedom is to be found in such a seemingly intrusive imposition as a grid mediating your contact with the world. Yet, as someone who lives in MR every day, I feel like I've discovered a way to live that returns my humanity to me. We exist in a contradictory world. Bastions of higher education and free thought turn out to be strongholds of conformity and even repression. The supposed freedom we have in democratic society is severely limited by our inability to walk down a street without breathing in the exhaust from thousands of cars while exposing our minds to countless advertising images (three thousand per day for the average citizen of the United States). As Greil Marcus so succinctly realizes, a reality is already imposed on us. The challenge now is to make that reality subjective, to figure out how to use technology to assert our right to individual and community realities in an age in which we perpetually move inward — from the product to the brand of product, from television to Web site WebCam. The move from outward to inward also represents fertile opportunity to re-imagine the entire project of freedom at the beginning of the new millennium.

Mediated Reality is a grid you impose on yourself, permitting a true cybernetic totality between environment and subject. It is the individual's entry point and guard post, a portal into a growing cyborgspace community that, at times, seems to subsume and overtake physical existence. However, it is also a recognition that the war to preserve individual freedom and consciousness has shifted ground. The old freedoms and dichotomies must be restated in the age of the cyborg. Just as our concept of privacy must change, so too must our understanding of what it is to be free, politically, intellectually, and morally. Unrestricted movement means nothing in an age in which our very minds are fettered by the trappings of commercial society. Can our right to live as we choose be equated with an environment in which our every move is monitored for the purposes of maintaining and enhancing a positive marketing environment?

As our humanistic space is increasingly violated by interior mechanisms, we seek to find similar interior spaces by which we can assert our own principles. This process is similar to the way we at once betray our privacy and carefully guard it. With the clear emergence of cyborgspace and the inevitable breakdown between various "realities," we will come to rely on interior free zones that, in time, will become our communities and our way to communicate. The cyborg era, then, will be an era in which we will respond with our own mechanisms, mechanisms that allow us to redetermine our right to free thought, our right to our dreams and fantasies, our right not to have our reality imposed on us by the ever-growing cadres of pollsters, marketers, publicists, and entertainment technology professionals. It may seem paradoxical to say that the battle to control interior cyborgspaces represents an opportunity in the real world. However, as Bukatman argues, "unlike the robot forms of the modernist era, wherein a mechanical body is substituted for the organic, the invisible processes of cybernetic information circulation and electronic technology construct a body at once material and immaterial — a fundamental oxymoron, perhaps, of postmodernity."[19]

With the onset of the World Wide Web and its connective links to an overall cyberspace media, we are shifting toward the inward spirals of an unconscious, invisible orbit. The true battle will be in the increasingly populated world(s) of cyborgspace. When the wearable user begins to perceive the world through a Mediated Reality skin, he or she will be entering a world in which the interior non-physical battle for expression and expansion finally begins. It will be a battle not about what we can own, but about what we can be. As such, it will change our very concept of shared space, which, more like a Web site than a TV show, becomes a place where people gather, where like-minded individuals at once give and take. Thus Australian Jerry Everard writes in *Virtual States*: "When technologies can be seen as the prostheses of the human form, extending our sight and hearing and sense of touch . . . so too technologies of social organisation will shift to accommodate the new range of human interaction made possible by such 'cyborgisation.' "[20]

Mediated Reality is the natural consequence of a cyborg world that attempts a difficult integration of opposing values: Physical reality versus cyborgspace; collective versus individual ways of living; technologies that control our lives versus technologies that can help us rein in the technologies that threaten to control our lives. As we pursue the right to be free of invasive technologies, we also pursue the right to transform institutions put in place in pre-cyborgspace eras. Thus the battle becomes about the right to talk to the government without first purchasing a language from a corporation, or the right to do research at a university without losing all claims to one's own thoughts and actions. The shift from VR to AR to MR is a complete restructuring, a bold announcement of our (new?) status as independent agents in technological society. It is the difference between being forever under corporate autocratic rule and establishing our own labs — in our dorm rooms, but also in our bedrooms, offices, parks and communities. The resultant discoveries may be the same, but the context and our ability to apply and interpret those discoveries is completely changed.

imaging the cyborg community

6

By becoming a computer, my hope has been to form a conceptual framework, as well as a practical embodiment, in which the individual can stand up to the combined corporate and governmental forces that increasingly seem to be working against the greater good. I am part of the Flesh Machine, and yet, I believe the Flesh Machine is also only a part of me. The cyborg is a necessary response, as we realize that the only way to protect ourselves against consciousness invasion is to use the tools of the machine against itself. Physical space, carved up, denuded, paved over and sold, has already been lost to us. The flesh has been harnessed, our lives adapted to the needs of the consumer state just as communities have sprawled and lost focus and meaning with the arrival of the automobile in everyday life. The coming battle, then, is not about how our physical selves will be harnessed. That has already happened. In our greed and short-sightedness, we collaborated and we lost. (Though, undeniably, we also gained.) Now the question becomes: What of this emerging new territory, this interior space of reality and perception? What if we can transcend physical space altogether, whether by altering what we see (making ads invisible) or by forming intangible communities based on the premise of interconnectivity — a world of mutual ownership and ideas where no one is, or could be, excluded?

The oxymoron of postmodernity is the realization that our mental interior spaces are, in fact, becoming the new terrains of communal and quasi-communal public space. The World Wide Web and the proliferation of hand-held and wearable electronic/ computational devices suggests a cyborg community that is, to be portentous, only a matter of time. And yet, this cyborg community may not be one that improves upon the human condition. Other forces work in opposition, attempting to apply the models of corporate culture to the freewheeling interiors of the Web and of Mediated Reality. Our collective shared imaginary cyborgspaces are constantly in danger of being paved over, fenced, and locked to everyone who cannot or will not pay admission.

I have already discussed some of the implications of software domination by the likes of Microsoft. I argued that by adopting "standards" that require the purchase of a particular brand of software, we have ourselves created a monopoly situation in which the company profits from our ignorance. Let me present an analogy: An equivalent in cyborgspace is a specially constructed public park, specially designed and fenced in, so that its gates would only open to those wearing Levi's brand blue jeans. Those wearing clothes manufactured by other vendors would not be allowed into the park. Those who made their own clothes, whether by their own loom or from cloth they purchased themselves, would also be denied access to this public park. Disabled individuals who needed to modify their clothing, say, someone with a broken leg in a cast who cut a slit in one pant leg, would also be denied access to the park. These people who are denied access to this park have still paid taxes. They've funded the construction of the park, and they pay for its maintenance, but they cannot use the park because they have not purchased and worn Levi's brand blue jeans to the park. Or, in the case of the handicapped individuals, access is denied because they've reverse-engineered or modified their Levi's jeans, making them incompatible with the software running the park's gates.

Such a situation sounds ludicrous, but that's essentially the current state of many "public" government-run Web sites. For example, I recently visited a Web site to obtain forms for starting a business, and these forms appear to require that I purchase special software from one specific corporation. Even the government-run Web site from which I obtained forms for application to a government-sponsored research program provides the forms only in a proprietary format for which special software needs to be purchased to fill out the forms. Applying for a U.S. patent? Well then, you'll need to purchase a copy of acroexch (Adobe Acrobat Exchange) to fill out the forms, since they're in the proprietary Adobe Acrobat format. If you're visually challenged, you can forget about entering this so-called public space, even though you may have paid taxes to build it. Many visually challenged computer users build their own special computers and write their own software, often coming up with innovative ways to "surf the Web," such as running the output of lynx through a text-to-speech converter or designing a custom Web browser that eliminates headache-inducing frames and reorganizes pages, filtering content and outputting with large font sizes. None of this is allowed in the "public" park.

Obviously, I would like to see public cyborgspaces that do not depend on the largesse of corporations for their existence. Which doesn't mean that new industries and economies will not develop around a cyborgspace community made possible by, among other things, the Mediated Reality perspective. For instance, MR sets forth a new computational framework in which the visual interpretation of reality is finely customized to the needs of each individual wearer of the apparatus. The computer becomes very much like a prosthetic device or like prescription eyeglasses. Just as you would not want to wear another person's undergarments or mouthguard, you may not want to find yourself wearing another person's computer. The traditional paradigm of one worldwide software vendor providing everyone with identical copies of an executable-only program should no longer apply. Instead, complete reconfigurability is needed and each user should be able to customize his or her own environment. Since many laypersons are not well versed in operating system kernel source code, there will be a growing need for system administrators and consultants.

In the wearable computer era, software will be free and users will buy support. There will be little problem with software "piracy," because the version of the software customized for one person will be of no use to someone with different needs. Because the computer will function as a true extension of the user's mind and body, it would not do the user any good to ingest software owned by someone else. The computer will function much like a "second brain," and in the true spirit of freedom of thought, it would be preferable that any commercial interests in the customization and contents of one's "second brain" be a work for hire (an interaction in which the end user owns the rights) rather than a software purchase or payment for service. There will be an exponentially growing need for personal system administrators as growing numbers enter the community of connected, collective, humanistic intelligence.

My goal here is not to denigrate software companies or any corporation. Instead of attacking software vendors, we need to blame ourselves. Why haven't we required our governments to make our public spaces accessible to all of us? Specifically, we should demand that any government Web page, along with any electronic forms therein, exist only in file formats and use only standards that are fully disclosed. We should simply begin by requiring ourselves, and by extension those we have elected to govern us, to use only formats for which there exists a scientific basis of total disclosure, and that can be read, written, and worked on with freely obtainable and fully disclosed (in source form) software. By extension, our publicly funded institutes, such as universities, as well as organizations doing publicly funded work, could be required to use file formats and other standards that are in the public domain. It would only be fair that our tax dollars go toward building public spaces that all of us can access, and public forums in which all of us can participate. Such accessibility, in and of itself, would go a long way toward encouraging the same practice in the corporate world. By adopting open source standards ourselves in our interior, public cyborgspaces, we are essentially restating the terms by which the non-physical community will be encountered in our collective web. This may well go much further toward solving what is essentially a control problem than the spectacle of, say, the U.S. government suing a software manufacturer that supplies it with the bulk of its own operating systems. At stake here is more than a readjustment of public policy; we are talking about providing the terrain for communities to flourish and thrive in. By preventing public spaces in cyborgspace, we are set back untold years, prevented from imagining new ways of interacting and being in shared media.

Proponents of Intellectual Property have used the word *piracy* to describe making "unauthorized" copies of informational "wares." It's as if they suggest that villains who attack an ocean-going vessel and kill all those on board are about equal in the degree of their crimes to those who make "unauthorized" copies of information "wares." I join Mitch Kapor in criticizing the equivalence between copying information and "piracy" as the entertainment/software industry's propaganda. In the age of the cyborg, in our search for new communal spaces, we must find a new way to share and exchange information. We must also recognize that just as "pirates" may steal intellectual properties, so too can corporations pirate our humanistic property (our ability to think clearly without interruption or interference) by invading and putting up barriers that exclude us from a cyborgspace that is, rightfully, infinite and beyond ownership. The theft of solitude allows an individual to benefit at the expense of others (for example, at the expense of the "commons"). I've already discussed my solution to this problem, which comes in the form of a simple engineering tool with which the individual may filter out unwanted real-world spam. Mediated Reality can do more than help us reclaim solitude in personal, private spaces. As advertising and private ownership creep into every facet of our lives, one important countervailing force will be our ability to form interconnected communities that can reassert the communal. As the commons expands on the Internet and contracts in our cities, we must take steps to ensure that at least some of our new communal spaces can be not only ad free, but also free from the virus of proprietary technology.

THE CYBORG COMMUNITY

The notion of a computationally mediated reality is rapidly emerging as a substantive force in our lives. Even the current hodgepodge approach to merging communications devices (such as portable telephones) with computational devices (personal organizers, personal computers, etc.) has already substantially changed how we live and communicate. Although these devices embody a loose and fluffy notion of "mobile multimedia" or the like, in truth they represent a computationally mediated grid that will be the natural extension of next-generation wearable computing. We have already seen a pivotal shift from mainframe computers to personal/ personalizable computers owned and operated by individual end users. This has represented a fundamental change in the nature of computing from large mathematical "batch jobs" to the use of computers as a communications medium. The explosive growth of the Internet is a harbinger of what will evolve into a completely computer-mediated world in which all aspects of life will be on-line and connected. With the onset of interconnected smart cyborgs, it is possible to envision new communities formed around new ways of interacting with the world. This allows the individual to go beyond singular experience, toward a symbiotic relation with a networked humanistic intelligence within a Mediated Reality environment. This, of course, will come about over time, and as part of the process in which cyborg communities develop and grow. The cyborg community, in which cybernetically linked mediated realities share space, will come about as a direct result of a collective and already advancing blurring between everyday "real life" and cyborgspace.

As I discussed in detailing my live WearCam experiment, images transmitted from my Wearable Wireless WebCam may be seamlessly "stitched" together on a Web page so that others can see my point of view. Because the communication is bidirectional, others can send me messages, for example, telling me the name of a person I've never met before who nevertheless can comment on my doings with a surprising degree of specificity. In addition to simply allowing others to annotate my "reality stream," I am allowing them to alter my perception of reality. I am participating in the creation of shared communities of two or ten or ten thousand people with the ability to interact directly with and through each other. Critics have raised objections to this process, citing everything from distraction (my eyes watching the screen even as I talk to you) to the crisis of information overload, causing crippling anxiety and stress as too much comes to us from too many directions. However, society is already getting used to the distracted look in people's eyes as they navigate a Mediated Reality world. When we are on the phone, on the Internet, watching TV, reading a magazine, or playing a video game, we are in at least two places at once. Is it so hard to imagine multiple overlapping communities of cyborgs who exist as fully in real life as they do in cyborgspace? Doesn't that already describe our lives? Perhaps the key differences in the cyborg age, then, will not so much be our right to access information but our right to disseminate and exclude information on our terms and as we see fit. We will formulate our own cyborgspaces (instead of visiting someone else's show, Web site, video game) and our own rules of censorship (we will censor the world according to our individual needs). Keep in mind that MR is designed to exclude as much as it can include. Sometimes, we will have to turn off. While today we retreat to an ever-diminishing wilderness to find a space that does not impinge on our humanistic property, WearComp allows us to walk down a busy street and not be assaulted by the ever-growing barrage of advertisements. This suggests how one might be "in" the community without being consumed by it.

At certain times we will need to block out distractions and focus. We have multi-tasking: People drive, talk on the cellphone, listen to a self-improvement CD on the car stereo, and eat a fast-food dinner all at once. At first, wearable computers might intensify this "problem." As M.D. Pesce notes: "Information has become our clothing, our food, our air, and free access to it has become a basic human right. Yet, at the same time, humans can be overwhelmed by information . . . and find themselves unable to make decisions within the infosphere."[1] The answer to this impasse, however, is not to preach the myths of technopoly and information overload. Rather, the solution will be to find ways to improve our ability to process and consume and decide what information should reach us on an individual basis. We have no other choice but to move forward if we are to reshape and maintain human possibility. We cannot stick our heads in the sand and wait to be told when the sky has cleared of billboards exhorting us to any number of seemingly contrary purposes. Being a cyborg is like having one's brain transplanted into the body of a toddler. The cyborg staggers around, not sure where he or she is going, always ready to topple over; there's too much to look at, too much ready information to process, too much to do. However, I'm learning quickly, to the point where I now make no distinction between the world inside my head and the world outside it. They are one and the same, and the sooner we realize that and come to terms with that truth, the sooner we can begin to live lives that are enriched — not diminished — by the vertiginous excesses of the mental environment. Only the most disheartened cynic can dismiss a baby's potential to grow, to explore, to see things no one else can. Living in a Mediated Reality as near to being under my complete control as is technologically feasible, I see that the old ways that constrict human possibility will inevitably be displaced. This is not some grandiose utopian vision of the future — for this displacement may, and probably will, lead to a long period of floundering and confusion — but it is a way to think about the future in which information — our lifeblood, our essential currency — is freed from the constraints of ownership in a time when an interwoven cyborg community communicates instantly and totally with its constituency. It isn't cyborgs assimilating us into their cold, hostile, amoral world that we should fear; after all, haven't we already been assimilated into that world? The cyborg, I believe, has the potential to rescue us. We will insist on our right to explore the terrain of cyborgspace as free agents capable of forming complex new communities.

THE ADIABATIC COMMUNITY

What will a cyborg community look like? Will it have a government? Will it have citizens, laws, elections? Will it, in fact, be more compelling and sensible than our current system of carving up plots of land and defending them with weapons? Certainly, we can hope that the coming cyborg age will bring us "nations" formed on shared ideals, instead of geography in which the accident of birth imprisons one as subject. But, in truth, I don't know how cyborg communities will grow and manifest themselves. They have already begun as Web sites where like-minded individuals form cyber proto-clubs that prove to be not just sites of information exchange but also terrains where friends meet to socialize, conspirators meet to conspire, and business types meet to strategize. Just imagine the uses for these types of spaces when we are on-line all the time, living in the virtual world as much as we do in the real world. Sites where you actually get inside the head of the creator and can interact in real time (such as my Wearable Wireless WebCam site) are the next small step. Another step will come when on-line cyborgs begin meeting in spaces of their own devising, each of them seeing through each other's eyes, their realities configured. Here we begin to realize the potential for individuality and commonality that a cyborg community could have. Christopher Kedzie's 1997 study of e-mail connections in a number of countries found "a strong correlation between increased interconnectivy and democracy."[2] "High technology can put unequal human beings on [an] equal footing," argues Sam Pitroda in "Development, Democracy, and the Village Telephone."[3] It is in the midst of these optimistic pronouncements that we begin to understand why the thinker Donna Harraway broke new ground when she positioned the cyborg revolution not as something to be feared, not as part of the corporate Flesh Machine, but as something with the potential to crumble the traditional barriers and hierarchies. At the same time, Harraway may be overly optimistic to think that changing our relationship to the body will necessarily free us from oppression. Boundaries in cyborgspace are ideological rather than geographical or racial. As we enter the post-corporeal era, our physical attributes (bodies) will matter less than our intellectual attributes (minds). Thus as racial tolerance increases to the point of universal acceptance of all body types, there will be, at the same time, a more critical look at ideals and beliefs. This has the potential to be liberating, but also to be limiting. Ultimately, unlike the corporeal limitations of identity (Your Papers Please) there will be the possibility of multiple identities and multi-threaded thought. What happens when some person declares themselves as their own country? Traditional geographically based countries are said to be at war when their physical boundaries overlap. Thus a declaration of independence (or sovereignty or freedom) from one's government (country) might have traditionally been a declaration of war. However, in the post-corporeal era, (cyborg) space is limitless, and there is room for multiple overlapping "countries" that can even be hidden from each other. Thus an individual may have dual citizenship in cyberspace. Moreover, a rich plurality of citizenships is possible, in which freedom to create new "nations" exists despite other allegiances and affiliations.

A community that begins as a place to exchange the best ways to filter out advertisements or produce your own on-line broadcast of the nightly news may indeed become something more than just an information connection — it may become a space, like a city, in its own right. Certainly, my own experience in cyborgspace suggests a compacting of physical and mental terrains, mergers, unification, and the gradual inability to tell one from the other. At the same time, the concept of the individual itself does not seem to be threatened — on the contrary, it may have greater currency, as "global" comes to represent not branding and conformity but uniformity of access and opportunity for diversity. As Manfred Clynes optimistically put it in an interview:

> Man's essence survives the vicissitudes of the body, with a brain of expanded functionality, with more highly evolved feeling, with further developed empathy. By the time that happens the very materials of the brain will have been changed to a degree, with a new freedom because its organizations will be less taken up with its own maintenance, and more with its consciousness, with communication to other consciousness, and communication with sources of information, music, art, experiencing new emotions. The web of Internet will truly become a body politic, loneliness banished for all, while maintaining individuality, privacy.[4]

There is a close parallel between the flow of information and the flow of heat (thermodynamics). Information theory and thermodynamics both involve concepts such as entropy and irreversibility. Once humanistic information (property) is stolen and disseminated, it cannot be put back. And yet, in the theory of thermodynamics, there is the relentless search for systems that are adiabatic, for processes that occur without gain or loss of heat. Just as we consider adiabatic systems in the theory of thermodynamics, we ought to be able to consider adiabatic existence from an informational point of view. Can information transfer occur without gain or loss?

Imagine a community of cyborgs — of wearable computer users mediating their reality — intimately connected to one another in thought, but having shared private thoughts. This, I believe, is the kind of community that the World Wide Web hints at, and that the wearable computer will bring to fruition: communities that function as entities in their own right, that allow — indeed, are based on — the free flow of information even as they establish borders and restrictions to preserve individual rights. A community that functions on the principle of full disclosure to all those within the community could declare itself an adiabatic entity. In its purest form, it will produce nothing beyond its borders and consume nothing beyond its borders. It will simply be.

Such a community challenges the notion of state identification (your papers are not in order, won't you please step aside?) and forces us to reconsider such horrible words as the *hive* and the *collective*. Would this be a static existence that limits innovation and progress? Not necessarily. There could — and should — be "production." However, production will largely take place in the realm of the virtual, following today's trend of seeing larger and larger numbers of people employed toward the production of entertainments and abstract ideas. An adiabatic community need not be an enclosed and rigid one. Just the opposite is the case: These can be vital, exciting, constantly changing mental communities that allow far more interaction and free-spirited dialogue and debate than today's cloistered world of conferences and journals.

Of course, even the most optimistic world of interconnected, forward-thinking, truly interactive and empowering communities (real and virtual intertwined) will have problems. The most obvious problem is the vast peoples of the planet who will be unable to participate in cyborg-space. And yet, though the Internet has been cast as the new game of a Western elite, it is also true that there is the potential for everyone on the planet to be affected by this changing terrain, just as few can now avoid the fallout of mass media — even those who lack the luxuries of TV, VCR, and stereo. Those with little or no access to the products of high technology are just as likely to be swept up in wave after wave of self-obsession, pop excess, technological ennui, and anxiety for a future in which we will be displaced, spoken for, polled, and perpetually reduced. Though at first the wearable computer and the cyborg revolution will be accessible to rela-tively few, the repercussions, as with the Internet, will be global. "The dif-ference between the haves and have-nots in the information society," writes Jerry Everard, "will not necessarily be those with the networks alone, but those who can find innovative ways to use those networks."5 This is why the cyborg revolution will and must continue, even as large numbers of people worry more about food and shelter and disease than broadcasting their own television shows. If we can find "innovative ways to use" the cyborg networks of the near future, we may also be able to find ways to improve a world held in thrall to global corporations whose claims to patents and intellectual property rights restrict, to use just one example, the flow of crucial prescription drugs to countries that most need them. Must the cyborg be dissociated from the plight of the hundreds of millions who live in poverty? One can envision a truer, more representative democracy and accompanying economy held together by a cyborgspace that does, indeed, concern itself with social justice (as opposed to merely paying lip service to it). These are not totally separate issues. At the same time, we must acknowledge that such a movement is somewhat in the future, and little consolation to those poverty-stricken workers paid $1 per day to make pricey running shoes for sale in the mall near you. At present, the benefits of cyborg technology are available only to those who are able to afford them. Still, in a cyborg age in which we have greater opportunities to communicate outside the relentless positivism of the market environment, we will also have more opportunities to be made aware of what our consumptive tendencies are doing to the rest of the planet. We will begin by putting our lives on-line, by becoming broadcasters and pundits, by sharing our VisualFilter spam kill files, so that advertisements can be filtered out collectively. This will give rise to ever-growing communities and empathies that, for the first time, will allow us to truly transcend tired nationalist principles. What does a border mean to a cyborg who lives at once everywhere and nowhere? As like-minded individuals establish cyborg meeting points they will emerge toward a plurality of identities and their own collective interpretations of a world in which cooperation is a practical and necessary part of everyday life — not just an idealistic concept children are taught in kindergarten. At the same time, we must be wary of losing our individual essence, of having our "I" turned into an "eye," impassively documenting instead of passionately participating.

THE RIGHT TO THINK

I am, more than anything else, an activist, a cyborg proponent of a new way to live. If this text does nothing more than incite speculation and discussion, I will have succeeded in opening up what has been so far a surprisingly closed dialogue. Who is conducting serious research into the nature of an increasingly cyborgized society? A handful of liberal academics who speak primarily among themselves, and a rarely criticized pool of profit-motivated manufacturers and their designers and researchers who speak, guardedly, through the mass media they own and dominate. If we are to move forward into an accessible and meaningful cyborg environment, we must bridge these gaps in our ability to talk about the technological future.

We must become inventors, theorists, writers, publishers, and even financial speculators, all at the same time.

In moving through the world, the WearComp system as my only constant, I have explored what I believe will come to be seen as a new era, as the start — not the end — of a new way to live. Is this the technology that will finally live up to the promise of enhancing free will and human possibility? I have to believe that it is, that, in fact, the wearable computer, if understood and made available, not as a uniform but, like the personal computer — as a tool to be used by anyone, however they see fit — will be a provocative conduit for transformation. The world will change, substantively, seismically. However, the world will also remain the same as it has always been. The cyborg revolution is not as much about reconfiguring the world as it is about reconfiguring individuals, changing our approach to the world.

To some, this cyborg transformation is horrible, and evokes the image of humanity trapped in a giant technological snare. To others, this is natural, the process of evolution taken to its inevitable conclusion. I don't consider wearable computers to be either an inevitable process of evolution and natural selection or the demise of human freedom at the hands of a history-less technological future. Technology is not natural, and to suggest that it is would be to suggest that individuals and societies have no role in the way technology is developed and used. At the same time, technology is not unnatural, and I feel most at home, most myself, when I am wearing and working on the WearComp system. Am I unnatural? Is every single person surfing the Web or using a cellphone or listening to a Walkman or wearing shoes unnatural? Robotics researcher Hans Moravec writes of humanity being "unleashed from the plodding pace of biological evolution . . . free to grow and confront immense and fundamental challenges in the larger universe."6 For him, evolution is too slow. Why should we wait for our bodies to shrink and our minds to expand and our foreheads to naturally develop ports we can plug into? However, cyberpunk sci-fi writer Bruce Sterling also has a point when he warns us that "Real people don't want to transcend the physical plane to live in some juiceless Plutonic cyberspace; what they want is to live right here and now and be young and sexy and beautiful for as long as posthumanly possible."[7] What, after all, can ever replace the corporeal pleasures that remain the fundamental essence of our short time on earth?

Reality is arbitrary, and words like *natural* and *unnatural* are rhetorical dialectics that prevent us from making the choices we need to make. Do we want a world of ubiquitous proliferating points of view? Or do we want a world of singular authority? In his book *Jihad vs. McWorld*, Benjamin Barber puts the dilemma of the present future this way: "Some stunned observers notice only Babel, complaining about the thousand newly sundered 'peoples' who prefer to address their neighbours with sniper rifles and mortars; others — zealots in Disneyland — seize on futurological platitudes and the promise of virtuality, exclaiming 'It's a small world after all!' Both are right . . ."[8] I quote Barber because our cyborg future is a global issue, which is to say it is a universal and far-reaching issue that cannot be reduced or simplified. To talk about the wearable computer is to talk about the future — and, of course, the present — of the human race. The cyborg has long captured the imagination because the cyborg has long been a metaphor for change, change that began in the early days of the industrial revolution and continues today, picking up speed like a truck rolling down a hill. Is it out of control? Is anyone behind the wheel? One thing is clear: We cannot continue merely jumping out of the way.

Coming straight at us is Augmented Reality and Mediated Reality. We have smart rooms and smart people. We have WebCams, photoborgs, ubiquitous surveillance, and methodical privacy invasion. Clearly, there is great potential for abuse of new wearable technologies. Yet, these very divisions suggest the potential and unpredictability of technology as it moves from being under institutional control to widespread use for any and all purposes. My goal as an inventor and researcher is to ensure that the balance of power is equal — despite all its contradictions. Still, the outcome is hardly clear. Parallel developments — both bad and good — will continue, at times meeting and even crossing, but never joining. Institutions consolidate their power over technologies even as more and more of us are empowered by personal and wearable technologies to put forward our own vision. Through it all, I hold to a central belief that the wearable, like the personal computer before it, will be intrinsically good. Personal technologies spawn personal choice. There is no such thing as too much information. The fragmenting "jihad" of conflicting territorial and historical conflicts versus the singular restrictive reality of a global economy that would pave over difference is not the only story. New communities linked together in virtual relationships suggest a novel paradigm, one in which differences and common interests unite and complement each other.

Marshall McLuhan's mentor Harold Innis argued that information is power, and that the way civilization transfers power explains how a civilization rises and falls. Which is to say, if you want to look at what happened to a civilization, you have to look at how information is being transferred. In that transfer you find the key to how power was developed, maintained, and lost. How would Innis analyze the state of information transfer in today's civilization? What would he say about our power structures? Today we transfer information at astonishing rates, not just between and about each other and our institutions, but also between our intelligent environment, what we tell our computers, houses, cars — and soon, very soon — our shoes, hats, and coats. The wearable computer, then, must be seen as the epicentre of proliferating data, ground zero, where we will store, share, and amass information. This is a new medium of information production, storage, and transference. A critic once summarized Innis's information theories in this way: "new information does not necessarily threaten an ensconced power elite. But a new medium for information does."9

Is it surprising that so many of the edifices we've depended on seem to be in processes of change, many for the worse, some for the better? The power centres are being challenged by personal electronics. Innis's theory is proving accurate and durable. Wearable computers are at the nadir of this challenge. Innis warned that a new medium's effects are difficult to predict. New media of information turn out to be contrary to their intent. Who could have predicted that to combat the camera we would all have to become cameras? Or that to combat the computer, we must all become computers? Can I say for sure that this technology will bring more good than harm, that the cyborg life is a good one? Of course I cannot. For better or worse, we will never be Moravec's "Mind Children," freed from the boundaries of the body to pursue the inner workings of the eternal celestial. Nor are we moving toward a shallow existence concerned only with material objects, a world in which we reject all attempts to explore the "juiceless" void of abstract thought and cyborgspace as interfering with our dedication to the pure everlasting physical pleasure. We are people, sustained and held to the planet, intent on our own lives and our struggles, perpetually split between our status as occupants of this planet and occupants of a virtual/mental sphere that extends our terrain into infinite dimensions.

Freud wrote that "man has, as it were, become a kind of prosthetic god. When he puts on all his auxiliary organs, he is magnificent; but these organs have not grown on him, and they still give him trouble at times."[10] We can think of Freud when cars crash, when the power goes off, when we are so intent on our lives as we wander the disembodied depths of cyborgspace that we don't notice those who starve for the right of free speech even as we glibly surf the Internet. We are not stronger or better than we were before. We are just different, troubled, blinded by our prostheses, by the magnificence of our plumage that nevertheless cannot prevent us from walking into walls. As D'Arcy Thompson notes in his 1917 contemplation of mathematics and nature, "I for one imagine that a pterodactyl flew no less well than does an albatross, and that the Old Red Sandstone fish swam as well and as easily as the fishes of our own seas."[11] We evolve, we change, we grow, we shrink; call it what you will. The wearable computer is crucial now because of the way technology has come to control our lives. If we could reshape the history of technology, perhaps we would do things differently, avoid the escalation that now requires us to clothe ourselves in circuitry to survive. Then again, changing our approach may have meant reducing our options. Cyborgspace is limitless. It is the only possible terrain in which we can expand continually without destroying the world and each other. So, technology brings us to unexpected places, even as it takes us away from places we once thought we would always be able to visit.

For most of my life, I've been a cyborg. I've lived in cybernetic unconscious tandem with a computer. I have sacrificed elements of "normal" existence for the privilege. I've waited patiently for society to accept my work and the cyborg revolution as the only possible response to a world in which too much power is concentrated in the hands of too few people. However, I now realize that this seismic shift in how we live won't come all at once, won't be announced by the talking heads on CNN and CBC Newsworld. In 1969, not long after McLuhan spoke of the electronic second skin, the French thinker Pierre Teilhard de Chardin wrote of "a network (a world network) of economic and psychic affiliations . . . being woven at an ever increasing speed."[12] Who could have imagined how quickly and literally his assertion would become undeniable? Just as, gradually, we have found ourselves surrounded by roads, just as, gradually, we have found that we depend almost entirely on computers to manage complex systems few of us really understand, just as, gradually, we have surrounded ourselves with cellular phones and PalmPilots and beepers and laptops and video cameras and personal watching/listening devices, gradually we will realize that we have conclusively and irreversibly entered the cyborg age. The question remains: What kind of network is being woven?

What kind of cyborg age will we live in? Despite a life often lived in isolation, despite being branded at various times a quack, a hack, and a freak,
I retain my idealism: Cyborg technologies that foster interconnected mental communities can, quite simply, "be" the world. The metaphor of the
"desktop" computer will be obsolete; it will be replaced with direct, constant, humanistic interaction — a new kind of reality in which each and
every (post)human being has equal opportunity to chart his or her destiny.

It's terribly depressing to think that we need a human-computer interface to suppress unwanted solicitations and invasions of mental space, and
find ways to reclaim the ageless process of narrative that is unique to the
human race. Nevertheless, it has come to this. In order, at the very least,
to preserve our right to moments of uninterrupted "free" thought, we
must battle the forces of media convergence that exist to promote our collective "identity" as citizen consumers. We already live much of our lives
in a disembodied collective cyborg or cyberspace that provides us near-
constant stimulation via electronic apparatus. However, our say in that
space (where the mass media encounters the individual) is limited both by
our inability to project our voice into the space and by the sense that this
is a crowded space already near bursting — why does the world need one
more story, song, Web site, dream? In truth, however, communal cyborg
space is unlimited — it is our personal mental space that is precious.
Preserving the right to think must be as much about protection as it will
be about projection. With a system such as WearComp, we are allowed
not just new entry points into paradigm communication shifts (such as
new ways to create and disseminate cultural ideas), but also new ways to
keep out the unwelcome by-products of the information age in the proliferating cyborg space that is melding and, in some cases, replacing our own
personal space.

The struggle to (re)claim media has been going on since the invention
of the printing press. Similarly, the struggle to find a new model by which
our increasingly disparate and intense leisure lives (inextricably intertwined

with a parallel mass culture cyborg consciousness) can be integrated into and used to make sense of other aspects of our lives — work, family, spiritual belief — has also been underway since, at the very least, Plato condemned poetry in his imaginary republic. Following the lead of his mentor, Socrates, Plato dismissed poetry not only because art was seen as a distraction from one's civic duties, but because he imagined the emergence of a written "field" of poetry to lead to just the kind of specializations and minimizations we have today. (Socrates argued against all written documents, arguing that they allowed the reader to possess and lay claim to knowing as opposed to actually having knowledge.) Thus Plato preferred the Socratic oral tradition in which the community shared a collective reality of literary texts passed on — and adapted — from one individual to another. In a way, Plato was correct in predicting that books would fragment communities and allow many who don't really "know" to nevertheless claim knowledge and shut out those who never had the chance to become experts. Plato's criticism of poetry, however, has come full circle: Art and entertainment, for too long in the hands of specialists and pseudo-experts, is now being returned to the individual determined to cast his or her voice into the mass media ocean. Personal Imaging has become a civic duty. As O.B. Hardison, Jr. so succinctly puts it: "Computers encourage a return to many of the mind habits of oral literature."[13]

This assertion of the right to speak — the inevitable shadow that follows the right to think wherever it goes — will lead to a further degeneration of our stance, our role, as isolated expert specialists mired in what Hardison thinks of as "the culture of the book."[14] We often hear researchers speak of fields of study as so-called "Computer Supported Collaborative Work." However, with the creation of the cyborg entity, we can imagine a much more widespread, freewheeling phenomenon, which I call Computer Supported Collaborative Living, or simply Computer Supported Collaboration (CSC). Similar to the approach to education found in the ExistEd concept, CSC is meant to break down the artificial boundaries erected between work and personal life. CSC is a way of living that implicitly challenges the increasingly artificial distinction between work and play. As Albert Einstein has said, "Love is a better master than duty."15 Divisions that lead us to judge ourselves solely by what we have accomplished in our professional lives (what we perceive as our duty) lead to mindless materialism and even mental illness. In the coming age, we will all be leisure specialists, at once maintaining our elaborate Web site devoted to the Six Million Dollar Man (Steve Austin as the kitsch prototype cyborg) even as we trade stocks, compose poetry, and painstakingly filter the stimuli of the outside world to preserve our ability to think clearly and without unnecessary obstruction. Meanwhile, old notions of work are plunged into crisis: On the frontiers of leisure, game programmers and celebrity skateboard riders are as likely to be found in the boardroom as they are to be found on the dance floor. The traditional work ethic makes little sense in a time when, as early as 1994, it was argued that 97 percent of all employment growth comes from what are optimistically referred to as the "knowledge" industries. Indeed, as Sandy Stone notes in her essay "Split Subjects," the shift away from the work ethic has been particularly evident in the high-tech workplace, which "incorporates a play ethic — not to displace the corporate agendas that produce their paychecks, but to complexify them . . . The people who play at these technological games . . . have seized upon advantages to make space for play in the very belly of the monster that is the communication industry."16 Similarly, Steven Levy, writing in his computer history work *Hackers*, argues that "games were the programs which took greatest advantage of the machine's power — put the user in control of the machine — made him the god of the bits and bytes inside the box."17

The notion of Computer Supported Collaboration, similar to the process of "learning by being," can only be successful if there is open communication, trust, and a gradual accumulation of knowledge, leading to personal and, ultimately, community entitlement. A new way to communicate, a new way to learn, a new way to create culture and thereby community, all point to a new way to "be." One of the most important aspects of this shift in being will be a fundamental reassessment of the dramatic divisions between our life roles at the end of the Industrial Revolution. In the coming years, perhaps the most tangible development to emerge from a humanistic intelligence–inspired cyborg (r)evolution, will be the breakdown of the divisions between our work and our leisure lives. We should think of this phenomenon as the beginning of the movement by which we reclaim our right to think.

Wearable cybernetics designed under the humanistic model tends to break down barriers and challenge divisions. Freed from the constraints imposed on us since the Industrial Revolution turned us all into assembly line tools, ironically it will be the communal networks of cyborgspace that will affirm our essential humanity. Equipped with a WearComp system, we will be outfitted with the ability to assert our own narratives and realities — a process that will take place on a continuous basis, whether we are working, playing, or doing something that is neither. While watching television, we will be able to voice our opinions and find a forum of our own, instantly sharing space with like-minded individuals around the world, and no doubt discovering in the process that our communal narrative precludes the need for things such as television.

Yet, none of this will come to fruition unless "the right to think" can be (re)introduced into everyday life. The right to think is something we've assumed, but it's a right that — after decades of corporate mind control via an invasive advertorial aesthetic — has been severely diminished. In an age in which thought is mediated by media, in which thought is, indeed, affected and even infected by media, it is necessary to recognize that the very concept of free thought, of an unhindered consciousness, must be called into question. Plot lines of sitcoms, advertising ditties, the rhetorical images of presidents riding in tanks, all somehow find their way permanently into our minds. If the eye is the window to the soul, shouldn't it have shades on it? Right now, we walk around with windows unshaded and unlocked, our minds open for anybody to throw in anything. The result is theft of our right to think. Billboards are theft. Nobody asked for my permission to put that image of Calvin Klein underwear into my head. When I argue that we must protect the right to think, this is what I mean: the right to, in any situation, in any circumstance, control, protect, and project our own thoughts.

With the protection of our right to think and engage in Computer Supported Collaboration, the precepts of industry are more systematically and meaningfully subverted, setting us on a new path of creating and being. As computers evolve from mainframe business machines to personal computers and eventually to personal cybernetics (wearable, prosthetic, or implantable devices), there will be a paradigm shift in which the boundary between execution of machine instructions and our own thoughts will blur. We live in a pivotal era. Computing machinery is moving into our prosthetic territories, and is beginning to function as part of our minds and bodies. The traditional view of the computer as a business machine is a hold-over from the time of the mainframe, and will need to change when the boundary between thinking and computing breaks down. The usual "office desktop" metaphor of computing will give way to a kind of reality user interface model of cyborg computing in which we collaborate with the computer on and off duty, our minds roving through cyborgspace communities, our own lives worthy and valid sources of wonder and entertainment (both for us and for others).

Such a development — in the case of millions who work in leisure-related activities already a partial reality — will be met with a fair degree of resistance. There will be calls to restrict the flow of information, the flow of freedom, to set boundaries on the cyborgspace just as boundaries and restrictions have already been imposed on the more limited Internet space. The cyborg self will need to fight for freedom of thought, or else be monitored by totalitarian Thought Police who fear the possibilities of a cybernetic evolution that will challenge, among other things, information hoarding, pseudo-democracy and the global war machine. Corporations will protest that cyborgspace is the equivalent of daydreaming on the job, reading on the job, writing poetry for your Web 'zine while earning $8 an hour as a faceless temp installed in a cubicle as transient as your job description. In an age in which dreams, fantasies, and alternative realities are big money, attempts to dub the coming creation of cyborgspace as "bad for business" will only serve to expose the limitations of a life system predicated on what is "good" for business. My experience as a cyborg inventor and educator has caused me to assert the inevitably of a fusion of business and life, creating a totality that has nothing to do with marketing, convergence, or corporate synergy and everything to do with sustainable environments (both physical and mental) that will allow us to bestow upon our children a world in which abstract ideas and free thought will matter more than how many cars are in the driveway. Technology critics have pointed out that employees who are given laptops to take home do an average of ten extra unpaid hours of work a week. However, it has also been noted that the move toward telecommuting is being cut back in the business world, as it is argued that employees who work from home are less productive. The only truth evident in these statistics is that everyone is looking for a way to enhance the effectiveness of employees through technology. The ideal, one supposes, is an automaton who simply never stops working (and doesn't need to be paid). Technological innovations have been used to reduce the gap between our work and our lives, with the intention of getting people to work harder more often. However, the disappearance of divisions between work and play can have another result: more fulfilled, coherent lives in which financial productivity is no longer the sole measure of success.

Today, the right to think is under siege. Information and technology is being hoarded, and the courts are being enlisted to rule on everything from attempts to restrict the flow of information across the Internet to attempts to patent human genome patterns. Ad filters and Personal Imaging are just opening salvoes in a war to control the paradigms of the cyborg age. Systematic attempts to repress the ideas and methods of cyborgspace — such as the move to censor the Internet and ban information exchange technologies (such as the now-neutered Napster, once a free Web-based community designed to facilitate the trading of songs) — attempt to preserve a status quo in which the hoarding of knowledge takes place regardless of the means or consequences. Nevertheless, though the retrograde and desperate forces of status quo oppression may succeed in the short term, many of the communal manners of being I have described in this book will soon be asserting themselves into the fabric of daily reality.

Each application for WearComp that I propose invariably leads to far-ranging new possibilities. Similarly, the applications I have discussed in this book also lead to counter-possibilities in which repression and regression become the legacy of the cybernetic age. The fact that the widespread availability of arts and entertainment products made possible by the digital age has actually created an alternative (pop culture) consciousness in us is indicative of the power of disembodied cyborgspace to transform what we understand to be important in our lives and in society. The coming arrival of an even more powerful interconnected cyborgspace that fuses media space with personal space and educative space will only hasten the triumph of leisure over work or, I should say, the full integration of work and play into a new cyborg terrain where we will be doing (being) both all the time at the same time.

I. FORMS AND DOCUMENTS

HUMANISTIC PROPERTY LICENSE AGREEMENT

If leaks of personal information are to be stopped, then they should be stopped at the source. Accordingly, I propose the Humanistic Property License Agreement, which I, and various others, require those wishing to produce for me an identification card to sign. The agreement establishes the terms under which our physical likeness can be used. I've used this form on several occasions in my everyday life. Naturally, responses to the HPLA have varied. The Massachusetts Institute of Technology decided to sign a Humanistic Property License Agreement when they took my picture for my ID card (and they even showed me that they deleted the picture afterwards). The University of Toronto decided to issue me an ID card without a picture rather than agree to the terms of the license.

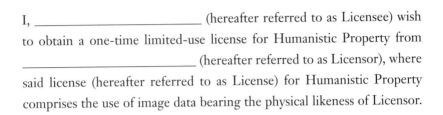

I, _____ (hereafter referred to as Licensee) wish to obtain a one-time limited-use license for Humanistic Property from _____ (hereafter referred to as Licensor), where said license (hereafter referred to as License) for Humanistic Property comprises the use of image data bearing the physical likeness of Licensor.

I understand that said image and data pertaining to said image is the property of Licensor, and shall remain so indefinitely. I further understand that this License permits me to acquire an electronic image (hereafter referred to as Humanistic Property) bearing the likeness of Licensee for the sole purpose of printing and providing Licensor with an identification card. I further agree that after issuing Licensee said identification card, that I may not save or record in any manner said Humanistic Property, or any portion thereof.

Furthermore, I assert that after a time period not to exceed five minutes after said identification card is printed, that said identification card shall be the sole record of said Humanistic Property, and that there shall be no other record of said Humanistic Property, whether retained mechanically, optically, electronically, or otherwise.

I understand that any such other record of said Humanistic Property is stolen Humanistic Property. I understand that my failing to permanently delete and erase all manner of said Humanistic Property other than one copy printed on said identification card shall constitute theft of said Humanistic Property. I further understand that failing to permanently delete and erase all manner of said Humanistic Property shall constitute an assignment of any material, media, and image storage system, whether mechanical, optical, electronic, or otherwise, that contains or contained stolen Humanistic Property, to Licensor.

I agree that said assignment of said material, media, and image storage system, whether mechanical, optical, electronic, or otherwise, that contains stolen Humanistic Property shall include, at Licensor's discretion, any components of Licensee's computer system that Licensor wishes to seize, including but not limited to hard disk drives, backup tapes, storage media, and computer networks. I assert that I have authority to make this assignment should stolen Humanistic Property have passed through any of the computer networks of the organization(s) of which I am a representative.

I further agree that the future existence of said stolen Humanistic Property shall constitute proof of said theft, whether said stolen Humanistic Property exists in any form within my organization or after transfer to another organization or entity, and that said existence of said stolen Humanistic Property shall be sufficient grounds for Licensor to seize any and all equipment which Licensee reasonably believes may contain or may have contained, transmitted, transferred, or processed said stolen Humanistic Property.

_____   _____

SIGNATURE   DATE

REQUEST FOR REMOVAL OF VISUAL MEMORY PROSTHETIC

I have often been told that regulations require me to remove WearComp. One of the ways I have responded has been by insisting that I could not remove the system until the Request for Removal form was signed.

This is an agreement (hereafter referred to as Agreement) pertaining to the safe inspection and handling of a visual memory prosthetic, visual filter, Laser EyeTap™ eyewear, EyeTap™ device, or visual information processor (hereafter referred to as Prosthetic), from a user, wearer, patient, or experimental subject (hereafter referred to as Wearer).

If Prosthesis includes means for directing light into an eye of wearer, or means and apparatus responsive to light that would otherwise enter an eye of Wearer (hereafter referred to as EyeTap), I agree to ensure that my inspection will not alter the optical path of any light passing through or produced by EyeTap, or that if I must alter the optical path of EyeTap (such as by moving EyeTap), I understand that Wearer may have acquired sensitivity to coherent light not processed by EyeTap, and that Wearer may be subject to dizziness, nausea, headache, or other effects caused by perturbation of the optical path of EyeTap, and I agree to assume responsibility for any adverse effects caused by my inspection.

I further agree to specify the following terms of my inspection, and agree to be bound by these terms: I will not subject Wearer to light levels in excess of _____ during my perturbation of said optical path. I will not subject Wearer to visual stimulus exceeding _____ during my perturbation of said optical path. I agree to assume responsibility for any damage caused to Prosthesis or Wearer as a result of my inspection. I further agree to nondisclosure and nonuse of any aspect of the Intellectual Property embodied in Prosthesis.

I assign any and all data I may derive, or cause to be derived, from my inspection of Prosthesis, including but not limited to data derived from devices with recording capability, and the media and systems upon which said media exist, to Wearer. If I jointly participate in an inspection of said Prosthesis, I agree to be jointly and severally bound by the terms of this Agreement.

_____   _____

SIGNATURE   DATE

REQUEST FOR X-RAY INSPECTION
OF VISUAL MEMORY PROSTHETIC

This is an agreement (hereafter referred to as Agreement) pertaining to the safe inspection and handling of a visual memory prosthetic, or other body-worn processor (hereafter referred to as Prosthetic), possibly including a physiological monitor, which may include direct connection to the body of a user, wearer, patient, or subject of experimental apparatus (hereafter referred to as Wearer). I request to have at least a portion of Prosthesis completely removed from body of Wearer, for purposes of my X-ray inspection of said Prosthesis. I wish to expose Prosthesis to a level of radiation not to exceed _____. I understand that Prosthesis is not a mass-produced product tested for withstanding X-rays, and therefore I agree to assume responsibility for possible adverse effect of X-ray exposure to Prosthesis. I agree to assume responsibility for any damage caused to Prosthesis as a result of my inspection. I further agree to nondisclosure and nonuse of any aspect of the Intellectual Property embodied in Prosthesis. I assign any and all data I may derive, or cause to be derived, from my inspection of Prosthesis, including but not limited to data recorded by computer systems or devices associated with the means and apparatus of X-ray inspection and the media and systems upon which said media exist, to Wearer.

_____   _____

SIGNATURE   DATE

REQUEST FOR DELETION (RFD)

In the past, when blatantly using WearComp/WearCam to capture video and transmit live to the Web, I have been told that I must cease my actions and immediately destroy the images I have recorded. I have responded by requesting that the employee read and sign the form below.

In the interest of employee safety, our employees are required to wear uniforms equipped with protective media to discourage others from exposing them to dangerous situations or environments (e.g. establishments where fire exits are chained shut illegally or the like), or to falsely accuse our employees of crimes (such as shoplifting and the like). Our employee uniforms capture images, photometric measurements, and/or other measurement information and the like, which may have been and may continue to be transmitted and recorded at remote locations. Furthermore, our employees are required to document, via more traditional photographic means, any incident in which there is a perceived or suspected safety hazard, or any incident in which there might be potential for a crime to be committed in the future (such as when an employee presents a company credit card, when an employee makes a purchase but is not given a receipt that provides proof of the purchase such that a false shoplifting accusation could be forthcoming, or when cash is being handled by one of our employees).

For YOUR protection, our employees are also required to photograph each person they interact with, as well as maintain a recording of the conversation, in order to pre-empt any disputes regarding return of merchandise. If you feel that one of our employees has documented something within your establishment that you do not wish to have remain on file in our image archives, or if you feel that your likeness should not remain on file in our archives you may submit a REQUEST FOR DELETION (RFD) to our employee, who will forward it to our Company Headquarters.

Your RFD, if properly completed in full, will be presented to a committee, and a decision will be made as to whether to expunge said image(s) or to flag said images as noteworthy (i.e. by submitting an RFD, you should be aware that it may in fact cause your likeness to be flagged as suspicious or of special interest to the permanent archives).

PART I:
DECLARATION OF REASON FOR RFD
(PLEASE CIRCLE ONLY ONE):

A   NATIONAL SECURITY:
You must be a government establishment or have government affiliation (such as government funding) to select this option.

B   COMPANY CONFIDENTIAL:
B1: A trade secret has been inadvertently documented by our employee.
B2: Strategic marketing plans have been inadvertently documented by our employee.
B3: Other company confidential _____
(please describe, use additional page if necessary)

C   Other _____ (please describe, use additional page if necessary)

PART II:

DECLARATION OF ABSTINENCE FROM WILLFUL
DESTRUCTION OF EVIDENCE OF A CRIMINAL ACT.

In recognition of the fact that measurement (photometric, radar, or otherwise) data captured by our employee may comprise evidence, in the context of a possible future criminal investigation against me or my establishment, I, the undersigned, declare that my REQUEST FOR DELETION is not for purposes of concealing criminal activity of myself or of others in my establishment.

I assert that my RFD is not intended to hide criminal activity of any kind occurring within my establishment, including, but not limited to, fire exits chained or otherwise fastened shut illegally, or criminal activity of myself. I further assert that my RFD is not for purposes of concealing or destroying evidence of harassment of a representative of Personal Safety Devices (PSD), or to conceal discrimination against a PSD employee.

NAME: _____

SOCIAL SECURITY NUMBER: _____

SIGNATURE: _____

RIGHT THUMB PRINT:

II. ART WORKS AND REFLECTIONIST EXPERIMENTS

THE CAMERA SERIES

Many of my interventions are technologically complex, and hard to duplicate without access to and familiarity with a wearable computer system. I wanted to come up with a series of "performances" that would be more accessible, and less technologically daunting. I envisioned the pieces below as programs of step-by-step instructions which could be done by anybody, regardless of their access to technology. Repeatability, a moralistic/humanistic resonance, and firsthand encounters that reflect the technological hypocrisies of society back upon those who passively conform to those hypocrisies, are all elements of the Reflectionist approach.

MAYBE CAMERA

- Take one rectangular piece of ⅛-in black or dark acrylic, cut to measure 3 x 4 inches.
- Obtain a bulky sweatshirt.
- Print the words "For YOUR protection, a video record of you and your establishment may be transmitted and recorded at remote locations. ALL CRIMINAL ACTS PROSECUTED!" in large letters, on the front of the shirt. Lay out the lettering so as to leave room for the acrylic between the two sentences.
- Affix the acrylic securely to the shirt.
- Wear the completed shirt into a department store or other location where video surveillance is used but photography is strictly prohibited (this criterion can be determined experimentally even before the

shirt is made, by entering the proposed establishment with a camera and taking pictures within said establishment in a somewhat obvious manner).

A large number of these shirts were made and worn by myself, together with groups of other people, on trips to various establishments such as department stores and gambling casinos.

For **your** protection a video record of you and your establishment *may* be **transmitted** and **recorded** at **remote** locations

ALL CRIMINAL ACTS PROSECUTED!!! Copyright (c) Steve Mann 19??

The "Maybe Camera" shirt.

PROBABLY CAMERA

- Obtain one miniature (12 inches in diameter or smaller) ceiling dome of wine-dark opacity, together with a camera and pan-tilt-zoom mechanism suitable for that dome.

- Affix dome to backpack, facing backwards, cutting appropriate mounting hole in backpack, leaving sufficient space, and installing appropriate housing for camera and pan-tilt-zoom mechanism. Leave the camera out for the time being.

- Insert a small battery-powered computer equipped with video-capture hardware and means of controlling the function of the pan-tilt-zoom controls automatically.

- Into the pack insert means of wireless communication to/from the Internet or to/from an Internet gateway/server.

- Prepare software to allow the function of the apparatus to be controlled remotely via a WWW page, with ability to capture and display images from the camera if the camera is present. Make this

WWW page world-accessible and known to various people around the world.

- Leave the work area and have someone else do the final assembly in your absence, according to the following instructions: Roll two dice. (1) If the dice total comes to two or three, insert into the dome a small lightbulb, affixed to the pan-tilt-zoom sensor but connected to it in no way; add sufficient ballast into the pack to make up the difference in weight between the bulb and the camera, so that the wearer cannot determine this difference by weight. (2) If the dice total exceeds three, insert the camera, properly mounting it and connecting it to a video digitizer. Verify its operation using a Web browser of your choice.

- Wear backpack together with shirt ("Maybe Camera"), into a record store, preferably Tower Records, where ceiling domes of wine-dark opacity are used. If asked if it is a camera, or what it is, indicate that you are not certain, but point out the domes upon their ceiling and indicate the similarity, so that perhaps it could be a light fixture. (Security guards at Tower Records have informed me that their ceiling domes of wine-dark opacity are "light fixtures.")

NO CAMERA

This conceptual piece involves video time-delay, to symbolize the disjointedness between cause and effect that video recording creates:

- Place pinhole camera and microphone into baseball cap, and record video from an establishment where photography, filming and the like are strictly prohibited, but where video surveillance is used and there are documented cases of hidden cameras having been used. While

recording video, talk to members of establishment, including manager. Ask whether or not they use video surveillance, and if so, why
they are videotaping you without your permission. Ask what their
ceiling domes of wine-dark opacity are, if any are present.

- Leave this establishment, and return with the following, but without
the camera: (1) flat-panel television screen affixed to shirt; (2) source
of previously recorded video material; (3) means of switching
between previously recorded material and standard broadcast
television channels.

- Play the previously recorded video on the television screen, and if you
are informed that photography, filming or the like is prohibited,
indicate that there is NO CAMERA, and that what you are wearing is
merely a television. Switch through the various channels, indicating
that one of them (the one playing the previously recorded material)
looks like it "must be a local channel — a VERY local channel."

SEAT SALE

*I had the opportunity to build the contraption described below, which has
been shown in various galleries around the world as part of the exhibit*
Telematic Connections: The Virtual Embrace.

Affordable reality is provided by way of a remote safety manager, remote
license server, or the like. A naturally occurring service is impaired by a
service saboteur which may be conditionally mitigated by way of license
purchase. Means and apparatus is provided to grant licenses only on certain conditions.

The "Seat Sale" chair has a comfort amplifier, in which comfort can be
downloaded over the internet. This helps to reduce seating costs and make

SeatSale on exhibit at the San Francisco Art Institute.

seating more widely available and more comfortable. A naturally occurring service is seating that happens ordinarily because there are lots of chairs left in various places. Thus seating happens quite naturally so that almost anyone can find a place to sit down. From park benches to your very own sofa, there is so much seating that it's dangerously close to extinction, in the same way that Napster has created so much music that music will soon be extinct since all musicians will soon starve to death causing there to be no more music.

Fortunately, though, forty-nine very sharp spikes are sticking out of the seat of the chair. This helps to sabotage the service reception interface which is the seat, by degrading the quality (comfort) of the seating service of seating. To purchase a one seat license, a user of the chair simply plugs

SeatSale on exhibit at the San Francisco Art Institute.

it into the Internet by way of electrical connection, which also provides power. A display comes alive, and displays a message to "SLIDE CREDIT CARD" into card reader to purchase a seating license. Once a seat is purchased, four solenoids, one for each corner of the matrix of 7 by 7 spikes, retract all forty-nine spikes down into the base of the seat. The base of the seat is preferably large and hollow for this purpose, and so that it can also house a small computer system that runs the license manager software.

DECON FACILITY: CYBORG TECHNOLOGY
VERSUS STATE SURVEILLANCE

A version of this proposed exhibit — one that did not require visitors to strip and submit to decontamination — was shown in the summer of 2001 at Toronto's TPW Gallery as Prior Art: Art of Record for Personal Safety.

Big Brother saves seconds and lives. The most insidious form of surveillance is that which purports to be for the benefit of the surveilled, hence the typical signage found on department store entrances "for YOUR protection, you are under video surveillance." Such doublespeak is commonplace, as if to justify the violation of privacy on the basis of security. Surveillance for hygiene and social control is also evident in the industry of mass decontamination facilities for rounding up and herding thousands of persons suspected of civil unrest or contamination. This exhibit's purpose is to juxtapose cyborg technology against state surveillance — the cyborg versus the stripped naked individual who no longer has access to personal technologies that

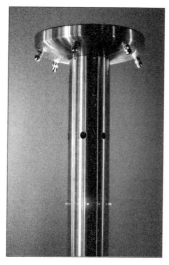

A six-station column shower within a hexagonal shower room is controlled by six NTSC RS 170 video motion detectors, combined with photometric stero body scanners.

Six video displays in the inner gallery allowed for monitoring of persons undergoing decontamination, to ensure compliance with decontamination procedures and safety policies.

can allow him or her to fight back against unwanted privacy invasion. In this exhibit, visitors to the gallery are confronted with a mass decontamination facility that includes the most modern Internet-connected sensor-operated showers with photometric stereo body-scanning machine vision capability. The exhibit is essentially a strip-down facility to remove cyborgian telematics from visitors entering the innermost gallery space.

Visitors to Decon are required to remove all personal telematic devices, cellphones, PDAs, pagers, and "wearables" (e.g. clothing, jewellery, etc.) and bag these personal items at the entrance. Once stripped of all manner of telematic elements, visitors proceed naked through the decontamina-

A decontamination officer's video view, by way of a smoked lexan viewing window into the men's shower room, shows that proper decontamination procedures are being safely followed.

tion showers and then to the drying area to receive a plain white uniform. Once inside the inner sanctum of the gallery, visitors can watch, on an array of monitors, others stripping and moving through the Decon facility.

SAFETY WALLETS

These days, you can patent just about anything. In 1999 I decided to sub-mit a patent that would cover a wide range of "inventions" dealing with new technological ways to respond to officials who demand that we show our identification while they hide behind the uniform of authority. Amongst these were a variety of "Safety Wallets."

"ANTENNA WALLET" is a safety wallet used to keep passports, identification, or other papers in order, as might be required by organ-izations that like to screen for or keep out undesir-ables. An antenna-100 keeps

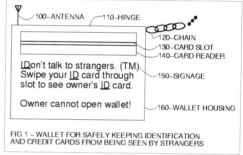

FIG 1 – WALLET FOR SAFELY KEEPING IDENTIFICATION AND CREDIT CARDS FROM BEING SEEN BY STRANGERS

the wallet on the Internet or the like, and a hinge allows it to open up but only after an identification of the person wishing to see the user's papers has occurred over the radio link provided by antenna-100. A tether (chain, cable, or the like) keeps the wallet attached to the user's body. Preferably tether is such that it can be threaded around the user's waist and then fed into the open wallet, such that access to the end is needed to detach the tether from the user, and access to the end requires opening the wallet. Alternatively, a special strap around the waist or ankle may be held in place by a cable similar to those used to lock down computers, which then is inserted into the wallet prior to closing it. Alternatively, the tether may be wireless, such that a person stealing the wallet will be subdued or marked with chemical means, such as that manufactured under the trade name Dye Witness™. A thief taking the wallet beyond reach of a corresponding wearable radio transmitter will simply cause the device to switch into a pro-tective mode of spraying with chemicals. Similarly, attempts to force open or bypass the lock on the wallet will result in similar discharge of chemi-cal disincentives. To open the wallet, an official must slide a government-issued ID card through slot in card reader as indicated by signage upon wallet housing. If the ID card is valid, and is found by way of antenna to not have been reported as stolen, then the locking mechanism of wallet housing is released so that the official can see that the wallet owner's papers are in order.

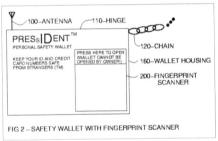

FIG 2 – SAFETY WALLET WITH FINGERPRINT SCANNER

"FINGERPRINT WALLET" is a version of the safety wallet invention that uses a fingerprint scanner instead of a card reader. The instructions simply direct the official wishing to see the owner's papers to press on a cer-tain portion of the wallet to open it. This portion of the wallet is really a miniature fingerprint scanner similar to those used in the BioMouse™ computer fingerprint scanner. The wallet checks to make sure the scanned fingerprint is a valid fingerprint and is not that of the owner, prior to releasing the mechanism that allows the wallet to open.

"URIDENT WALLET" shows an embodiment of the wallet that cannot be opened by drug users such as drug-using criminals wearing SS uniforms. In order to open the wallet, it is necessary that someone other than a member of the urIDent™ wal-let owner's collective urinate into the urine tester. Urine tester verifies the drug-free aspect of the individual asking to see the owner's papers. In this case wallet housing may be

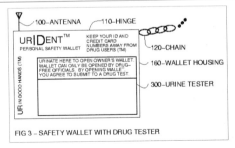

FIG 3 – SAFETY WALLET WITH DRUG TESTER

opened after cleaning off excess urine. Wallet housing is equipped with a seal, to keep the papers inside from getting soaked in urine.

"DNA WALLET" depicts a safety wallet with DNA sampler. Officials carrying stolen identification would no doubt be terrified of this wallet, because of the DNA sampler. However, law-abiding non-corrupt offi-

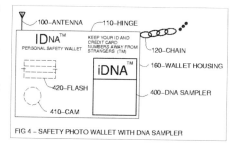

FIG 4 – SAFETY PHOTO WALLET WITH DNA SAMPLER

cials have nothing to fear, and simply insert a DNA sample, causing wallet housing to be unlocked so they can open it. Much to their pleasant surprise, they will be photographed with camera when the wallet opens. Flashlamp makes certain the precious moment is captured in the best colour rendition possible. Camera transmits images over antenna to a plurality of remote locations in various countries around the world, so that a dishonest official will have a hard time destroying all of these images, and therefore runs a higher risk of getting caught. Honest officials will no doubt enjoy being photographed. It is most certainly only the dishonest or corrupt officials who fear accountability. Thus it may suffice to have only the flashlamp without the camera, so as to scare away criminals. In fact, in many of these embodiments, a large number of fake units that look like the real ones, with only a few real units, would suffice to frighten corrupt officials, forcing them to remain on their best behaviour at all times since they never know whether or not they are being remotely monitored or the like.

COMPUTER SUPPORTED COLLABORATION (CSC) — A way of living in which individuals and communities engage in perpetual collaboration and information sharing linked through wearable computers with the capacity to mediate reality.

CYBERNETICS — The term coined by mathematician Norbert Wiener in 1948 to describe the feedback loop of information as it interacts in society. Wiener defined cybernetics as the "study of messages as a means of controlling machinery and society."

CYBORG — The term coined by Manfred E. Clynes and Nathan S. Kline in 1960. Taking their cue from the term Cybernetics, and inspired by the possibility of space travel, the two visionaries imagined a human being that would merge unconsciously with technology. Their vision was of a human being as part of a technological feedback loop functioning unconsciously to extend certain predetermined processes.

DIFFUSIONISM — The strategy by which problems that technology creates in society are addressed through technological innovations and inventions, in essence, battling the machine with the machine. In diffusionism, new, widely disseminated technologies are invented to combat social ills that are created by prior technologies.

DUSTING — WearComp application in which a cybernetic photographic process of painting with light vectors is created by electronic flash. Dusting requires the unification of the mind, the body and the computer-controlled flash/ cybernetic capture process.

ENGWEAR (ELECTRONIC NEWS GATHERING WEARABLE SYSTEM) — A version of the WearComp system specifically designed for the gathering and dispensation of current events. Allows the wearer to broadcast a variety of media including video and audio instantly in real-time to the World Wide Web.

EXISTED (EXISTENTIAL EDUCATION) — An approach to education, specifically education in computers and technology, in which the student essentially "learns by being." The student is encouraged and directed to become one with the subject which he or she is exploring/studying.

EXISTENTIALITY — Existentiality denotes the degree to which the individual has control of personal technology systems — does the technology allow for the creation of sustainable personal spaces? A wearable computer system that allows the user to control all input and outputs has existentiality. A "smart" room that automatically adjusts lighting and environment regardless of the occupant's wishes does not provide existentiality.

EYETAP — The primary input/output device into the WearComp wearable computer system. Allows the user to view the world as images imprinted onto the retina by rays of laser light controlled through several linked computers. The WearComp user "sees" through miniature cameras, with the image filtered into the computer system before finally being projected into the eye. The EyeTap allows the eye to function as both a camera and a display with text and graphic capabilities. In this way, eye and camera, mind and computer, are joined.

HUMANISTIC INTELLIGENCE — A philosophical approach to developing technologies that holds that users of technology should have complete control over the technology they are using. Humanistic Intelligence holds that technology should always be controlled by, and be responsive to, the user.

HUMANISTIC PROPERTY — A term coined to describe the mental space that surrounds the individual. The mental space that each individual occupies and thus owns. What one sees, what one hears, what enters one's senses, as well as what one produces without conscious thought or effort.

KEYER — A device similar to a home computer mouse that allows the WearComp user to input into the system. Usually kept in a pocket, the smallest keyer is a push-button switch the user can press for a short time (a "dot") or a long time (a "dash") to key letters using a code, such as Morse code, at maybe fifteen words per minute if the user has some reasonable degree of experience. A single push-button keyer is sufficient to allow the experienced WearComp user to send and receive e-mail, take photographs, make calculations, and instruct the computer to screen out all ads for cigarettes.

LIGHTSPACE — An early motivating application of the WearComp system, the goal of lightspace was to experience an altered perception of reality by exploring a large range of possible forms of illumination while observing a scene or object from different viewpoints. Lightspace was essentially a photographic project that sought to capture the essence and possibility of altered perceptions by trapping momentary shifts in perception through the medium of photography. Experiments in lightspace, which required the invention of a link between mind, body, and camera and the ability to program complex sequences of events, led to the invention of the WearComp wearable computer system.

MEDIATED REALITY — Mediated Reality is the technological process by which the WearComp user can mediate all visual input and output. Mediation includes overlaying virtual objects on "real life", and taking away or otherwise visually altering objects.

PERSONAL IMAGING — The branch of personal technology systems that deals with the construction of realities. This is a camera-based computational framework in which the camera behaves as a true extension of the mind and body, after a period of long-term adaptation.

REFLECTIONISM — A strategy of social criticism in which technology is used to explore the technological tools of everyday life, reflecting technology back at society with the aim of making individuals confront and realize the hidden biases and impacts technology has on society.

SHOOTINGBACK — Documentary Webcast video on privacy invasion and surveillance video shot by Steve Mann using the Wearable Wireless WearCam WearComp application.

VICARIOUS SOLILOQUY — A method of giving presentations and lectures using the WearComp system. In this method, the audience sees not the lecturer, but what the speaker is seeing, i.e. what the speaker is looking at projected on a large screen. This essentially puts the audience "inside the head" of the speaker, with whom they share a first person perspective.

VISUAL MEMORY PROSTHETIC — In this WearComp function, visual information is temporarily recorded in a memory buffer. The Visual Memory Prosthesis can help the user to forget or not see at all, as well as remember and enhance vision. Visual Memory Prosthesis can be used as a safety system: If something atypical happens, sensors pick up the sudden change in the user's heart rate and the video record of the event will be pulled from the buffer into permanent storage. In the Visual Memory Prosthetic, the user's brain is using the machine as a second brain, and the machine uses the user's brain as a second central processing unit (CPU).

WEARABILITY — Wearability denotes how much free movement an individual has when utilizing a personal technology system. A personal technology system has wearability if it allows independence through freedom of movement (including the ability to "put on" and "take off" the technology). A walkman has wearability, as does an artificial heart, but an iron lung or a mainframe computer lack wearability. Wearability, of course, does not automatically mean that the wearer will actually have autonomy in action and thought.

WEARABLE WIRELESS WEARCAM — A\WearComp application that allows the user to broadcast everything he or she sees in real time to the World Wide Web. From 1994 to 1996 Steve Mann wore the Wearable Wireless WearCam continuously.

WEARCOMP — The wearable computer invented by Steve Mann. This is a fully mobile data processing system attached to the body, with one or more input and output devices.

WEARTEL — A WearComp videoconferencing application in which two users communicate by seeing each other's point of view/perspective.

CHAPTER 1

1 Don Tapscott quoted in Jerry Everard, *Virtual States* (London: Routledge, 2000), p. 3.

2 Mark O'Brien, "Is the Body Obsolete?," *Whole Earth Review* (#63, 1989), p. 36.

3 Margaret Morse, *Virtualities* (Bloomington: Indiana University Press, 1998), p. 127.

4 Christopher Isherwood, *Goodbye to Berlin: A Berlin Diary* (London: Hogarth Press, 1939), p. 1.

CHAPTER 2

1 Natalie Jeremijenko, "Database Politics and Social Simulations," http://tech90s.net/nj/transcript/nj_05.html

2 Hans Moravec, *Mind Children* (Cambridge: Harvard University Press, 1988), p. 59.

3   Margaret Morse, *Virtualities* (Bloomington: Indiana
    University Press, 1998), p. 8.

4   Seth Shulman, *Owning the Future* (Boston: Houghton
    Mifflin, 1999), p 112.

5   Anne McIlroy, "Scientist's Sacrilege: Making Money,"
    Globe and Mail (January 3, 2001).

6   Moravec, *Mind Children*, p. 16.

7   O.B. Hardison Jr., *Disappearing Through the Skylight*
    (New York: Viking, 1989), p. 301.

8   Moravec, *Mind Children*, p. 85.

9   Critical Arts Ensemble, *Flesh Machine* (Brooklyn:
    Autonomedia, 1998), p. 5.

10 Critical Arts Ensemble, *Flesh Machine*, p. 5.

11 Walter A. McDougall, ... *the Heavens and the Earth:
    A Political History of the Space Age* (Basic Books:
    New York, 1985), p. 7.

12 Norbert Wiener quoted in William Kuhns, *The Post-
    Industrial Prophets: Interpretations of Technology* (New York:
    Weybright and Talley, 1971), p. 164.

13 Norbert Wiener quoted in William Kuhns, *The Post-
    Industrial Prophets: Interpretations of Technology*, p. 218.

14 Manfred E. Clynes and Nathan S. Kline, "Cyborgs and
    Space," from *The Cyborg Handbook*, edited by Chris Hables
    Gray (New York: Routledge, 1995), p. 31.

15 Donna Harraway quoted in Chris Hables Gray and Steve
    Mentor, "The Cyborg Body Politic and the New World
    Order," *Prosthetic Territories: Politics and Hypertechnologies*,
    edited by Gabriel Brahm and Mark Driscoll (Boulder:
    Westview Press, 1995), p. 231.

16 DARPA Web site, www.DARPA.mil/mto/smartmod/
    factsheets/sccms.html

17 Calvin Coolidge quoted in *The History and Development of Advertising*, Frank Presbrey (Garden City: Doubleday, 1929), p. 76.

18 David Channel, "The Vital Machine," from *The Cyborg Handbook*, edited by Chris Hables Gray, p. 12.

19 Chris Hables Gray and Steve Mentor, "The Cyborg Body Politic and the New World Order," in *Prosthetic Territories: Politics and Hypertechnologies*, edited by Gabriel Brahm and Mark Driscoll (Boulder: Westview Press, 1995), p. 231.

20 Bill Buxton, "Ubiquitous Media and the Active Office", Nikkei Electronics (in Japanese), no. 632 (March 1995), pp. 187–195. (In English at www.billbuxton.com/ubicomp.html)

CHAPTER 3

1 Donna Harraway quoted in "Cyborgology," from *The Cyborg Handbook*, edited by Chris Hables Gray (Routledge: New York, 1995), p. 1.

2 Joseph Dumit, "Brain-Mind Machines and American Technological Dream Marketing: Towards an Ethnography of Cyborg Envy," from *The Cyborg Handbook*, edited by Chris Hables Gray, p. 348.

3 Judith Gaines, "Cyberclothes," *Boston Globe* (Sept. 23, 1997).

4 Robert Hooke, *Micrographia*, quoted from http://wearables.www.media.mit.edu/projects/wearables/timeline.html#1665, originally published 1665.

5 Chris Hables Gray, Steven Mentor, Heidi J. Figueroa-Sarriera, "Cyborgology," from *The Cyborg Handbook*, edited by Chris Hables Gray (Routledge: New York, 1995), p. 1.

6   Thomas Bass, "Dress Code," *Wired* (April 1998).

7   Linda Hales, "Take a Walk on the Cyber Side," *Washington Post* (September 9, 2000), p. C02.

8   Charmed Technology Web site, www.charmed.com

9   Hester Abrams, "Geeks Go Chic with Wearable Computers," Reuters (September 24, 2000).

10 Gina Smith, "Bionic Man is on the Horizon," ABC News (June 23, 2000).

11 Michelle Lloyd, "The Loneliness of Cyborgs," http://home.fuse.net/mllwyd/cyborgs.html

12 Marilyn Morley, "Technology to Wear," *Montreal Gazette* (May 29, 1999), p. J8.

13 Adam Rogers and N'gai Croal, "Steve Mann Looks at the World," *NewsWeek* (July 17, 1995).

14 Samantha Hill, "Introducing the Bionic Man," *Time Magazine*, Vol. 154, No. 15 (October 11, 1999).

15 Paul Bannister, "Web Man Walking," *National Enquirer*, (January 27, 1998), p. 10.

16 Allan Newell quoted in Mark Stefik, *The Internet Edge* (Cambridge, Mass.: MIT Press, 1999), p. 258.

17 Thomas Bass, *Eudaemonic Pie* (Boston: Houghton Mifflin, 1985), p. 219.

18 Scott Bukatman, *Terminal Identity* (Durham: Duke University Press, 1993), p. 230.

19 Allan Kaprow, *Essays on the Blurring of Art and Life*, ed. Jeff Kelley (Berkeley: University of California Press, 1993), p. 187.

20 J.G. Ballard quoted in Scott Bukatman, *Terminal Identity*, p. 31.

21 O.B. Hardison Jr., *Disappearing Through the Skylight*, p. 5.

22 Glenn Zorpette and Carol Ezzell, "Your Bionic Future," *Scientific American* (September 1999).

23   Natalie Jeremijenko quoted in Courtney Eldrige, "Better Art Through Circuitry," *New York Times Magazine*, (June 11, 2000), p. 25.

24   Jennifer Gonzalez, "Envisions Cyborg Bodies," from *The Cyborg Handbook*, edited by Chris Hables Gray, p. 271.

CHAPTER 4

1   Earl Miller, "Jenni's Web," *Fuse*, vol. 23 , #2 (September 2000), p. 23.

2   Earl Miller, "Jenni's Web," *Fuse*, p. 23.

3   Edward Rothstein, "Turning Public and Private Inside Out," *New York Times* (November 18, 2000), p. A21.

4   Michel Foucault, *Discipline and Punish* (New York: Vintage, 1995), p. 170. (Originally published in France, 1975.)

5   Michel Foucault, *Discipline and Punish*, p. 201.

6   Ken Robins and Les Levidow, "Socializing the Cyborg Self: The Gulf War and Beyond," from *The Cyborg Handbook*, edited by Chris Hables Gray (Routledge: New York, 1995), p.124.

7   Ursula Franklin, "The Real World of Technology," Massey Lecture Series, 1989. http://masseylectures.cbc.ca

8   Margaret Morse, *Virtualities* (Bloomington: Indiana University Press, 1998), p. 182.

9   Phil Patton, "Caught," *Wired* (January 1995).

10   James Gorman, "The Size of Things to Come," *New York Times Magazine* (June 11, 2000), p. 21.

11   Daniel Golden, "The Face of the Future," *Boston Globe Sunday Magazine* (June 30, 1996).

12   MIT Media Laboratory, http://ilu.www.media.mit.edu/vismod/demos/smartchair/html

13   Mark Stefik, *The Internet Edge* (Cambridge, Mass.:
     MIT Press, 1999), p. 268.

14   Steven Kother, "The Genius Who Sticks Around Forever,"
     New York Times (June 11, 2000), p. 10.

15   Posting to Wear-Hard Listserv, June 1999, http://
     wearables.blu.org/wear-hard/19997252.html

16   "Celebration School Issues Students Wearable Java
     Computers," *Business Wire*, March 17, 1999.

17   "Smells Like Teen Credit," *New York Times Magazine*,
     (November 5, 2000), p. 30.

18   Robert O'Harrow Jr. and Liz Leyden, "U.S. Helped Fund
     License Photo Database," *Washington Post*, (February 18,
     1999), p. A1.

19   Barrie McKenna, "E-tailer Shakeout Punctures Privacy,"
     Globe and Mail (July 20, 2000), p. T1.

20   Stephen Labaton, "Learning to Live with Big Brother,"
     New York Times (July 23, 2000).

21   Louis Brandeis quoted in Stephen Labaton, "Learning to
     Live with Big Brother," *New York Times* (July 23, 2000).

22   John Fitzgerald quoted in Mick Hans, "Cameras Catch Red-
     Light Runners: Cities Install Photo-Enforcement Systems at
     Problem Intersections," *Traffic Safety* (Jan./Feb. 1997), p. 8–12.

23   Lynda Hurst, "The Little Brothers Are Watching You,"
     Toronto Star (August 12, 2000), p. J3.

24   Critical Arts Ensemble, *Flesh Machine* (Brooklyn:
     Autonomedia, 1998), p. 26.

25   Michel Foucault quoted in Scott Bukatman, *Terminal
     Identity*, p. 38.

26   Sandy Stone, "Split Subjects, Not Atoms; or How I Fell in
     Love with My Prosthesis" from *The Cyborg Handbook*, edit-
     ed by Chris Hables Gray, p. 400.

27 Peter Cheney, "Is Pornography Out of Control?," *Globe and Mail* (December 2, 2000), p. F5.

CHAPTER 5

1 Jeff MacGregor, "What's Wrong With TV? Just Do the Math," *New York Times* (August 9, 1998), p. 27.

2 Kalle Lasn quoted in Simon Choise, "Takin' It to the Net," *Globe and Mail* (June, 12, 1999).

3 Paul Hoffert, *All Together Now* (Toronto: Stoddart, 2000), p. 14.

4 Android Andy Warhol quoted in Scott Bukatman, *Terminal Identity*, p. 328.

5 *Space Jam* dialogue quoted in Naomi Klein, *No Logo* (Toronto: Knopf Canada, 2000), p. 57.

6 Paul Hoffert, *All Together Now* (Toronto: Stoddart, 2000), p. 177.

7 MIT Epistemology and Learning Group, http://el.www.media.mit.edu/groups/el/elthemes.html

8 Jerry Everard, *Virtual States* (New York: Routledge, 1999), p. 129.

9 Scott Bukatman, *Terminal Identity*, p. 195.

10 David Shenk, *The End of Patience* (Bloomington: Indiana University Press, 1999), p. 7.

11 Paula Rooney, "Research Facility Pioneers Advanced Computer Interfaces," *Computer Reseller News* (Nov. 13, 2000).

12 Critical Arts Ensemble, *Flesh Machine*, p. 23.

13 Margaret Morse, *Virtualities* (Bloomington: Indiana University Press, 1998), p. 184–185.

14 Timothy Leary quoted in Scott Bukatman, *Terminal Identity*, p. 139.

15 William Gibson quoted in Kevin Kelley, "Cyberpunk Era," *Whole Earth Review* (1989, #63), p. 79.

16 Jennifer Gonzalez, "Envisioning Cyborg Bodies," from *The Cyborg Handbook*, edited by Chris Hables Gray, p. 267.

17 Scott Bukatman, *Terminal Identity*, p. 33.

18 Greil Marcus, *Lipstick Traces* (Cambridge, Mass.: Harvard University Press, 1989), p. 99.

19 Scott Bukatman, *Terminal Identity*, p. 208.

20 Jerry Everard, *Virtual States*, p. 75.

CHAPTER 6

1 M.D. Pesce quoted in William R. Macauley and Angel J. Gordo-Lopez, "Advancing Cyborg Textualities for a Narrative of Resistance," from *The Cyborg Handbook*, edited by Chris Hables Gray, p. 436.

2 Christopher Kedzie study quoted in Mark Stefik, *The Internet Edge*, p. 241.

3 Sam Pitroda quoted in Mark Stefik, *The Internet Edge*, p. 239.

4 Manfred Clynes quoted in Chris Hables Gray, "An Interview with Manfred Clynes," from *The Cyborg Handbook*, edited by Chris Hables Gray, p. 52.

5 Jerry Everard, *Virtual States*, p. 75.

6 Hans Moravec, *Mind Children*, p. 1.

7 Bruce Sterling, "Is the Body Obsolete?," *The Whole Earth Review* (1989, #63), p. 50.

8 Benjamin Barber, *Jihad vs. McWorld* (New York: Ballantine Books, 1995), p. 4.

9   William Kuhns, *The Post-Industrial Prophets: Interpretations of Technology*, p. 153.

10 Sigmund Freud quoted in Chris Hables Gray and Steve Mentor, "The Cyborg Body Politic and the New World Order," in *Prosthetic Territories: Politics and Hypertechnologies*, edited by Gabriel Brahm and Mark Driscoll (Boulder: Westview Press, 1995), p. 231.

11 D'Arcy Thompson quoted in O.B. Hardison, Jr., *Disappearing Through the Skylight*, p. 45.

12 Pierre Teilhard de Chardin quoted in O.B. Hardison, Jr., *Disappearing Through the Skylight*, p. 288.

13 O.B. Hardison, Jr., *Disappearing Through the Skylight*, p. 260.

14 O.B. Hardison, Jr., *Disappearing Through the Skylight*, p. 260.

15 J. Moyer and G. Fierheller, "Managing in an Information Highway Age," *Business Quarterly*, vol. 58, #3 (1994), p. 73.

16 Sandy Stone, "Split Subjects, Not Atoms; or How I Fell in Love with My Prosthesis" from *The Cyborg Handbook*, edited by Chris Hables Gray, p. 401.

17 Steven Levy quoted in Scott Bukatman, *Terminal Identity*, p. 196.

ACKNOWLEDGEMENTS

My life as a cyborg evolved from a personal hobby dating back to my early childhood. Therefore, I must thank, first and foremost, my parents, for raising me, being with me early on in this development, and for continuing to stay with me, tapping into my right eye, through radioteletype, remote visual guidance, www, etc., offering me patience, support, encouragement, and love, as well as advice from and into my visual field of view, without which life's stress may well have made this book impossible.

I thank my brother, Richard, for his assistance throughout my childhood days and in the early developmental stages, in much of the debugging of systems (such as the early pushbroom "duster" softwear, font tables for it, etc.), and more recently advice from afar. He also contributed extensively to WearComp2, and somewhat to WearComp7 and WearComp8.

My sister, Beth, provided much in the way of artistic direction in the early days of my "dusting" efforts, thus contributing to the artistic vision of the lightspace concept.

My grandparents taught me as a young child the skills I needed to accomplish the building of the many prototypes of my various inventions. My grandfather taught me how to weld and work with sheet metal, as well as all the skills of the machine shop, and my grandmother taught me how to knit and sew so that I could make my own "smarter" clothes.

I thank my wife Betty, for fourteen years of "5, 4, 3, 2, 1, dust." Thanks for helping me catch each packet of happiness, however brief.

Thanks to Antonin Kimla, who gave me the stepping relays to build my first wearable lightpainting computer, and later the funding to do it right (with solid state components). Thanks to Ron Lancaster for his enthusiasm in math class, helping get me out of (and into) trouble, and for donating lots of components for building my early rigs. Thanks to Dr. Carter, who helped me interface my lightpainting pushbroom to my 6502 wearable, and Kent Nickerson, who helped with some of my miniature personal radar units. All three are from McMaster University, each had a significant impact on this work.

Much of the early work on biosensors and wearable computing was done with, or at least inspired by, work I did with Dr. Ghista, and later refined with input from Dr. DeBruin, both of McMaster University.

Dr. Max Wong of McMaster University supervised my undergrad project, designing an RF link between two 8085 wearable computers, which I had assembled for my "photographer's assistant" project.

Thanks to Dr. Simon Haykin, my M. Eng advisor, who inspired my love of "Radar Vision."

My Ph.D. advisor, Rosalind W. Picard, served as a wonderful mentor and role model, along with the other members of my thesis committee at MIT, as well as B.K.P. Horn and Marvin Minsky, all of whom offered sound advice and constructive criticism that has shaped my thinking and improved my work.

Thanks also to Charles Wyckoff and Kim Vandiver of the Edgerton Center, who helped sustain my fascination with electronic flash.

Olivier Faugeras, through his course and our after-class discussions, had much to say in helping me decide what to focus on.

Michael Artin instilled in me a love of algebra and Lie groups, and tolerated my desire to apply exact science (algebra) to the inexact world.

Gilbert Strang instilled his love of linear algebra, Victor Guilleman his love of harmonic analysis, and Irving Segal his love of metaplectomorphisms of the position-momentum (or time-frequency) space.

Hiroshi Ishii helped keep me on a scholarly track and helped me in many other ways. Ted Adelson sustained my natural scientific curiosity.

Julia Sher invited me to lecture at the Massachusetts College of Art, where the class discussion afterwards significantly affected my thinking.

Thanks to Jonathan Rose who has more recently become a major source of inspiration and common sense.

I would also like to thank my students: James Fung, Felix Tang, Corey Manders, Chris Aimone, Tomas Hirmer, Taneem Ahmed, Adnan Ali, Jason Boyer, Daniel Chen, Peter Dalacostas, Derek Fearnley, Milan Milicic, Rafael Van Daele-Hunt, and Laura Wood.

Many useful comments have come from the thousands of people I have met in my day-to-day interactions, through the apparatus — either face-to-face (on the street, etc.), or through the Net of which my body is, in some ways, a part. These people — too numerous to mention or even identify — have responded with comments ranging from harsh criticism to insightful ideas, all of which have in some way shaped my thinking.

Finally I thank God for letting there be light, in the wide sense, including those portions of the electromagnetic wave spectrum that have kept me in touch with my loved ones by way of wireless communications systems.

Steve Mann and Hal Niedzviecki would also like to thank the following people for their commitment to this book: At Doubleday Canada, Maya Mavjee. At Westwood Creative Artists, Bruce Westwood and Hilary Stanley. Darren Wershler-Henry provided research material, editing and singular insights. Sam and Nina Niedzviecki provided research and enthusiasm. Rachel Greenbaum supported this project from the outset, and offered invaluable commentary throughout, both on the book's form and on the implications of a cyborg world.